The Emil and Kathleen Sick Lecture-Book Series
in Western History and Biography

The Emil and Kathleen Sick Lecture-Book Series
in Western History and Biography

Under the provisions of a Fund established by the children of
Mr. and Mrs. Emil Sick, whose deep interest in the history and
culture of the American West was inspired by their own experience
in the region, distinguished scholars are brought to the University
of Washington to deliver public lectures based on original research
in the fields of Western history and biography. The terms of the gift
also provide for the publication by the University of Washington
Press of the books resulting from the research upon which the
lectures are based. This book is the seventh volume in the series.

The Great Columbia Plain:
A Historical Geography, 1805–1910
by Donald W. Meinig

Mills and Markets: A History of the
Pacific Coast Lumber Industry to 1900
by Thomas R. Cox

Radical Heritage: Labor, Socialism, and Reform
in Washington and British Columbia, 1885–1917
by Carlos A. Schwantes

The Battle for Butte: Mining and Politics
on the Northern Frontier, 1864–1906
by Michael P. Malone

The Forging of a Black Community:
Seattle's Central District, from 1870
through the Civil Rights Era
by Quintard Taylor

Warren G. Magnuson and the
Shaping of Twentieth-Century America
by Shelby Scates

The Atomic West
edited by Bruce Hevly and John M. Findlay

The Atomic West

EDITED BY

Bruce Hevly

AND

John M. Findlay

Center for the Study of the Pacific Northwest

in association with the

University of Washington Press, Seattle and London

Library of Congress Cataloging-in-Publication Data
The atomic west /
edited by Bruce Hevly and John M. Findlay.
p. cm. — (The Emil and Kathleen Sick lecture-book series
in western history and biography ; 7)
Includes index.
ISBN 0-295-97749-3 (cloth : alk. paper).
ISBN 0-295-97716-7 (pbk. : alk. paper)
1. Atomic bomb—West (U.S.)—History.
2. Nuclear energy—United States—History.
3. Nuclear energy—United States—Industrial
applications—History.
I. Hevly, Bruce William.
II. Findlay, John M., 1955–   .
III. Series.
QC773.3.U5A85   1998   98–39504
363.17'99'0978—dc21   CIP

To the memory of

Stanley Goldberg (1934–1996)

Contents

Contents

Acknowledgments

B ecause this anthology has taken some time to make its way into print, people have begun joking about its long half-life. While we detect no signs of decay in the potency of the chapters that follow, it is nonetheless a relief to thank at long last those who have assisted in the project.

The following chapters had their start in 1992 as papers at "The Atomic West, 1942–1992: Federal Power and Regional Development," a symposium sponsored by the Center for the Study of the Pacific Northwest at the University of Washington. The meeting was considerably enhanced by support from the National Science Foundation; Ron Overmann of the NSF proved particularly helpful in overseeing our grant (SBE-9122643). The Museum of History and Industry in Seattle, through the efforts of Wilson O'Donnell and Sheryl Stiefel, graciously cosponsored the symposium. The Department of History contributed valuable resources at a time when the Center was just getting started; Marge Healy and Jennifer Alexander proved especially helpful in organizing and running the meeting. And we learned a great deal from the many people who attended.

The conference and this book have both benefited from considerable support from the Emil and Kathleen Sick Lecture-Book Series in Western History and Biography. This generous endowment teams up the Department of History and the University of Washington Press to encourage good scholarship in regional history. The collaboration it entails has been a pleasant experience. Julidta Tarver, managing editor of the Press, has been both patient and persistent in her support of the project from its inception. She found anonymous referees for the manuscript who made valuable suggestions for revision. Leila Charbonneau brought greater cogency to the chapters through skillful and humane copy-editing.

At the Center for the Study of the Pacific Northwest, Kim McKaig good-naturedly kept the book project organized and on track, and took care of countless details to ensure its completion. James B. Morrison created the maps of the Atomic West, eastern Washington, and the Great Basin; Dan O'Neill contributed the map of Alaska.

As this book has made its way into print, the authors' research has appeared in other forms. Dan O'Neill's chapter was originally published in somewhat different form as "H-Bombs and Eskimos: The Story of Project Chariot," *Pacific Northwest Quarterly* 85 (January 1994): 25–34. We appreciate the *Quarterly*'s permission to redo the essay. Thomas Wellock's chapter comes from his book *Critical Masses*, and the University of Wisconsin Press has kindly agreed to let us share it.

It troubles us deeply that one of the contributors to this collection is not alive to see it in print. Stanley Goldberg died in October 1996. His chapter, which his family graciously has permitted us to publish here, attests eloquently to his gifts as a historian. What is less apparent are the warmth and wit and level of engagement with the issues surrounding America's nuclear history that he possessed. Stan was like a magnet at our 1992 symposium: others gathered around to hear what he had to say and discuss our findings with him. He drew provocative conclusions for us, and challenged us to think anew about our responsibilities as scholars and citizens. Dedicating the book to Stan's memory is but one small way to acknowledge a lifetime of contributions.

The Atomic West

The Atomic West

Region and Nation, 1942–1992

Bruce Hevly and John M. Findlay

O n December 2, 1942, in a prototype reactor on a University of Chicago squash court, a team of scientists under the leadership of the Italian physicist Enrico Fermi created the world's first self-sustaining nuclear reaction. Nobel Prize winner Arthur Holly Compton, who oversaw the Chicago research effort, witnessed the event and then called chemist James Bryant Conant in Washington, D.C., to report this critical step in the race to beat Nazi Germany to the atomic bomb. According to his recollections, Compton had to convey his message across unsecured telephone lines, and at the same time apologize because the breakthrough had come a week ahead of schedule and Conant had missed the opportunity to be there.

"Jim," Compton said, "you'll be interested to know that the Italian navigator has just landed in the new world. . . . [T]he earth was not so large as he had estimated, and he arrived . . . sooner than he had expected." Conant replied in the spirit of the code: "Were the natives friendly?" "Everyone landed safe and happy," answered Compton.[1]

Comparing advances in physics to the discovery of a new world, the two scientists likened the exploration of the atom to the westering process in America that had begun with Christopher Columbus's voyage 450 years before. In 1942 the pursuit of the atomic bomb was also tied to the American West in a much more concrete fashion. By the time Compton told Conant about the success of the latter-day Italian navigator, the U.S. Army Corps of Engineers had already selected a western site—Los Alamos, New Mexico—for one of the Manhattan Project's key scientific laboratories, and it was preparing to designate another—Hanford, Washington—as the place for manufacturing plutonium for atomic bombs.

Compton's remark that "Everyone landed safe and happy" calls to mind the hopes and fears accompanying exploration of a new scientific frontier. Since early in the twentieth century, Europeans and Americans had held dramatic expectations for the coming of atomic power. The heat and radiation spontaneously emitted by newly discovered substances such as radium, uranium, and polonium, as well as the penetrating radiation released by X-ray equipment, led to a series of utopian and dystopian predictions. Some looked forward to an atomic age, successor to the age of iron and steam, in which abundant power would be the key to economic expansion, leisure, and the eradication of poverty and class strife. Others warned of a coming period of apocalyptic warfare in which "radium bombs" delivered by aircraft might turn cities into rubble, bringing civilization to an end and, perhaps, a new beginning. Prospectively, the power of the atom seemed to promise one of two clear fates: heaven or hell on earth.[2]

It is fitting that the American West played such a prominent role in determining the fate of the atom. The region, like nuclear power, has generally been a realm of dramatic hopes and fears, a place often likened to hell or to heaven, and a setting shaped by collisions among deeply held expectations and between expectation and reality.

One expectation consistently held for the West by federal officials was that it contained ample wide-open spaces for a great variety of experimental activities. That most of those spaces belonged to the U.S. government only made it easier to act on that expectation by putting them to atomic uses. The different federal entities in charge of nuclear weapons programs—the Army between 1942 and 1946; the Atomic Energy Commission (AEC) between 1947 and 1974; the Energy Research and Development Administration (ERDA) between 1974 and 1977; and the Department of Energy (DOE) after 1977—all chose western locales for numerous atomic tasks, especially the dirtier ones. They generally regarded the region as relatively empty, and they valued that undeveloped space for its apparent capacity to buffer people from the dangers associated with making and testing nuclear weapons and storing hazardous wastes.

The Atomic West thus emerged primarily through federal initiatives. But westerners themselves—old-timers and new arrivals both—toiled to make nuclear power a reality and to shape the forms it would take.[3] Through the mid-1970s, the Atomic West succeeded in marrying the purposes of nation with those of the region.

4

All the activities associated with the political economy of nuclear energy eventually took place amid western landscapes. Federal agencies inaugurated them in two significant spurts, one from 1942 to 1945 and the other from 1947 to 1955. During the Second World War, the U.S. Army Corps of Engineers built at Los Alamos a weapons laboratory where atomic bombs were designed and assembled. It simultaneously built and operated the Hanford Engineer Works, which manufactured and stored plutonium. Combining Hanford's raw material with the know-how developed at Los Alamos, the United States ushered in the atomic age with the first detonation of an atomic bomb at the Trinity site near Alamogordo, New Mexico, July 16, 1945; and it brought an end to World War II with the atomic bomb dropped on Nagasaki, Japan, August 9, 1945.[4] Of course, completion of the Manhattan Project depended upon the contributions of organizations in every part of the country; uranium produced at Oak Ridge, Tennessee, fueled the bomb dropped over Hiroshima, on August 6.[5] But the "empty" West garnered more than its share of new and prominent atomic facilities.

After a lull in 1946, the onset of the Cold War accelerated weapons production as well as research and development of new atomic technologies. Consequently, the AEC further advanced the Atomic West, substantially increasing both Hanford and Los Alamos in size beginning in 1947. It also narrowed their functions and reassigned some of the tasks they had performed during World War II to new, more specialized facilities in the West. To test new reactor technologies, the AEC founded the National Reactor Testing Station along the Big Lost River in Idaho in 1949.[6] In 1951 it began detonating nuclear weapons at the Nevada Test Site, fifty miles northwest of Las Vegas. By 1963, about a hundred aboveground nuclear explosions had occurred there.

In 1952 the AEC signed an agreement with the University of California to establish a second western weapons laboratory at Livermore, California. The new institution added to the ties between America's atomic weapons program and the University of California, which already managed the weapons lab at Los Alamos and had undertaken additional work for the AEC on its Berkeley campus. Programs devised at Livermore led to further plans for the West. Project Chariot, conceived by Edward Teller in 1957, proposed to reengineer part of Alaska through underground detonations of nuclear devices. Teller's plan did not come to pass, but nuclear tests were held at Amchitka, in the Aleutian Islands

MAP 1. The Atomic West

National Wildlife Refuge, in 1965, 1969, and 1971. Additional tests were conducted in Colorado and New Mexico.[7]

Elsewhere in the West, the Rocky Flats plant, just outside Denver, was built in 1952 in order to mill plutonium from Hanford into weapons components. Rocky Flats and other sites shipped materials to the Pantex facility in the Texas panhandle, also constructed in 1952, where the AEC now assembled nuclear weapons. Many of these devices became the warheads for missiles that were stationed throughout the country, but particularly in the states of the Great Plains and Rocky Mountains. After 1946, moreover, in response to an AEC program of incentives, mines and mills in the Rocky Mountain states increasingly generated a domestic supply of uranium, one of the raw materials that went into both nuclear weapons and, eventually, nuclear power plants.[8] Meanwhile, civilian nuclear power, developed throughout the country, took on special significance in western regions hopeful that abundant energy would spur industrial development; in this process the federal government played the role of referee, albeit one with considerable interest in the game's outcome.

All of these western nuclear activities generated waste products, and most facilities were engaged (if only passively) in programs of waste storage and management throughout the Cold War period.[9] In the 1980s, when the United States grew more concerned about the environmental and health effects of the wastes generated in the making of bombs, it looked again primarily to western sites in order to address the problems. Facilities such as Hanford, which had by itself generated an enormous amount of waste over the years, began to devote more resources to managing their own pollution. By the end of the decade, clean-up became the primary mission at Hanford, Rocky Flats, and other western sites. Meanwhile, the DOE began to design new national repositories in Nevada and New Mexico for radioactive wastes. The federal government thus brought into the 1990s its tradition of relying inordinately upon the American West as the location for its nuclear programs.

When the Army and AEC began building the Atomic West, public criticism of their programs remained largely muted. In the 1970s and 1980s, by contrast, the federal government encountered growing opposition to these activities. And, as the estimation of the impact of federal weapons programs changed, it became common to interpret them as something imposed by the federal government upon westerners without their consent. It is certainly true that the U.S. government, for a variety of reasons, did not disclose fully the dangers associated with the weapons facilities it placed in the region.[10] But it is also the case that very few westerners objected to the establishment and growth of an Atomic West between the mid-1940s and the mid-1970s. They also tended to view their region as "empty," although for them the term connoted economic underdevelopment. Federal investment in weapons programs promised to fulfill the region's long-frustrated hopes for growth and prosperity, and to help end its colonial status vis-à-vis the East.

Many westerners hoped that industry would both bring new jobs to the region and fit in with the natural environment, providing workers with opportunities for the advantages of life as well as easy access to recreation and open spaces. In fact, creation of the Atomic West accelerated the processes of urbanization and industrialization in western America, moving it a little closer to the dreams of some of its boosters while doing little to protect it from the environmental and cultural changes feared by others. With growth also came greater autonomy from the eastern corporations that had seemed so powerful before World War II, yet the Atomic West was hardly liberated from the East. Now Washington, D.C., rather than Wall Street, more often called the shots, although westerners proved remarkably adept at influencing government decisions about their region.[11] While federal power initiated, managed, and bankrolled the nuclear programs, westerners for most of the postwar period generally helped to shape them. Their advocacy of nuclear power plants served as a measure of their enthusiasm for atomic technologies.

Beginning in the mid-1970s, however, the climate of opinion changed. The harmful effects of federal weapons programs for the West began to gain attention, and doubts surfaced concerning the financial and environmental prospects of nuclear power plants. Contrary to federal officials' vision of a largely vacant area, the West was never nearly empty enough. It contained too many residents who would, inevitably, be exposed to the pollution released by nuclear weapons programs. It also contained intricate ecosystems which, far from making for an "empty" place, ensured that radioactive and chemical wastes would be absorbed into, distributed about, and concentrated within the landscape in quite complicated ways. Over the last two decades, many came to argue that the environmental effects of nuclear weapons programs have pushed the West closer to hell than to heaven. The marriage of nation and region had become strained. Divorce offered no realistic option, of course, but by 1992 the growing tensions marked the end of an era for the Atomic West.

For all that has happened since 1942, neither utopia nor disaster has come to pass as predicted (although, arguably, small groups within the West have experienced some of one or the other). In retrospect, a clear vision of the consequences of atomic power in the West—a determination whether federal nuclear weapons programs made the place more like heaven or hell—is hard to achieve. Indeed, we do not propose that such evaluations are strictly the province of historians. We do contend that, for those engaged in the current debates, a history of the Atomic West can provide a necessary measure of detail, complexity, and, especially, context.

Taken together, the essays in this volume illustrate the value of detail, complexity, and context for students of the Atomic West. The chapters got their start as papers presented at a symposium held at the University of Washington, Seattle, in September 1992. The event marked the fiftieth anniversary of the Manhattan Project's arrival in the West, a suitable occasion to take stock of how the atom and the West have affected one another.[12] The symposium occurred at a time when controversy over the legacy of the Atomic West was cresting. Both new revelations and pending litigation were compelling the region to rethink its nuclear past.

The Atomic West symposium aimed to help along the process of rethinking by demonstrating the usefulness of different contexts for understanding the past, each derived from a different historical perspective. In considering the Atomic West, historians need to consider scholarship from at least three academic specialties. The history of nuclear power was initially of primary interest to historians of American politics and government, and to historians of science and technology. Only more recently has it attracted the attention of historians of the American West, who have begun to study the atom in regional terms. The latter have been drawn to the subject more than before because of a recognition of the importance of federal intervention in settling and shaping western North America since the early nineteenth century, and because of a growing interest in the American West of the twentieth century.[13] In organizing a conference on the subject of the Atomic West, then, one goal was to bring together what had been essentially separate strains of analysis. Work in political history, history of science and technology, and western American history, it was assumed, would benefit from a cross-pollination of questions, methods, sources, and assumptions. Yet, as the essays here demonstrate, such crossbreeding has not created a unified or hybrid nuclear history.

Historians, of course, are not the only ones writing new stories about the Atomic West. Scholars from other disciplines have also contributed to the discussion (and to this anthology). Moreover, the chorus of voices speaking of the Atomic West includes many besides scholars. Ever more prominent are the active participants from the past who offer their reminiscences, drawing on experiences that were not public knowledge during the Cold War. Also, formerly passive participants now demand to be heard. Downwinders are concerned that the facts be known about their exposure to hazardous fallout from atmospheric weapons tests, to the radioactivity and waste products generated in the course of manufacturing plutonium and mining uranium, and to other health risks of America's nuclear programs. Scientific investigation and class-action litigation will contribute additional chapters to the history of the Atomic West.

The chapters that follow have been grouped chronologically. Parts One and Two conform roughly to the first and second spurts of growth, during World War II and the early Cold War, when the federal government created and enlarged the Atomic West. Part Three shifts the focus from the central government to westerners and their increasingly critical response to nuclear programs. Some critics of the Atomic West had emerged by the early 1960s, but the main protests came during and after the 1970s.

In considering the creation of the Atomic West, it is important to keep in mind that wartime building projects occurred within an already established framework. New Deal programs had laid down in the West a foundation upon which federal intervention in the economy, for the purposes of providing power, transportation infrastructure, and the means for economic development, had begun to reshape patterns of settlement and industry.[14]

In the book's first section of three essays on the Manhattan Project, Robert Ficken and Carl Abbott discuss the role of preexisting regional conditions that helped shape the project's final form. Ficken shows how the Army placed the Hanford Engineer Works at a site where New Deal efforts to make use of the Columbia River had already established a powerful federal presence. The problem for many nearby residents was that Hanford's great need for electric power interfered with more locally controlled plans for expanded irrigation and cheap electricity, as promised by the builders of Grand Coulee Dam. Abbott analyzes the construction of the federal towns of Richland and Los Alamos as bedroom communities for nuclear workers. Built during World War II to support the Manhattan Project, these cities drew upon a planning language developed through the course of the New Deal. After the war, the ideas guiding the redesign of the two communities changed to a more suburban-oriented dialect, in keeping with the times.

Stanley Goldberg focuses less on New Deal precedents than on wartime exigencies. He shows how a crucial event at Hanford, the "speedup" of early 1945, mirrored the entire Manhattan Project's rush to build and use a plutonium bomb before the end of the war. Goldberg proposes that a set of internested, complementary goals—to validate General Leslie Groves's war service, justify the project's expense and diversion of critical resources, and bring the war to a speedy conclusion—spurred on the effort to produce plutonium from Hanford's reactors, despite sizable economic and environmental costs.

The three essays in Part One point to a federal government imposing conflicting sets of values on the West. As Ficken and Abbott show, the Manhattan Project built upon and borrowed from New Deal thinking about economic development and the creation of community. Federal planners of the 1930s provided tools with which the Army of the 1940s began to fill in the empty spaces assumed to exist in the West. At the same time, however, these ideas that promoted community and development contradicted the utility of emptiness which was central to the decision made by Leslie Groves to order a speedup at Hanford in the spring of 1945. The consequences of accelerated production of plutonium—in particular a significant increase in the radioactive contaminants emitted by the plant in the course of separating plutonium from irradiated reactor fuel— were consistent with a vision of the area as empty land, but not with the emerging communities of the Manhattan Project or with the emerging development of the Columbia Basin Project. Such complexity comes into the historical picture only through the exploration of local contexts.

The Manhattan Project was a crash effort, not really suitable for reconciling different western visions. At war's end the United States put its continuing commitment to nuclear technology on a different, long-term footing. After 1946 the civilian Atomic Energy Commission, which replaced the U.S. Army's Manhattan Engineer District, oversaw the design of nuclear explosives and reactors and the production and procurement of fissionable materials. It operated under the direction of a board of presidential appointees who served after Senate confirmation and acted in close consultation with Congress and with military and scientific advisory panels.

The AEC's development, testing, and stockpiling of nuclear weapons soon took place within the context of the Cold War and the rise of the national security state, a "state within a state" dedicated to the necessity of a constant mobilization within the dangerous world as perceived by most Americans and their leaders for the two decades after World War II. As Dean Acheson expressed it in 1947, Americans were taking measure of "the fact that the business of dealing with the Russians is a long, long job. . . . [I]t can only be done by the United States getting itself together, determining that we cannot maintain a counter-balance to the communistic power without . . . money, imagination, American skill and American technical help and many, many years."[15]

Embracing the concept of national security, according to historian Daniel Yergin, required "that the country assume a posture of military preparedness; the nation must be on permanent alert. There was a new emphasis on technology and armed force," including the development of an industrial system in support of nuclear weapons.[16] A few public figures such as Henry Wallace questioned some of the axioms on which the national security state rested, but the great majority of the American people and their political leaders supported it through the successive crises in Iran, Greece, Korea, the Mediterranean, and Southeast Asia. Atomic spies, missile gaps, and windows of vulnerability became the stuff of political campaigns, and the counterbalance of nuclear forces was accepted as the recipe for the prevention of all-out war between the superpowers. It thus fell to the Atomic Energy Commission to mobilize the Atomic West for additional national service.

In Part Two, three essays describe some of the features of AEC operations in the postwar West. Two are concerned with the building of institutions for the application of intellectual capital to the development of nuclear weapons. Government-owned, university-operated laboratories occupied sites where western landscapes served to attract scientific talent, and these labs provided western states with an opportunity to stake a claim on federal support for science that might otherwise go to institutions closer to Washington, D.C.

Gregg Herken analyzes the establishment of a cooperative arrangement between the government, academia, and industry by examining how U.S. nuclear weapons laboratories were put on a permanent footing as part of the long-term mobilization of the national security state. Academic sponsors such as the University of California had initially undertaken to operate military laboratories as a wartime exigency; there was no obvious justification to keep the institutions under their wing after the war ended. Herken explores why university leaders made a continuing and expanded commitment to remain involved with American nuclear weapons programs.

Ferenc Szasz adopts a biographical approach in surveying the career of James Tuck. A British recruit to the Manhattan Project, Tuck went from Cambridge University to Los Alamos during World War II and, after a brief return to England, headed back to New Mexico to make a career at the Los Alamos Scientific Laboratory. An enthusiastic booster of fusion power, Tuck represents a figure well known in the history of the American West: an outsider who became an important part of a new community and who saw in it a model for the future.

In the final essay in this section, Barton C. Hacker takes up the issue of the atmospheric fallout from nuclear weapons tests. He describes the ways in which information about possible hazards from the tests was compiled and points to how a monopoly of information served to buttress a system in which the U.S. government made decisions on questions of public health without local involvement. His interpretation is of direct relevance to the ongoing disputes over the consequences of the government's Cold War activities for western citizens.

A common theme in these three essays is the intersection of national and regional currents. At times, differences in power between actors representing the federal government and local concerns were substantial, as Hacker shows. But institutions such as the University of California and individuals such as Edward Teller and James Tuck came to the bargaining table with considerable stock in trade, and they influenced the outcome of federal investment in the West. Although they were the agents of federal power in one sense, they also represented distinct interests rooted in the West and, to some degree, independent of Washington, D.C.

If the Cold War as understood by federal officials composed the general political and cultural context for the postwar development of nuclear technology, the American West framed that technology with a distinctive context of its own. The region experienced dramatic growth after 1940, due largely to wartime and postwar migrations which were in turn stimulated by federal defense spending. Westerners never simply waited for government to promote regional development, however; they also undertook a series of efforts to develop an industrial base capable of supplementing, or perhaps even surpassing, the extractive industry, agriculture, and food processing that had provided so much regional employment over the previous century. Such growth industries as aerospace and electronics not only marked the continuing effect of the federal presence in the economy but also altered relationships between the extractive and the manufacturing West, the rural and the urban West.[17] Demographic and economic growth, furthermore, heightened regional demand for additional electrical power to support the new populations and industries. Nuclear energy, which began to be developed for commercial use in the late 1950s, was regarded as one logical answer to the region's kilowatt needs.

By the early 1970s, the consequences of western demographic and economic expansion in turn would be challenged by the nascent environmental movement, particularly powerful in the West, which often set itself against the forces of development.[18] Environmental concerns lay behind much of the growing skepticism toward nuclear power in the American West after 1960, and this skepticism is a focus of the final section of the book.

Part Three consists of four essays on groups opposed to the development of nuclear technology. Each case demonstrates the local dynamics of dissent against systems constructed to develop nuclear weapons and nuclear power. The essays by Dan O'Neill and Matthew Glass provide an understanding of the mixture of activist cultures that emerged when plans for extending the national security state challenged well-established meanings associated with western landscapes by local inhabitants. As O'Neill argues, some Alaska Natives found that their unwillingness to sacrifice their home country for the sake of the nuclear tests planned for Project Chariot resonated with the commitments of some biologists, anthropologists, and ecologists. Even within the AEC's Washington, D.C., headquarters, a faction argued for a detailed cost-benefit appraisal before undertaking new nuclear tests, a development that did not readily endorse the desires of Chariot's proponents at the Lawrence Livermore Laboratory. Glass discusses the way in which an area in the Great Basin represented a sacred landscape to two disparate

14

groups—the Western Shoshone and the Mormon community centered in Salt Lake City. Each opposed the plan to site MX nuclear-armed missiles in the region. Westerners were no longer so predisposed to favor economic growth, even in "underdeveloped" areas, without looking at the environmental, social, and cultural costs. Their skepticism presented new challenges to federal officials who previously had not encountered so many doubters. In the 1980s and 1990s this turnabout in regional thinking came to plague DOE efforts to design large nuclear waste repositories in Nevada and New Mexico.

The cause of nuclear energy suffered from similarly diminished support. Since before the New Deal the increased production of electrical power had been seen as one key to greater economic development of the western United States. By the time civilian nuclear power became a realistic possibility, westerners had honed their rhetoric concerning power and its importance, especially in public power states such as Washington. As Daniel Pope and Thomas Wellock demonstrate, when a western antinuclear movement emerged in the 1970s to question the common assumption equating progress with abundant electrical power, it had to rely on peculiar political and cultural resources characteristic of local contexts. In California, those opposed to the construction of additional nuclear power plants drew upon both the potential of the initiative system and the emerging strain of antimaterialism within California's suburban white-collar culture. In Washington State, those opposed for environmental or moral reasons to nuclear power found that they could make a more effective argument by appealing to the economics of nuclear energy. They acted not only through referendum but also by pressuring the constituent segments of the Washington Public Power Supply System—the local public utility districts that had to underwrite construction bonds for costly, nuclear-powered generating plants.

Preoccupation with national security during World War II and the Cold War, and utopian predictions about the benefits of abundant energy, had encouraged investment in nuclear technology by the United States. After the 1960s, however, neither set of motivations remained uncontested. To Natives in Alaska, or Western Shoshones and Mormons in the Great Basin, what did "defense" mean if not the preservation of the landscapes with which their particular histories had been bound? And as abundance became a hallmark of the postwar economy, important segments of the community recalled that they expected their energy to be delivered on neo-Edenic terms: inexpensively, and without adverse environmental consequences. The promises of the atom with respect to "defense" and "abundance" were increasingly interpreted according to the local meanings attached to those ideals. As a consequence, the paths of nation and region increasingly diverged.

While America's nuclear programs need to be understood in light of developments in America's military, diplomatic, scientific, and political establishments, as most previous work has attempted to do, they should also be perceived in terms of the *places* they affected—places that in turn affected them. The chapters that follow demonstrate the importance of understanding the contexts, spatial as well as chronological, in which nuclear technologies were developed and debated, embraced or rejected. Regional and local contexts are essential for arriving at a more complex and complete history of American involvement with nuclear technology for energy and military power.

NOTES

1. Arthur Holly Compton, *Atomic Quest: A Personal Narrative* (London: Oxford University Press, 1956), 144. For a more thorough description of the organizational structure of the Manhattan Project and the plutonium effort based in Chicago, see Stanley Goldberg's chapter in this volume. Accounts of the first self-sustaining chain reaction are numerous: see Richard Rhodes, *The Making of the Atomic Bomb* (New York: Simon and Schuster, 1986), 435–42; Emilio Segre, *Enrico Fermi, Physicist* (Chicago: University of Chicago Press, 1970), 128–30; and Robert G. Sachs, ed., *The Nuclear Chain Reaction—Forty Years Later* (Chicago: University of Chicago Press, 1984).

2. Spencer R. Weart, *Nuclear Fear: A History of Images* (Cambridge: Harvard University Press, 1988), part 1. See also George Basalla, "Some Persistent Energy Myths," in *Energy and Transport,* ed. George Daniels and Mark Rose (Beverly Hills, Calif.: Sage Publications, 1982), and Basalla, "Energy and Civilization," in *Science, Technology and the Human Prospect,* ed. Chauncey Starr and Phillip Ritterbush (New York: Pergamon, 1980).

3. Patricia Nelson Limerick coined the term "Atomic West," which we have borrowed for the name of this volume. See her essay, "The Significance of Hanford in American History," in *Washington Comes of Age: The State in the National Experience,* ed. David H. Stratton (Pullman: Washington State University Press,

1992). One discussion of how westerners shaped federal efforts to their own ends is John M. Findlay, "Atomic Frontier Days: Richland, Washington, and the Modern American West," *Journal of the West* 34 (July 1995): 32–41.

4. An overview of the Manhattan Project is best provided by two works which pay little attention to region: Rhodes, *The Making of the Atomic Bomb* (see note 1 above), and Richard G. Hewlett and Oscar E. Anderson, Jr., *A History of the United States Atomic Energy Commission,* vol. 1, *The New World, 1939/1946* (University Park: Pennsylvania State University Press, 1962). On Los Alamos, see James W. Kunetka, *City of Fire: Los Alamos and the Atomic Age, 1943–1945,* rev. ed. (Albuquerque: University of New Mexico Press, 1979). On wartime Hanford, see S. L. Sanger, *Hanford and the Bomb: An Oral History of World War II* (Seattle: Living History Press, 1989); second edition published as *Working on the Bomb: An Oral History of World War II Hanford* (Portland: Portland State University Continuing Education Press, 1995). On the Trinity test, see Ferenc Morton Szasz, *The Day the Sun Rose Twice: The Story of the Trinity Site Nuclear Explosion, July 16, 1945* (Albuquerque: University of New Mexico Press, 1984).

5. During the war, a major new, nonwestern atomic installation was Oak Ridge, Tennessee, which is covered by Charles W. Johnson and Charles O. Jackson, *City Behind a Fence: Oak Ridge, Tennessee, 1942–1946* (Knoxville: University of Tennessee Press, 1981).

6. Jack Holl, "The National Reactor Testing Station: The Atomic Energy Commission in Idaho, 1949–1962," *Pacific Northwest Quarterly* 85 (January 1994): 15–24. In 1949 the government also spun off Los Alamos's Sandia branch laboratory as an independent engineering laboratory under the management of AT&T. See Necah Stewart Furman, *Sandia National Laboratories: The Postwar Decade* (Albuquerque: University of New Mexico Press, 1990).

7. The chapters by Gregg Herken and Dan O'Neill in this volume discuss, respectively, the relationship between the University of California and the AEC, and Project Chariot.

8. Michael A. Amundson, "Home on the Range No More: The Boom and Bust of a Wyoming Uranium Town, 1957–1988," *Western Historical Quarterly* 26 (Winter 1995): 483–505, offers a case study of the uranium industry in the West.

9. Key elements of the story of waste products generated by nuclear weapons tests are covered in two volumes by Barton C. Hacker: *The Dragon's Tail: Radiation Safety in the Manhattan Project, 1942–1946* (Berkeley: University of California Press, 1987); and *Elements of Controversy: The Atomic Energy Commission and Radiation Safety in Nuclear Weapons Testing, 1947–1974* (Berkeley: University of California Press, 1994).

10. Some of the issues are covered by Howard Ball, *Justice Downwind: America's Atomic Testing Program in the 1950s* (New York: Oxford University Press, 1986);

Hacker, *Elements of Controversy* and *The Dragon's Tail;* and the more popular Michael d'Antonio, *Atomic Harvest: Hanford and the Lethal Toll of America's Nuclear Arsenal* (New York: Crown Publishing Group, 1993).

11. Roger Lotchin, *Fortress California, 1910–1961: From Warfare to Welfare* (New York: Oxford University Press, 1992), illustrates how western urbanites lobbied the U.S. government for local investments in defense plants and military bases. See also Findlay, "Atomic Frontier Days." Thomas Wellock's chapter in this volume details efforts to lobby on behalf of nuclear power plants.

12. As a group, the chapters here are representative neither of the conference that engendered them nor of the entire spectrum of topics deserving the attention of historians or already receiving it. Four other papers presented at the meeting have also been published together in a special issue of *Pacific Northwest Quarterly* 85 (January 1994) devoted to the "Nuclear Northwest." Others have appeared elsewhere, or represent parts of larger projects being developed.

13. On these themes in recent western American history, see Richard White, *"It's Your Misfortune and None of My Own": A History of the American West* (Norman: University of Oklahoma Press, 1991), parts 2 and 4; cf. Gerald D. Nash, *The American West Transformed: The Impact of the Second World War* (Bloomington: Indiana University Press, 1985).

14. See especially Richard Lowitt, *The New Deal and the West* (Bloomington: Indiana University Press, 1984).

15. Daniel Yergin, *Shattered Peace: The Origins of the Cold War and the National Security State* (Boston: Houghton Mifflin, 1978), 5.

16. Ibid., 196.

17. Simon Ramo, *The Business of Science: Winning and Losing in the High-Tech Age* (New York: Hill and Wang, 1988), is one participant's account; Ramo was educated at Cal Tech and returned to California after World War II to work in the military electronics industry. John M. Findlay, *Magic Lands: Western Cityscapes and American Culture After 1940* (Berkeley: University of California Press, 1992), and Carl Abbott, *The Metropolitan Frontier: Cities in the Modern American West* (Tucson: University of Arizona Press, 1993), depict the transformation of the West, especially in cities, after 1940.

18. White, *"It's Your Misfortune,"* 552–53, 569–72; Samuel P. Hays, *Beauty, Health, and Permanence: Environmental Politics in the United States, 1955–1985* (Cambridge and New York: Cambridge University Press, 1987).

I. BUILDING A FEDERAL PRESENCE

Grand Coulee and Hanford

The Atomic Bomb and the
Development of the Columbia River

Robert E. Ficken

Writing to political friends in March 1943, an indiscreet congressional staffer revealed details of the nation's most hush-hush military undertaking, a project bound to have a transforming impact on the Pacific Northwest. The contract drawn and signed between the U.S. Army Corps of Engineers and the Du Pont Company, the large chemical corporation, was "so big and so secret," wrote the private secretary of Congressman Walt Horan of Washington State, "that the orders on it which went from the President to General [George C.] Marshall and on down left that space blank which told what it was all about." The arrangement dealt with "no ordinary defense plant or powder plant."[1] Although the exact purpose was no clearer close to home, the sudden flurry of activity on the pancake-flat wedge of land between the Columbia and the lower Yakima Rivers was indeed dramatic. "The Du Pont people and the Army have taken over 650,000 acres," wrote an astounded observer, and "[the] people of White Bluffs, Hanford and other communities have been given 30 days to evacuate."[2]

These writers were unaware that the object of their interest was a key component of the Manhattan Project to develop an atomic bomb. The site for production of plutonium to be used in the bomb must, according to criteria laid down by General Leslie Groves, be remote from population centers and close to substantial quantities of electricity and fresh water.[3] The inhospitable countryside around Hanford, the location of a generally unsuccessful early twentieth-century irrigation venture, satisfied all requirements. The small number of local ranchers and orchardists were easily removed, the Columbia River flowed past in mighty volume, and the recently completed Grand Coulee Dam was ready to meet the demand for power.[4] The atomic bomb, said the popu-

21

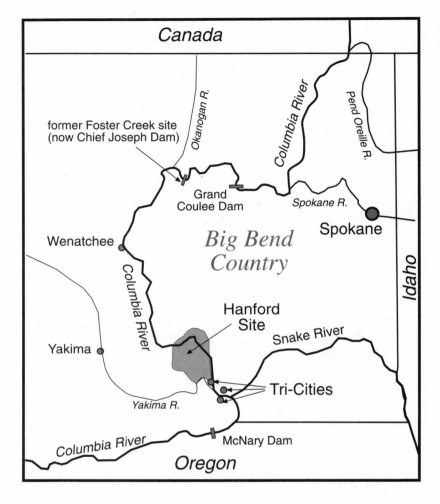

MAP 2. Hanford and the Columbia Basin, Washington

lar writer John Gunther in 1947, was "a kind of apocalyptic, demonic child of the Columbia."[5] The terrifying weapon was also the unintended offspring, one of many ironic descendants, of the long campaign for a giant dam on the upper river. It was, moreover, the progenitor, directly and in symbolic terms, of the full-scale hydroelectric development of the Columbia.

Gunther's "demonic child" traced its lineage back to the period of the First World War and rival home-front plans for reclamation of the arid Columbia Basin. One of these plans, born in the small towns of the Big Bend, called for building a mammoth dam on the Columbia and pumping impounded water into the vast natural irrigation reservoir of the Grand Coulee.[6] The other, generated in Spokane with the influential blessing of the Washington Water Power Company, proposed construction of a so-called gravity canal from the distant Pend Oreille River.[7] In July 1920, the state Columbia Basin Survey Commission—in a finding soon endorsed, for a considerable fee, by General George Goethals of Panama Canal fame—reported in favor of the latter approach. The United States Reclamation Service, fully aware that this conclusion was based more on political calculation than solid engineering data, advised against federal involvement, thus stalling the project for years due to lack of funding.[8]

Serious promotional work resumed in 1929, thanks to the shrewdness of Washington's four-term Republican senator, Wesley L. Jones. Recollecting that a congressional resolution authorized Corps of Engineers "multipurpose" studies of the nation's navigable streams, Jones called on the Army for a detailed survey leading to development of the Columbia. Eager to please a senior legislator and willing to poach upon the preserve of the Bureau of Reclamation, the military responded with the major engineering document known informally as the 308 Report. Completed in its original form in 1931, the study determined, to the satisfaction of all objective observers, that a Grand Coulee dam would be the superior means of watering the Columbia Basin, largely because of the subsidy that would be provided to irrigation by the sale of electricity. The report also posited a series of eight dams on the river, from the giant coulee structure farthest upstream to Warrendale closest to Portland.[9] To the chagrin of local interests, however, President Herbert Hoover privately voiced a strong objection to the findings, on the basis of cost and the need to avoid exacerbating the nation's farm surplus problem. Following the presidential lead, the War Department overruled the recommendations of its field engineers.[10]

Grand Coulee was resuscitated by Franklin D. Roosevelt's 1932 campaign pledge to build the nation's "next great hydro-electric development" on the Columbia River.[11] Early the following year, a new Columbia Basin Commission, appointed by Governor Clarence D. Martin, set about the task of securing federal funds for a dam to be constructed by the state of Washington. Meeting with Senator Clarence Dill, President Roosevelt imposed his own design on the project. To hold down initial costs, the structure must be in the form of a "low dam," with completion to the originally planned height delayed until some unspecified date. Reclamation, still considered by most local supporters the principal benefit of the dam, must be "deferred until such time as existing lands suitable for agriculture have been taken up."[12] Although objecting to these deviations from longtime planning, the state commission had no choice but to accept the president's wishes in the matter.[13] Similar hard logic applied in October 1933 when Secretary of the Interior Harold Ickes, custodian of the $63 million in public works funding allocated to the project, insisted on a federal takeover of the dam. Grand Coulee was transformed, out of fiscal necessity, from a locally built and maintained operation, to be run in the interests of the Big Bend, into the property of the United States.[14]

After close to a year of preparatory labors, construction began in late 1934. In 1935, a change order, pushed by the Bureau of Reclamation on the basis that current project economics made the "low" structure non-competitive with the Army's Bonneville Dam, provided for completion of the original "high dam."[15] Despite occasional political complications, work proceeded in an orderly fashion on what visiting journalists variously described as "the biggest thing on earth," the "great dam," and "the eighth world wonder."[16] Finished in the fall of 1941, with three operating generators in place, Grand Coulee was indeed an impressive monolith. The dam, formed from over nine million cubic yards of concrete, rose 500 feet above the riverbed and held the Columbia back all the way to the Canadian border, a distance of 150 miles. The cost, too, inspired awe, the final official figure of $196 million representing a threefold increase over Roosevelt's truncated design of 1933.[17]

Longtime supporters of Grand Coulee had two prime worries as the dam neared completion. Their intent, dating back to the original formulation of the project, had been to make the Columbia Basin a self-contained unit, free of outside economic or political domination. Industry, located close to the power plant, would provide markets for the produce of farms opened on reclaimed lands. The creation of the Bonneville Power Administration (BPA) as a "provisional" marketing agency threatened the conviction of dam proponents that "this project should be guided by the people of the immediate area concerned." Interest groups in the vicinity of the dam, asserted the Wenatchee publisher Rufus Woods, "will do a better job because it is before them by day and by night."[18] Headquartered in Portland, mixing the output of Grand Coulee with that of Bonneville Dam and at work by 1941 on a regionwide transmission network, the BPA undermined the dream of local control and the belief that locally produced electricity should go to local consumers.[19] The "postage stamp" rate structure, moreover, under which customers paid $17.50 per kilowatt-year for primary power regardless of distance from the generating stations, removed the incentive for manufacturers to build at or near Grand Coulee.[20]

Concern over the role of the Bonneville Power Administration was matched by fear that there would be few customers, no matter what organization acted the part of salesperson. Throughout the 1930s, champions of the Columbia River dams relied on long-term projections of energy consumption and on wishful thinking to refute negative forecasts regarding power sales. Build it, they argued in effect, and the demand will come. J. D. Ross, the first director of the BPA, denounced those "crepe hangers" who considered Bonneville and Grand Coulee prospective "white elephants." New electricity, he insisted, automatically generated markets: "No great hydro power plant ever goes begging." Yet Ross himself, in his previous position as head of Seattle City Light, had asserted that the coulee dam's management would be unable to sell enough electricity to recover the cost of construction.[21] Planning new projects for the interior Pacific Northwest, the Corps of Engineers stressed the paramount need for dams and locks to promote year-round navigation on the Columbia-Snake route between Portland and Lewiston. "Further development of the Columbia River in the interests of power will not be required for many years to come," reported Colonel Thomas Robins, the senior Corps officer in the region.[22]

In a classic example of the importance of timing to historical development, the Second World War rescued Grand Coulee and Bonneville from the danger of becoming "white elephant" scandals. The dams, in turn, made possible a virtual economic revolution. On the eve of Pearl Harbor, three-fourths of the wage earners in the Pacific Northwest labored in the timber industry and in agriculture, traditional activities dating back to the pioneer era of the mid-nineteenth century. For all practical purposes, major industrial activity was limited to production of lumber, pulp, and paper. Four thousand persons, a relative handful compared to later standards, worked in Seattle for Boeing, one of America's several struggling aircraft concerns. Shipyard employment in Washington and Oregon stood, altogether, at fewer than two thousand workers. Until 1940, when a manufacturing center linked to Bonneville commenced production, the closest aluminum plant was in California. The winds of war, driven by a mighty current from the federal dams, swept away this backwoods setting. "Low-cost power from the Columbia," as the Pacific Northwest Regional Planning Commission pointed out in 1943, had "a revolutionary effect upon the industrial development of the region."[23]

The $40 billion expended by the federal government in the West during the war years produced enormous change from the Rockies to the Pacific, from the Mexican border to remote Alaskan outposts. Between 1940 and 1942 alone, over 200,000 newcomers took up jobs in the defense industries of Puget Sound and the Columbia River. Shipbuilders employed 170,000 laborers in 1943. Boeing employment reached 50,000 in 1944, a year in which the company produced $600 million worth of airplanes for the government, or nine times the value of the output for all Seattle manufacturing enterprises in 1939. Wages soared as the draft, enlistments, and the demand for civilian workers overwhelmed the supply of men and women. The population of the Pacific Northwest increased by a fifth over the entire wartime era, but personal income mounted by 162 percent.[24]

Of special importance, Washington and Oregon became major producers of aluminum with five plants, all financed by the federal government. By the end of the war, these outlets turned out, depending on the study consulted, between 37 and 45 percent of the nation's supply of the strategic metal.[25] The availability of cheap Columbia River electricity was, according to the National Resources Planning Board, "the chief drawing-card" attracting manufacturers to the Pacific Northwest. Inexpensive power more than offset the inconvenience and cost involved in transporting raw materials essential to the production of aluminum from distant sources of supply.[26] The industry required 17,000 kilowatt-hours of energy to manufacture a single ton of aluminum and was responsible for much of the massive war-generated increase in electricity consumption.[27]

Hanford, though, was arguably the most dramatic and certainly the most secretive consumer of the Columbia's energy. The initial movement of laborers and equipment into the desert of eastern Washington was quickly noticed by the newspapers, from nearby Pasco to the Puget Sound area and elsewhere. Appealing to publishers on the basis of patriotism, Manhattan Project officials soon erected a cordon of voluntary censorship around the construction site.[28] Private discussion continued unabated, however, especially with respect to the significance of the mysterious goings-on at the Hanford Engineer Works. "They will immediately take all the surplus power from Grand Coulee Dam," a veteran development advocate learned from representatives of Du Pont, the federal contractor. Based on the mistaken belief that Du Pont was erecting an enormous smokeless powder factory, this forecast was nonetheless accurate. Once up and running, the plutonium plants required the entire output of two generators at the Grand Coulee powerhouse.[29]

Together, the Hanford Works and the new aluminum industry placed a severe strain on the existing power network of the interior Northwest. The defense plants, pointed out the Wenatchee newspaperman Rufus Woods, "require service night and day, week in and week out and month in and month out," producing in total "a 100 percent power load" on Grand Coulee. To meet the demand, three generators originally assigned to Shasta Dam in California were shifted north in 1942 and another three units were installed in 1943.[30] Nine weeks after the attack on Pearl Harbor, the Bonneville Power Administration recommended, in addition to expanded capacity at existing projects, the building of two or more of the dams slated for the Columbia under the Army's old 308 Report blueprint. Work must also be expedited, claimed the BPA, at Hungry Horse on the Flathead River of Montana, a distant project capable of enhancing downstream energy production on the Columbia.[31]

Reporting findings submitted by the Corps of Engineers in August 1943, the War Department added to the impression that a power emergency detrimental to America's strategic interests loomed in the Pacific Northwest: "The construction of Bonneville and Grand Coulee Dams and the development of war industries utilizing electric energy generated at these projects has demonstrated the need for the ultimate development of the full water resources of the entire Columbia River Basin."[32] Local booster groups, taking advantage of the situation, demanded new federal undertakings on the river. Self-appointed legislative champions of the Columbia, like Republican Congressman Walt Horan, meanwhile applied pressure in the nation's capital.[33]

Absorbing huge amounts of power and acting as a particularly graphic symbol of the general wartime absorption of energy, Hanford helped throw open the doors to the all-out utilization of the Columbia plotted in the 308 Report. Survey work began in 1942 at Foster Creek, the next dam site downstream from Grand Coulee, and at Umatilla below the mouth of the Snake. The demand added by construction of the plutonium works accentuated the significance of these new dams. Although the final plan for Foster Creek Dam called for the expenditure of $108 million, more than twice the amount posited in previous forecasts, the Army recommended that Congress promptly appropriate the necessary funds.[34] Even with reversion to peacetime rates of electricity consumption, advised Colonel Conrad Hardy, the officer responsible for the study, the output of all existing Pacific Northwest plants would be absorbed within a few years. Unless the needs of the immediate future were properly cared for in the present, Hardy concluded, "the industrial development of the region may be seriously handicapped." The argument was appealing and the need obvious, leading to congressional authorization of Umatilla (renamed McNary Dam after Oregon's late Senator Charles McNary) in 1945 and of Foster Creek (renamed Chief Joseph Dam) in 1946.[35]

Wartime construction planning dealt with more than just power-generating dams. Engineers and local boosters alike considered the Columbia an unpredictable and inefficient resource. Water flowed at the lowest level in winter, when demand was greatest. In spring and early summer, when long days and mild temperatures reduced the need for electricity, the river reached its highest mark. This circumstance was intolerable, at least to the engineering and developmental mentality, wasting an estimated four-fifths of the Columbia's potential energy. The solution was, in theory, simple. "Storage," wrote a military engineer, B. E. Torpen, in the closing days of the war, "is the key to complete development of the Columbia River."[36]

Impounded behind dams for release during normal low-flow periods, stored water increased all-year power generation downriver. The concept, though obvious, was implemented only in the face of economic, geographic, and political obstacles. Engineers such as Torpen mourned the lost opportunity to build "one large dam at The Dalles, creating an inland lake larger than Puget Sound and several hundred feet deep." Such an undertaking, which would, among several unsalutary consequences, flood Hanford, was no longer feasible. Attempts to drown out alternate locations on the Columbia faced opposition from increasingly militant fisheries organizations. The canyons of the Kootenai, the Clark Fork–Pend Oreille, the Spokane and other mountain tributaries, streams generally outside the purview of previous planning studies, were the most viable options.[37] Federal officials based in Seattle and Portland ignored, in the interest of overall regional progress, the possibility that residents of Idaho and Montana might protest destruction of their environment for the benefit of Washington and Oregon.[38]

Planning for the construction of storage dams also brought the United States into conflict with Canada, producing a long-simmering dispute. A third of the total water supply of the Columbia drainage came from north of the border.[39] "The heavy run-off and mountainous topography of the headwaters," reported an American engineering study, "make the Canadian portion of the Columbia River favorable for large storage reservoirs." Such projects "would firm the power at all points below the respective reservoirs." The concept of treating the entire river system as a single entity, without regard to international boundaries, was technically sound and naturally appealing to the United States. Residents of British Columbia, however, where flooding was a minor problem and existing power needs were adequately served by plants in the Fraser River Valley, saw no benefit for themselves in boosting the efficiency of Grand Coulee and other south-of-the-line generating stations.[40]

Different perspectives emerged most clearly in a dispute over the proposed Libby Dam on the Kootenai River of northwestern Montana, a project featuring cross-border stream impoundment.[41] To facilitate work on this prime storage undertaking, the United States in March 1944 requested the International Joint Commission, a body created by the Boundary Waters Treaty of 1909 for just such purposes, to resolve the issue of common river development. The IJC, in turn, appointed a board of American and Canadian engineers to carry out the necessary technical investigation.[42] Meeting for the first time in July, the panel focused on the Kootenai in general and on Libby in particular. Operating on the "basic principle" that "the boundary is to be ignored in setting up the physical elements of the best plan," the board eventually endorsed the Corps of Engineers proposal as the superior alternative, technically and economically.[43] "Basic principles," though, ignored the capacity of adverse public opinion in British Columbia to delay construction for three decades.[44]

Ventures launched in wartime, as the history of Libby Dam suggests, were pursued in the peacetime Cold War era. Grand Coulee, together with Bonneville, drove metals factories, aircraft plants, shipyards, and the Hanford Works, making a signal contribution to victory over the Axis.[45] The dams also set in motion economic and population trends leading to further development of the Columbia and its tributaries, Umatilla and Foster Creek being but the third and fourth steps in implementing an enlarged version of the 308 Report. Building on tendencies evident prior to Pearl Harbor, moreover, defense-generated demand completed the reorientation of Grand Coulee from a local-state to a regional-federal undertaking. "We have gone right smack into centralization instead of decentralization," complained Rufus Woods. "All the benefits from the set-up," agreed one of the publisher's colleagues, ". . . flow off to Portland."[46] In a telling symbol of the new order of things, Wenatchee, the urban center of the Big Bend country, was bypassed by BPA transmission lines linking Grand Coulee with Hanford, the lower Columbia, and Puget Sound.[47]

Drawing large amounts of power and enjoying highest-priority status, Hanford also reshaped and interfered with other federal programs. The Columbia Basin Irrigation Project, as conceived by the local sponsors of Grand Coulee, targeted over a million acres of land for reclamation. Wheat ranchers, however, withdrew some 300,000 acres prior to the July 1945 vote of landowners on the necessary preconstruction Bureau of Reclamation water contract. Remaining property holders assumed a larger per capita burden in repaying their allotted portion of the cost of Grand Coulee Dam and attached works.[48] The burden was increased in the spring of 1949 when the Atomic Energy Commission, worried about the possibility of downwind soil contamination from Hanford, ordered the removal of 173,000 acres in the Wahluke Slope area from the project. On behalf of irrigation advocates, Rufus Woods protested the order of AEC chairman David Lilienthal, claiming that the decision "takes out a large portion" of land equal in extent and quality to "the wonderful Yakima Valley." Although the fiscal consequences for both settlers and the Bureau of Reclamation appeared onerous, considerations of national security and the public health made the proclamation final.[49]

Meanwhile, a postwar economic boom, fueled by defense spending, produced a rapidly accelerating demand for electricity in the Pacific Northwest. Annual per capita consumption increased from 1,500 kilowatt-hours in 1940 to 7,100 in 1955. In the latter year, eight plants in Washington and Oregon produced half the nation's aluminum and accounted for half the electricity consumed in the region.[50] Attempting to keep pace with demand, five new federal dams came on line during this period: Hungry Horse on the Flathead, Albeni Falls on the Pend Oreille, and Chief Joseph, McNary, and The Dalles on the Columbia. Three public utility district (PUD) projects on the upper Columbia, moreover, were completed. Even with these substantial additions to capacity, however, the Bonneville Power Administration predicted regionwide brownouts by the mid-1960s. Seeking a long-range solution to an impending crisis, a federal task force called in 1953 for construction of at least twenty-three power-producing dams in the Columbia Basin.[51]

Federal, state, and local agencies were especially interested in developing the Columbia between Priest Rapids and the reservoir of McNary Dam. The vehicle for this development was a 1957 proposal by the Washington Public Power Supply System, a consortium of utility districts, for a high Ben Franklin Dam near Richland. Designing the optimum plan for implementation of the WPPSS scheme, the Corps of Engineers recommended construction of a $342 million project, capable of producing 352,000 kilowatts of electricity.[52] Citing the dangers of contaminated soil and water, the Atomic Energy Commission interfered with survey work and protested the entire Ben Franklin plan as a threat to Hanford. "The majority of the anticipated problems," reported a high-ranking Army official, "would result from a rise in groundwater elevation reducing the stability of foundations under larger structures, reducing the effectiveness of underground radioactive waste disposal systems, and changing the underground flow pattern so as to permit the seepage of wastes in undesirable locations." Conceding the probability of "adverse effects" on Hanford, the Corps and WPPSS abandoned Ben Franklin, leaving the stretch of river above Richland in an undeveloped state.[53] In the ultimate environmental irony, the presence of a nuclear reservation responsible for radioactive pollution of the Columbia led eventually to the designation of the Hanford Reach as a National Wild and Scenic River.

Grand Coulee was itself built in a river of ironies. Planned as the means of reclaiming the vast Columbia Basin, the dam was built in the 1930s without irrigation features. Conceived to protect local interests from outside domination, the structure emerged from the political process as the property of the United States, constructed and operated by one federal agency, the Bureau of Reclamation, and subject to the marketing dictates of another, the Bonneville Power Administration. Meant to advance peaceful pursuits—farming, mining, and milling—the dam became instead an integral part of the modern military-industrial complex, its energy transformed into aluminum and plutonium. On the Columbia, Grand Coulee and science, mixed together by happenstance, gave birth to the "demonic child" and brought Washington from the periphery to the forefront of the new and uncertain Atomic West.

NOTES

1. Karl Stoffel to Kirby Billingsley, March 12, 18, 29, 1943, Rufus Woods Papers, Wenatchee World, Wenatchee, Washington.

2. Billingsley to Stoffel, March 9, 16, 1943, Kirby Billingsley Papers, North Central Washington Museum, Wenatchee.

3. On the vital importance of electricity to the selection of Hanford, see War Production Board to Bonneville Power Administration, May 11, 1944; Leslie R. Groves Memorandum for UndersecWar, August 11, 1944, both Manhattan Engineer District Records, Record Group (RG) 77, National Archives, Washington, D.C.

4. See introductory entry, F. T. Matthias Diary, Corps of Engineers History Office, Fort Belvoir, Virginia.

5. John Gunther, *Inside U.S.A.* (New York: Harper and Brothers, 1947), 119.

6. *Wenatchee Daily World,* July 18, 1918. At the time, there were no dams on the Columbia River. The only power generated on the upper river came from a small irrigation company plant at Priest Rapids. See Hydro Electric Plants . . . Above the Mouth of the Snake, September 1921, Seattle District Records, U.S. Army Corps of Engineers, RG 77, Seattle Federal Records Center.

7. Marvin Chase to A. P. Davis, February 10, 1919, Columbia Basin Survey Commission Records, Washington State Archives, Olympia. On the competing plans, see Bruce C. Harding, "Water from Pend Oreille: The Gravity Plan for Irrigating the Columbia Basin," *Pacific Northwest Quarterly* 45 (1954): 52–60; Bruce Mitchell, "Rufus Woods and Columbia River Development," *Pacific Northwest Quarterly* 52 (1961): 139–44. The history of the struggle for Grand Coulee Dam belies the hydraulic theorizing of Donald Worster, in which a forceful federal bureaucracy imposes reclamation on an unsuspecting local citizenry. See Donald

Worster, *Rivers of Empire: Water, Aridity, and the Growth of the American West* (New York: Pantheon Books, 1985).

8. *The Columbia Basin Project* (Olympia: Frank M. Lamborn, Public Printer, 1920); George W. Goethals Report on Columbia Basin Irrigation Project, March 20, 1922, copy in Willis Batcheller Papers, University of Washington Libraries, Seattle. For a sample of Bureau of Reclamation views, see D. C. Henny, James Munn, and C. T. Pease to Chief Engineer, December 13, 1920, Department of the Interior Records, Office of the Secretary, 1907–1936, RG 48, National Archives.

9. Wesley L. Jones to Roy R. Gill, January 25, February 26, March 22, 1929, Wesley L. Jones Papers, University of Washington Libraries, Seattle. Prior to the intervention of Senator Jones, Major John S. Butler, the officer in command of the Seattle Corps District, argued against a role for the Army on the upper Columbia. The military engineers, said Butler, ought to avoid the "duplication of effort" involved in taking on a subject best handled by "another department of Government," the Bureau of Reclamation. Butler to Chief of Engineers, December 26, 1928, Seattle District Records; December 14, 1928, Rivers and Harbors Files, Records of the Office of Chief of Engineers, 1923–1942, RG 77, Washington National Records Center, Suitland, Maryland. The report was published as *Columbia River and Minor Tributaries,* 73d Cong., 1st sess., 1933, H. Doc. 103. Revisions made by senior Corps officials resulted in a final list of ten dams. Bonneville Dam eventually supplanted the Warrendale site originally favored by the engineers.

10. Brief of Conversation with President Hoover, October 8, 1931; Report on Meeting with the President, October 1931; James O'Sullivan to Rufus Woods and William Clapp, March 6, 18, 26, and April 7, 1932, all Woods Papers. Charles Hebbard to Gill, November 6, 1931, Roy R. Gill Papers, Washington State University Library, Pullman.

11. The speech also sparked a drive in Oregon for construction of Bonneville Dam. *The Public Papers and Addresses of Franklin D. Roosevelt,* 13 vols. (New York: Random House, 1938–50), 1:727–42. See also Philip J. Funigiello, "The Bonneville Power Administration and the New Deal," *Prologue* 5 (Summer 1973): 89.

12. A. S. Goss to Clarence D. Martin, April 17, 1933, James O'Sullivan Papers, Gonzaga University Library, Spokane. C. C. Dill to Martin, April 17, 19, 21, 26, 1933; to O'Sullivan, April 19, 1933; Franklin D. Roosevelt to Dill, April 20, 1933, all Clarence D. Martin Papers, Washington State University Library, Pullman. Roosevelt's letter to Dill, detailing the points discussed, has been published in Edgar B. Nixon, ed., *Franklin D. Roosevelt and Conservation, 1911–1945,* 2 vols. (Hyde Park, N.Y.: Roosevelt Library, 1957), 1:158–59.

13. Woods to E. F. Banker et al., November 10, 1933; Banker to W. Gale Matthews, May 2, 1933; Matthews to Harvey Smith, April 28, 1933, all in Columbia Basin Commission Records, Washington State Archives, Olympia. Willis Batcheller to O'Sullivan, April 21, 1933, O'Sullivan Papers.

14. Minutes, October 20, 31, 1933; O'Sullivan to Martin, October 28, 1933, all in Columbia Basin Commission Records. O'Sullivan to Woods, October 28, 1933, O'Sullivan Papers. Woods to Dill and John Bowen, October 26, 1933; to Batcheller, November 6, 1933, Woods Papers. Dill to Martin, October 28, 1933, Martin Papers.

15. Elwood Mead to Harold L. Ickes, December 19, 27, 1934, May 11, 20, and June 4, 1935, Department of the Interior Records, Office of the Secretary, 1907–36. Grand Coulee began as a $63 million project funded by the Public Works Administration. The state of Washington provided $377,000 for engineering studies and clearing of the dam site. Congress authorized the dam in 1935, and construction was thereafter financed by annual appropriations.

16. Richard L. Neuberger, "The Biggest Thing on Earth," *Harper's* 174 (1937): 247–58; Stuart Chase, "Great Dam," *Atlantic Monthly* 162 (1938): 593–99; Robert Ormond Case, "The Eighth World Wonder," *Saturday Evening Post* 208 (July 13, 1935): 23 ff. For detailed coverage of the dam's construction, see Paul C. Pitzer, *Grand Coulee: Harnessing a Dream* (Pullman: Washington State University Press, 1994), chaps. 6–13. Also see Richard Lowitt, *The New Deal and the West* (Bloomington: Indiana University Press, 1984), 163–70.

17. S. O. Harper to Marshall Dana, July 6, 1935, National Resources Planning Board Records, RG 187, Seattle Federal Records Center.

18. Woods to Paul J. Raver, July 21, 1943, Woods Papers. The BPA was established in 1937 as a means of temporarily resolving debate over whether an existing federal agency or the proposed Columbia Valley Authority should be responsible for selling power from Bonneville Dam. Grand Coulee, nearing completion, was placed under the marketing jurisdiction of the BPA in 1940. On the creation of the BPA, see Charles McKinley, *Uncle Sam in the Pacific Northwest: Federal Management of Natural Resources in the Columbia River Valley* (Berkeley: University of California Press, 1952), 157–62; Herman C. Voeltz, "Genesis and Development of a Regional Power Authority in the Pacific Northwest, 1933–43," *Pacific Northwest Quarterly* 53 (1962): 65–69.

19. Construction of the transmission system is covered in Charles E. Carey, "The Bonneville Project," *Proceedings of the Fifth Pacific Northwest Regional Planning Conference, April 27–29, 1939* (Portland, 1939?), 131; *Columbia River and Tributaries,* 87th Cong., 2d sess., 1962, H. Doc. 403, vol. 2, app. C, part 1, 4–5; part 3, 1; McKinley, *Uncle Sam in the Pacific Northwest,* 170–72.

20. Woods to Arthur Langlie, October 4, 1944, Woods Papers. BPA rate policies are summarized in Paul J. Raver's address to Seattle Rotary Club, December 4, 1940, Warren G. Magnuson Papers, University of Washington Libraries, Seattle. Also see McKinley, *Uncle Sam in the Pacific Northwest,* 167–68; Funigiello, "Bonneville Power Administration," 91–92.

21. Ross to Roosevelt, May 31, 1938, Rivers and Harbors Files, Records of the Office of Chief of Engineers, 1923–1942 (see note 9 above). On Ross's career with the BPA, cut short by his death in 1939, see Funigiello, "Bonneville Power Administration," 89–93.

Ross's change of position reflected an altered bureaucratic perception. At City Light, he sought federal funding for the Seattle utility's Skagit River power project and viewed Grand Coulee as a rival for both financing and eventual customers. Ross to Guy Myers, January 17, 1934; to Ralph A. Horr, January 25, 1934; to Ross Tiffany, August 4, 1934; to Charles H. Ireland, August 18, 1934, Seattle Lighting Department Records, University of Washington Libraries, Seattle.

22. Thomas M. Robins to Chief of Engineers, June 30, 1937, in 75th Cong., H. Doc. 704; to Chief of Engineers, March 3, 1934; Report of Technical Advisory Committee, March 24, 1934; Proceeding of Conference on Power Uses, December 14, 1934, all North Pacific Division Records, U.S. Army Corps of Engineers, RG 77, Seattle Federal Records Center.

23. National Resources Planning Board, *Pacific Northwest Region: Industrial Development* (Washington, D.C.: Government Printing Office, 1942), 19, 21, 22, 29–30; *Pacific Northwest Development in Perspective* (Portland: Pacific Northwest Regional Planning Commission, 1943), n.p.

24. Gerald D. Nash, *The American West Transformed: The Impact of the Second World War* (Bloomington: Indiana University Press, 1985), 17, 79; National Resources Planning Board, *Pacific Northwest Region,* 4–5, 19, 30; *Columbia River and Tributaries,* app. C, part 5, 23. Hours worked in Washington State increased by 24 percent between 1940 and 1946, but payrolls were up 105 percent. *Employment Trends in Basic Industries, Sept. 1940–Aug. 1946* (Olympia: State Department of Conservation and Development, 1947), 10.

25. *Columbia River and Tributaries* (see note 19 above), app. C, part 6, 4; *Columbia River and Tributaries, Northwestern United States,* 81st Cong., 2d sess., 1950, H. Doc. 531, 65, 3110, 3154; National Resources Planning Board, *Pacific Northwest Region,* 29; Gerald D. Nash, *World War II and the West: Reshaping the Economy* (Lincoln: University of Nebraska Press, 1990), 101.

26. National Resources Planning Board, *Pacific Northwest Region,* 29; Nash, *American West Transformed,* 29. On the general subject of power's role in war mobilization, see Philip J. Funigiello, "Kilowatts for Defense: The New Deal and the Coming of the Second World War," *Journal of American History* 56 (1969): 604–20.

27. *Columbia River and Tributaries,* app. C, part 6, 3; *Columbia River and Tributaries, Northwestern United States,* 3156; Federal Power Commission Staff Report on Proposed Umatilla (McNary) Dam, February 1946, file 1505–22, Upper Columbia Basin, Seattle District Office, U.S. Army Corps of Engineers. As an example of

aluminum's drain on power, 40 percent of the energy sold by the BPA in August 1947 went to the industry. Memorandum, September 12, 1947, Columbia Basin Commission Records.

28. Matthias Diary, March 10, April 19, 23, 25, 27, May 3, and June 5, 12, 1943.

29. Billingsley to Stoffel, March 16, 1943, Billingsley Papers; Marc Reisner, *Cadillac Desert: The American West and Its Disappearing Water* (New York: Viking, 1986), 170.

30. Woods to Walt Horan, August 23, 1943; to Henry Carstensen, January 13, 1943, Woods Papers.

31. Bonneville Power Administration Service Report, February 12, 1942, Magnuson Papers; C. R. Moore to Division Engineer, February 27, 1942, Rivers and Harbors Files, Records of the Office of Chief of Engineers, 1923–1942. Locally based Army engineers, figuring an anticipated postwar depression into the equation, still regarded one new Columbia River dam as an absolute necessity by 1950. H. G. Roby to Wood, July 26, 1945, Accession 68A-1926, Records of the Office of Chief of Engineers, 1943—Washington National Records Center (hereafter Acc. 68A-1926, Chief of Engineers Records).

32. Robert A. Lovett to Cordell Hull, August 23, 1943, Acc. 68A-1926, Chief of Engineers Records.

33. Herbert J. Wild to District Engineer, April 16, 1942, Rivers and Harbors Files, Records of the Office of Chief of Engineers, 1923–1942; Horan to Carstensen, June 3, 1944, Walt Horan Papers, Washington State University Library, Pullman.

34. Conrad P. Hardy to Division Engineer, August 15, 1945, file 1505–22, Upper Columbia Basin; Horan to Robins, November 2, 1945, and Robins to Horan, November 15, 1945, Horan Papers.

35. Hardy to Division Engineer, August 15, 1945, File 1505–22, Upper Columbia Basin. On Umatilla Dam, see William F. Willingham, *Army Engineers and the Development of Oregon: A History of the Portland District, U.S. Army Corps of Engineers* (Washington D.C.: Government Printing Office, 1983), 150–51. Foster Creek was eventually named Chief Joseph Dam in a clumsy attempt to appeal to Indians on the adjacent Colville Reservation.

36. B. E. Torpen memorandum, Storage for Power, Columbia River Basin, August 1945, file 1505–2, Upper Columbia Basin.

37. B. E. Torpen, "Power and Columbia River Storage: Projects in the Region's Potential," December 12, 1951, Columbia Basin Inter-Agency Committee Records, University of Washington Libraries, Seattle. Storage dams generated electricity, but their primary function was the impoundment of water for release in the interest of efficient operation of downstream plants.

38. On the rise of opposition in Idaho and Montana, see J. P. Alvey to Hugh B. Mitchell, June 13, 1946, Hugh B. Mitchell Papers, University of Washington Libraries, Seattle.

39. Background on International Columbia River Investigations, n.d., Acc. 68A-1926, Chief of Engineers Records; Paul J. Raver, "The Challenge to Statesmanship," *Pacific Northwest Quarterly* 49 (1958): 99.

40. "Columbia River and Tributaries, Northwestern United States," 395; Background on International Columbia River Investigations, n.d., Acc. 68A-1926, Chief of Engineers Records; *Columbia River and Tributaries,* 1:128.

41. Complicating the situation, the 1846 treaty resolving the Oregon boundary dispute obligated the United States to take no action restricting navigation on the Columbia. Although the federal government had authority over navigable waters south of the border, moreover, the Dominion of Canada delegated this responsibility to the provinces, giving greater weight to the impact of popular opinion in British Columbia. *Columbia River and Tributaries, Northwestern United States,* 351–53; W. O. Silverthorn to L. L. Wise, January 7, 1955, Columbia Basin Inter-Agency Committee Records; V. Meek to Robins, August 8, 1945, Acc. 68A-1926, Chief of Engineers Records.

42. Background on International Columbia River Investigations, n.d.; Lovett to Hull, August 23, 1943; Robins to Hardy, April 7, 1945; Hardy to Weber, September 19, 1945, all Acc. 68A-1926, Chief of Engineers Records. Silverthorn to Wise, January 7, 1955, Columbia Basin Inter-Agency Committee Records.

43. Interim Report on Kootenay River to the International Joint Commission, November 1, 1950; L. H. Hewitt to G. L. Beard, enclosing Preliminary Notes, July 1, 1949, both File 1505–22, Libby Project, Seattle District Office, U.S. Army Corps of Engineers; to Theron Weaver, March 11, 1949, Acc. 68A-1926, Chief of Engineers Records.

44. Congress authorized construction of Libby Dam in 1950, but the failure of diplomacy brought preliminary work to a halt in 1955. Conclusion of a Kootenai River agreement in 1961 allowed planning to resume, and the dam was finished in the mid-1970s. Silverthorn to Wise, July 7, 1955, Columbia Basin Inter-Agency Committee Records; Comprehensive Framework Study, 110, Pacific Northwest River Basins Commission Records, University of Washington Libraries; *Portland Oregonian,* March 16, 1961, clipping in Northwest Public Power Association Records, University of Washington Libraries.

45. For one of many arguments stressing the contribution of Grand Coulee to victory, see Billingsley to Mitchell, May 21, 1946, Mitchell Papers.

46. Woods to Emil Hurja, August 7, 1941, Woods Papers; Billingsley to Stoffel, March 16, 1943, Billingsley Papers.

47. Woods to Raver, April 21, 27, 1942, Woods Papers.

48. *Wenatchee Daily World,* July 28, 30, 1945; Paul C. Pitzer, "Visions, Plans, and Realities: Irrigation on the Columbia Basin Project" (Ph.D. diss., University of Oregon, 1990), 77–80, 83–85.

49. *Wenatchee Daily World,* April 20, 1949; Michele Stenehjem Gerber, *On the*

Home Front: The Cold War Legacy of the Hanford Nuclear Site (Lincoln: University of Nebraska Press, 1992), 107–10.

50. *Columbia River and Tributaries,* 1:10–11, 13, 46, 48; app. C, part 5, 37–38, 45, 170, 183; part 6, 1, 3–7, 13.

51. Ibid., app. C, part 1, 1; Westby and Gedney Memorandum, April 17, 1958, file 1505–22, Upper Columbia Basin; T. H. Lipscomb to Gus Norwood, September 21, 1950; Fernald et al. to Scheufele, September 10, 1953, both Northwest Public Power Association Records.

52. The project name was an amalgam of Benton and Franklin Counties. Plan of Survey, Ben Franklin Project, April 29, 1960, file 1517–08, Survey Reports, Seattle District Office, U.S. Army Corps of Engineers.

53. The failure of the Ben Franklin project also led to the fateful decision of WPPSS, based on BPA predictions of impending power shortages, to proceed with construction of five nuclear plants, three slated for Hanford. *Columbia River and Tributaries,* 1:228, 230–232; Robert Young to Division Engineer, March 15, 1960; Plan of Survey, Ben Franklin Project, April 29, 1960; Cassidy to Kenneth J. Bousquet, January 25, 1961, all file 1507–08, Survey Reports.

General Groves
and the Atomic West

The Making and the Meaning of Hanford

Stanley Goldberg

Most histories of the atomic bomb concentrate on the efforts to solve technical conundrums and escape seemingly blind alleys in the struggle to make the bomb a reality. The basis for tribute is often the technical competence and ingenuity of the scientists and engineers who figured out how to manufacture the nuclear fuels and develop the components that went into the first bombs in time for use during the Second World War.

Many historians are awed by the technical accomplishments of Manhattan Project scientists, engineers, and technicians. I view the Manhattan Project as a very large, complex industrial organization in which solving technical problems was but one aspect of completing the first bombs by the end of the war. As I have argued elsewhere, a major motivating force in making sure that the bomb *was* used during the war was the self-interest of General Leslie R. Groves, the military head of the project; and similar motives impelled some of the civilians in the War Department to whom Groves reported.[1] From the moment he was placed in command of the Manhattan Engineer District (MED), commonly referred to as the Manhattan Project,[2] Groves did everything possible to ensure that the atomic bomb was built and used before the war's end. His allies in this effort were Secretary of War Henry Stimson, Assistant Secretary of War Robert P. Patterson, Head of the Office of Scientific Research and Development (OSRD) Vannevar Bush, and Bush's second in command, James B. Conant. In effect, Groves was their agent. Consciously or not, they made sure that all the right doors were open to him.

Whether or not the Japanese would have surrendered without an Allied invasion if the bomb had not been used is not a subject considered in this article. What I will show is that Groves and his War Department superiors took all steps possible to be sure that the atomic bomb played a role in bringing the war to an end. Indeed, they were fearful that the war would end *before* the bomb was used.

Other motivations for using the bomb at the end of the war, it has been argued, were to put the Russians on notice regarding postwar adventurism and to end the war before the Soviet Union could get a firm foothold in the Pacific theater. There is ample evidence to support such views concerning other motivations, and this article will not attempt to analyze their relative weights. My concern here is to examine the means used to complete construction of the project's major industrial and laboratory facilities, document how Groves pressured the management of those installations to produce enough fissionable material as quickly as possible to ensure that atomic bombs would be ready for use, and show how he then pressed his representatives on the island of Tinian to make haste to send the atomic bomb–carrying B-29s on their way to Hiroshima and Nagasaki.[3]

Groves mercilessly drove all Manhattan Project facilities. His hand is particularly evident at the Hanford Engineer Works (HEW) located along the Columbia River in south-central Washington State. This site manufactured and purified plutonium, the fuel for the cores of the implosion bomb tested at the Trinity site at Alamogordo, New Mexico, in July 1945 and dropped on Nagasaki three weeks later. This essay focuses a good deal of attention on the management of Hanford, but that should not be taken to suggest that Groves's approach there differed from the methods he used at other MED facilities.

The use of the atomic bomb against Japan had at least as much to do with politics internal to the United States, and with politics internal to the American military bureaucracy, as it did with the beginnings of our international competition with the Soviet Union or with our war against Japan.

LESLIE GROVES

Just before being appointed to head the Manhattan Project, Groves was deputy chief of the Construction Division of the Army Corps of Engineers. His rise to that position had been meteoric. Promoted from captain to major in July 1940, by November he was a colonel and effectively in charge of all new Army construction within the United States. Groves himself had demanded the rank of colonel, reasoning that otherwise he would not command the necessary respect and authority from Army subordinates or from the civilian contractors who would answer to him. His services were so much in demand that the orders for his promotion were on President Roosevelt's desk within twenty-four hours.[4]

In moving from major to colonel (bypassing the rank of lieutenant colonel), Groves jumped over the seniority claims of officers from eight West Point classes, and some of them were not pleased. Groves couldn't have cared less, for typically his only concern was to get the job done right and on time—whatever the job was, whatever it took to do it. His forte was untangling bureaucratic and administrative messes by zeroing in on the nub of a problem. He had a solid understanding of engineering practice, and when he moved into unfamiliar territory he did his homework with a vengeance. He was bluff, brooked no nonsense, and displayed little tact. He always appeared genuinely self-assured, and once he made a decision he never second-guessed himself or showed any evidence of being worried about the consequences.

Most people did not see another side of this confident personality. Groves had a solid intuition about people. He could quickly size up a new acquaintance and decide whether that person would be a help or a hindrance. These attributes supported his administrative style, which centered on keeping the size of his organization to a minimum. On the one hand he freely delegated authority; on the other, he demanded competence and loyalty from those he hired. His judgment rarely failed him in this regard. When it did, he was ruthless in getting rid of the person. During World War II, those officers and enlisted men who worked for MED whom Groves decided had to go—either because he judged them to be incompetent or because he suspected, but could not prove, that they talked too much about what they were working on— would be summarily ordered to a new posting, often in the Aleutian Islands or an equally remote place, making it unlikely that loose talk would go anywhere. In one case, Groves was convinced that a physicist was passing information to the Soviets and insisted that he be drafted and sent through basic training. Each time the man's unit was ordered to the Pacific theater, he would be transferred to a new unit just starting basic training.[5]

He delegated authority without hesitation because he believed that responsibility without authority undermined morale. But he built his organization in such a way that he could identify and confront the responsible individual at any level. Groves and his very small staff directed operations efficiently.[6] Those who shouldered the responsibilities in a manner that advanced his program admired and appreciated his administrative style because he left them alone to do their jobs. Those who failed to meet his expectations found him monitoring their work, then interfering with it, and, if matters did not improve quickly, they were demoted or transferred. Their attitudes ranged from fear to loathing and hatred. Few were neutral.

Aside from his work on the atomic bomb, Groves is best known for supervising the construction of the Pentagon (1941–42), a role he was fiercely proud of and defended throughout his life against any charges of waste or mismanagement. But the Pentagon was just one of the projects he controlled and directed. At the height of war mobilization in the summer of 1941, he was responsible for managing construction contracts that were being assigned at the rate of $600 million a month—roughly $6 billion dollars a month in 1994 dollars. There is ample evidence that Groves kept on top of it all.[7]

GROVES TAKES CHARGE

Groves's appointment as head of the Manhattan Project came in September 1942, just after the peak in mobilization construction had passed. For him the assignment was a bitter disappointment. Anticipating the upcoming North African campaign, he wanted command of a Corps of Engineers combat regiment. Success in that kind of command was the surest road to rapid promotion. Groves loved his country but he also was very ambitious, and among the peers he had outraged he was extremely unpopular. In fact, by the spring of 1942, Groves's superiors were under heavy pressure to get rid of him.[8]

Responsibility for managing the program to build an atomic bomb had been turned over to the Army Corps of Engineers in June 1942. Previously, the program, which had been devoted almost entirely to laboratory work, had been lodged within the organizational structure of the National Defense Research Committee (NDRC), which itself was to evolve into the Office of Scientific Research and Development (OSRD) on July 1, 1941. The head of NDRC, Vannevar Bush, had designated his second-in-command James B. Conant to oversee the Uranium Project, then known by the code name S-1. The decision to turn responsibility of the project over to the Army Corps of Engineers stemmed from Bush's conviction that whether or not the United States knew how to produce a practical fission weapon, it had to make an all-out effort to do so. The evidence available to him suggested that Germany was well on its way to making a fission bomb, and he recognized that it would be catastrophic if this should happen before the United States had its own nuclear weapon. Before the war, opponents of the idea of a massive effort to build an atomic bomb had argued that to make an all-out attempt would violate the basic premise for deciding which technical projects would receive attention and support: only projects that could be utilized in *this* war should receive attention. In the summer and fall of 1941, Bush engineered at least the appearance of a consensus among consultants that an atomic bomb could be completed in time to be used during the war.[9]

Bush's choice of the Corps of Engineers to complete the project was based in part on the fact that it possessed the talent and equipment to build the factories that would be needed as the project moved from research and development to manufacture. An equally important reason was that the required funding could be easily hidden in the Corps' massive wartime budget. Until the summer of 1942, work on the atomic bomb had been paid for out of emergency funds that Congress had authorized for President Roosevelt, but Congress had not been involved or consulted on this particular use of the funds. By mid-1942 the atomic bomb project had become too expensive to fund in this way, and however it was to be funded, Bush wanted to make sure that the details of the project were kept from Congress, not so much because he did not trust congressmen to keep it secret, but because he was sure that congressional oversight would create unacceptable delays.[10]

When responsibility for the project was formally turned over to the Corps of Engineers in June 1942, it was placed under the command of James C. Marshall, a competent but easy-going administrator. Marshall's approach was sure, but cautious and hesitant. The Corps' Real Estate Division had recommended a site for the project's factories in a 57-square-mile parcel of land along the Clinch River in eastern Tennessee. But Marshall sat on that recommendation and by September 1942 Bush was concerned over lack of obvious progress within MED. Major sums of money had been committed, yet nothing of consequence seemed to be happening. He demanded that Colonel Marshall be replaced. Groves's superiors saw their chance to kill two birds with one stone. They could push Groves out of the way and also satisfy Bush's demands, noting that they had appointed the man everyone acknowledged as knowing— better than anyone else in their command—how to get things done.

Bush, however, was quite unprepared for Leslie R. Groves, who appeared in his office on September 17, 1942, and announced that he had been appointed to run MED. Groves went on to say that he would not take official command until after his promotion to brigadier general had been approved. (The recommendation was made on September 17 and was approved and announced on the 23rd.) Bush was convinced that Groves's overbearing attitude would have disastrous consequences.[11]

Groves's style is revealed by his activities between the time he left Bush's office and the day his appointment became official. In his Manhattan Project memoir he noted that on September 19 he paid a visit to Donald Nelson, head of the War Production Board. At the start of the Manhattan Project in June, when Colonel Marshall had requested a high manpower and matériel priority, the request had been brushed aside. Both Nelson and General Lucius Clay, deputy chief of staff for requirements and resources, were skeptical and they gave the project an AA-3 rating; high, but not high enough. It was the standard priority rating for construction projects.[12] This meant that there would be delays in the acquisition of apparatus and machinery made of essential materials. Marshall was unhappy about the rating but had quietly accepted it. Now, Groves related, he confronted Nelson and told him that MED's secret work was much too vital to the war effort to be saddled with a AA-3 rating. Groves also told Nelson that he, Groves, required authorization to assign whatever rating was required to get the job done. When Nelson flatly refused, Groves unhesitatingly told Nelson that he would have to tell President Roosevelt that his director of war mobilization disagreed with the president's judgment that the Manhattan Project was the most important program of the war and he would therefore have to recommend to the president that the project be canceled. It was a typical Groves bluff, and he left Nelson's office with a letter from Nelson— dictated by Groves—which read: "I am in full accord with the prompt delegation of power . . . through you to the District Engineer, Manhattan District, to assign a AAA [the highest] rating, or whatever lesser rating will be sufficient to those items the delivery of which in his opinion, cannot otherwise be secured in time for the successful prosecution of the work under his charge."[13]

Several days later, on September 23, Stimson convened a status review meeting. Attending were Groves; Patterson; Chief of Staff General George C. Marshall; Head of Services of Supply (SOS, the umbrella organization for the Corps of Engineers) General Brehon Somervell; and his chief of staff, General Wilhelm Styer. Also at the meeting was the Navy representative to the Manhattan Engineer District, Admiral William R. Purnell, as well as Conant and Bush. In the middle of the meeting Groves suddenly got up and asked to be excused. If nothing more significant was to be considered, he explained, he was leaving for Tennessee to examine firsthand the parcel of land recommended as the site for the project. It was a bold but typically Grovesian move. Calculated or not, this was probably the moment when Bush and Conant began to understand why Styer and Somervell had been so confident that Groves was the right man for MED.[14] Within twenty-four hours of leaving the meeting, Groves ordered the Corps of Engineers Real Estate Division to begin land-taking procedures for the 57-square-mile parcel of land that was to become Oak Ridge.

COURTING DU PONT

Bush's original scheme for the atomic bomb project assumed that the entire factory complex for producing nuclear fuel and building the bomb itself would be located at one site. The Army had decided to locate that site in eastern Tennessee, the Oak Ridge parcel.[15]

But Conant, who always insisted that work on the bomb should be restricted to activities that would result in a weapon for the current war, was highly skeptical that enough plutonium could be made in the time required.[16] Even before the Manhattan Project, in spite of opposition from the scientists within the project, Conant had advocated exploiting industrial expertise from the private sector because he believed the scientists had no experience and no special talent for such a large-scale task. Thus, in August 1942, he secured the temporary services of a Du Pont chemical engineer to help assess the degree to which Arthur Compton, director of the Uranium Project's Metallurgical Laboratory (Met Lab) at the University of Chicago, had mapped out a realistic schedule to design and construct plutonium reactors and separation plants.[17]

That is where the situation stood when Groves went to Chicago on October 5, 1942, to begin visiting all the major facilities of his newly acquired command. He was appalled at what he found. When appointed, he had been told that the basic studies of isotope separation, plutonium manufacture, and bomb physics had been completed and all that would be required was to construct the factories necessary to do the job and organize and oversee the work force. What he found instead was uncertainty, doubt, and what he would have termed ignorance. Not only had the reactors for the production of plutonium not been designed, there had not even been a demonstration that a sustained nuclear chain reaction could be achieved. Nor were there any designs for the factories needed to separate the plutonium, once produced, from uranium. In fact, there was not even a bench-top model for this task.[18]

What probably disturbed Groves most was the attitude and working habits of the scientists whose efforts were supposed to guide the decisions on manufacture. Groves was an engineer. In his own work he relied on estimates based on calculations made with as much precision as possible. While such specifications might be the hallmark of the scientist at his or her lab bench, especially when having to distinguish relatively small differences between large numbers, in projecting a plan of research and development it was common practice for scientists to be satisfied with order-of-magnitude estimates (one order of magnitude being a factor of ten). Such practices unnerved Groves and many of his Army engineer colleagues. Orders of magnitude are not very helpful if you are engineering the foundation for a building or a bridge pier.[19] So it is understandable that Groves might have been dumbfounded when one of the scientists told him that the amount of uranium 235 required for the bomb, to one order of magnitude, would be five kilograms. Groves considered such an estimate—between half a kilogram and fifty kilograms per bomb—to be of little help in estimating the size or cost of the installation required.

The emotional clash between Groves and the scientists at Chicago on this first visit has been detailed in many accounts of the Manhattan Project.[20] Underlying disagreements on substance and style were virtually unbridgeable gulfs between two cultures. For his part, Groves tended to be defensive among those with advanced degrees.[21] At one point during his visit, Groves announced to the group that while he might not have a doctorate, he had gone to school full time for ten years after leaving West Point. He saw this as equivalent to two Ph.D.s. The remark was reported to have passed in stony silence.[22] Imagine the embarrassment of the assembled scientists, most of whom probably saw the Ph.D. as nothing more than a required union card.

The scientists, on the other hand, were already restive under the rigid compartmentalization of information that had been imposed on the project as early as 1940. In their view this policy was antithetical to effective research. They were convinced that restricting the free flow of information among scientists would significantly delay their work.[23] But Groves made it clear, much to their displeasure, that not only would he continue the policy, he would enforce it with renewed rigor. The real issue underlying the complaints of the scientists ran deeper, to their sense that the project, which they had controlled at the start, was being turned over to an institution—the military—which had neither scientific expertise nor administrative skill.

In fact, turning the project over to the Corps of Engineers was only the beginning. Groves intended to contract out all industrial-scale aspects to private industry. It was the way he always worked. Initially, in his capacity as deputy chief of construction for the Corps, he had recommended to James Marshall that Stone and Webster, a large international construction company, be designated as prime contractor for the Manhattan Engineer District: they had a good deal of experience engineering scientific projects and had performed well in the many contracts they had executed for Groves. Taking his cue from Conant's initiative with Du Pont, before visiting Chicago, Groves had already met several times with E. G. Ackart, Du Pont's chief engineer—the idea being that Du Pont would subcontract through Stone and Webster to design, build, and operate the industrial-scale chemical works needed to separate the plutonium created in the nuclear reactors from its parent element, uranium. And on October 3, 1942, two days before Groves first visited Chicago, Du Pont signed a contract to design and build the separation plants.[24]

After his Chicago meeting with Compton and the scientists, Groves realized that even Conant had not fully comprehended the scale of operation required for the project to succeed.[25] Groves's experience told him that the project would be far too large to be managed effectively by a single prime contractor, even one with the resources and manpower of Stone and Webster. And his initial contact with the scientists convinced him that they could never engineer the required structures and industrial-scale processing equipment.[26]

Groves was determined that Du Pont should become prime contractor for the entire plutonium project, including design and construction of the reactors and the separation plants as well as the subsidiary operations, such as preparation of the uranium metal for insertion into the reactor. At first Du Pont officials tried to beg off, partly on the grounds that they knew nothing about nuclear engineering. But Groves was not willing to take no for an answer. He pointed out to them that no one had any experience in this field. And in the end he made appeals directly to Du Pont's president and the board of directors of the company on the basis of patriotism and the importance of the project to winning the war.[27] It was an argument which Du Pont could not win. Even so, Groves had to concede several conditions before Du Pont was willing to take on responsibility for the plutonium project. Still smarting from the "Merchants of Death" label the company had acquired in the 1930s when it was charged with profiteering on the sale of arms and munitions during World War I, Du Pont insisted on being paid no more than one dollar over costs.[28] The company also insisted on being allowed to send a team of scientists and engineers to Chicago to evaluate what had been accomplished thus far. And though by the early part of November, Du Pont had all but agreed to Groves's importuning, the board resisted making a final commitment until a review of the entire MED program could be carried out by a suitable panel of experts—the Lewis Commission, named after its chair, MIT chemist W. K. Lewis. Du Pont itself was represented on the committee, probably Groves's strategy to increase Du Pont's involvement even as it deliberated. On December 1, 1942, the company entered into a formal cost-plus-fixed-fee agreement to design (subject to Met Lab approval), build, and operate all plutonium production for MED.[29]

Many leading Met Lab scientists were irate. They insisted that Du Pont did not have the competence to undertake such a task. They also argued that forcing them to educate and work with such an enormous bureaucracy would stall a project already crippled by Groves's compartmentalization rules. These complaints continued throughout the war and beyond.[30] In 1964, Kenneth D. Nichols reported:

48

I can remember Enrico Fermi protesting: "We don't need this great organization; they are too conservative. If you people will just hire for me the laborers and supply them with brick, I'll tell them where to lay it." . . . I remember later going over to Arthur Compton and Arthur said, "Sometimes I'm inclined to agree with Fermi. If we just had somebody to design the water works and roads, I think I'd almost be willing to back him." I said, "Well, Arthur, I'm a hydraulics expert and I have built a lot of roads and runways. I can design the waterworks and the roads. Let's do it." Then he started to laugh. He kept his feet on the ground. He was a great man, but he wanted us to listen to him.[31]

This was no laughing matter for many of the scientists. They correctly perceived that they were being marginalized to dispensing technical advice.[32] Several times after the war, Groves vehemently denied that he had ever described the scientists who worked on the project as "the biggest collection of crackpots ever assembled."[33] Whether he had or not, folklore among the scientists reflected the tension that arose during the war between Groves and his Corps of Engineers personnel on the one hand and the scientists on the other. If Groves considered most of the scientists, but especially those in Chicago, to be undisciplined, impractical prima donnas, for their part the scientists considered Groves to be a largely uneducated, blustery, rule-following automaton, who commanded respect only by virtue of his rank and who had little idea of the environment required for creative laboratory or theoretical scientific work.

DECIDING TO BUILD HANFORD

By the time Du Pont had formally committed itself, both Groves and Du Pont engineers had realized that siting the industrial plutonium facilities at Oak Ridge was not feasible. The issue was largely one of safety. A greater expanse of land would be required to isolate the reactors from the separation plants and the entire complex from population centers. The 57-square-mile reservation at Oak Ridge in eastern Tennessee was just too small to site factories for uranium separation and plutonium manufacture. And for Groves, a site for the industrial production of plutonium was a top priority.

During the second week in December 1942, Groves gave Lieutenant Colonel Franklin T. Matthias, who had been doing odd jobs for Groves for several months, a special assignment: to proceed to Wilmington, Delaware, where Du Pont and Met Lab scientists and engineers were meeting to hammer out the criteria for the new site. Matthias was to take no notes but was to remember what he heard. Returning to Washington that night, he was to call Groves from the train station. (Groves had had his eye on Matthias as a person who might be able to shoulder considerable responsibility and gave him small jobs of ever-increasing importance to test his capabilities.) Matthias made the call and was amazed when the general drove his car down to the station. Once Matthias was in the car, Groves asked him what he thought of the meeting. "Well, I think I have to read some of Buck Rogers' comics to get mentally conditioned," was Matthias's response. At that point, Groves explained the whole project to him. Groves then said that Matthias and two Du Pont engineers would start out the next morning to locate a spot somewhere in the country that met the site criteria.[34] Besides ample sources of electricity and water, those criteria included:

- The area encompassing the piles (reactors) and separation plants should be a rectangle of approximately 12 miles by 16 miles.
- The laboratory should be situated at least 8 miles away from the nearest pile or separation plant.
- The employees' village should be no less than 10 miles upwind to the nearest pile or separation plant.
- No town of as many as 1,000 inhabitants should be closer than 20 miles from the nearest pile or separation plant.
- No main highway or railroad should be closer than 10 miles to the nearest pile or separation plant.[35]

These criteria represent the state of knowledge, at the beginning of 1943, based on virtually no experience, concerning radiation hazards to be expected in a worst case (Chernobyl-like) disaster.

Matthias and his Du Pont colleagues made scaled templates reflecting these criteria. They studied geological survey maps and located several potential sites. It was immediately clear to all of them, the moment they saw it, that their ideal site centered on the small village of Hanford, Washington, along the banks of the Columbia River, not far from the

Bonneville and Grand Coulee generating stations. Back in Washington, D.C., on New Year's Eve, 1942, Matthias told Groves, who quickly ordered the Corps of Engineers to buy the roughly 660 square miles of arid south-central Washington orchard land that was to become the Hanford Engineer Works (HEW).

Though he said nothing specific, Groves must have been very pleased with Matthias's work. According to Matthias:

> [In January and part of February 1943] I was doing a lot of things like getting the airlines to knock . . . [the Hanford Reservation] out of their routes and get the government to make it [a] non-flyable area. I had to get the Army and Navy both to give up some gunnery and bombing practice ranges that we had selected as part of the property. I did a fair amount of planning with the Du Pont Company about the contract and how to administer it.
>
> One day, about the middle of February, General Groves asked me to come in, and he said, "I have been told that I can have any Corps of Engineers officer I want to run the Hanford project, anyone that is not tied up in a combat assignment. . . . I wish you'd check around and give me some recommendations."
>
> And I said, "All right." I started out, and I got to the door that was part open.
>
> And he said, "By the way, if you don't find anybody I like, you're going to have to do it yourself."
>
> And I stopped right away, and I said, "General there isn't anybody I can recommend." So he appointed me right then.[36]

THE MAKING OF HANFORD

Under normal circumstances, there is a well-established routine for transforming a laboratory procedure that takes place under abstract conditions (for example, a chemical reaction in a test tube) into full-scale industrial production. That process, often referred to as "scaling up," is usually a two-step process the exact details of which depend greatly on the nature of the relationship between the raw materials used and the desired end product.[37] The first stage is to develop a "pilot plant" operation—a small-scale experimental trial unit which serves to guide technique and gauge probable cost. Pilot plants are considered the surest and quickest way of transforming laboratory investigations into commercial applications. They provide crucial information on whether a proposed sequence of operations will yield the desired product. Scaling up is not simply a matter of linear multiplication, however. The conditions in the laboratory may not be suitable for bulk, assembly-line environments. Therefore, a second stage in the scale-up process is the "semiworks"—a manufacturing plant operating on a limited commercial scale to provide final tests of a new product or process and produce market samples.

The equivalent of a laboratory-bench experiment for making plutonium was the 400-ton graphite moderated uranium pile (reactor) which was constructed in a squash court under the west stands of the University of Chicago's football stadium—Stagg Field. The experiment was dubbed CP-1 (Chicago Pile No. 1). It was hardly a bench-top piece of work in the normal sense of the word. The feasibility of a self-sustained, controlled uranium fission reactor was demonstrated when that pile went "critical" on the afternoon of December 2, 1942. Under normal circumstances, the next step would have been to build a pilot plant and then a semiworks. At CP-1, when it went critical, was a Du Pont vice-president and Lewis Committee member, Crawford Greenewalt. As a bright young engineer, he had overseen the $20 million scale-up gamble Du Pont took to transform the test-tube production of nylon into an assembly-line industrial process.[38]

Even before responsibility for designing, building, and operating the plutonium facilities had been turned over formally to Du Pont, Groves had vetoed a plan for the Met Lab scientists to run "pilot" and "semi-works" plutonium production. With Conant's approval, he decided that there would be no pilot plants or semiworks for most of the processes required to produce the materials for atomic bombs.[39] He recognized the inherent risk in making that decision, but it had to be taken if the bomb was to be ready "in time." "In time" could have at least two meanings. First, Groves shared with many of the scientists the fear that Germany was ahead in the race to develop an effective fission bomb. From that perspective, "in time" meant "before the Germans." In addition, frustrated in his desire for a regimental command, the ambitious Groves was determined to use the successful completion of the Manhattan Project— including use of the bomb to ensure victory—to advance his own career ambitions. From that perspective, "in time" meant "before the end of the war."[40]

On reflection, it is clear that the decision to omit the two key steps in the process of transforming laboratory experiment into commercial production would not ordinarily have been a decision made by the administrative head of the organization. That the decision was made by Groves— a person with no special knowledge in nuclear physics or chemical engineering—reveals how he had taken over the management of *all* phases of the project.[41] Groves's original orders were to build the necessary facilities to manufacture the nuclear fuel and the bomb, to stand in readiness to aid the scientists as their needs demanded, and to take such steps as were necessary to maintain secrecy and provide security.[42] Those around him soon saw that Groves had transcended those limited responsibilities.[43] His own rendition of his orders was more like "To build the atomic bomb in the shortest time possible and thereby end the war."[44]

Despite the scant experience accumulated, anywhere, in the art of isotope separation or plutonium production and purification, there were two compensating factors supporting Groves's gamble:

- Cost was no object. Therefore whenever Groves was faced with a choice between two or more techniques none of which were, on paper, clearly superior, he ordered parallel industrial development of all the alternatives.
- Manpower and matériel demands of the Manhattan Project had top priority. During the war, competition for skilled manpower and for scarce strategic resources (such as copper, steel, and rubber) among competing programs was intense. Maintaining its number one position among all competing programs was sometimes not easy, but Groves was always successful in beating back the Manhattan Project's competition.

Cost Was No Object

Funding for the Manhattan Project was buried within the massive Corps of Engineers budget in order to avoid congressional inquiries. Costs of a particular process were not a consideration, as Groves's approach to uranium separation illustrates. At the time he took over the project in September 1942, three techniques for separating uranium 235 from uranium 238 held promise: electromagnetic, gaseous diffusion, and gaseous centrifuge processes were being actively pursued. Among most of the scientists working on the project, looking at the long term, the gas centrifuge was favored while electromagnetic separation was thought to be the most wasteful. Groves was not interested in the long term at that moment, and stopped gas centrifuge development because that program seemed the least aggressively run. He ordered full-scale development of both gaseous diffusion and electromagnetic isotope separation at a time when neither system had been tested and shown to be viable. By the end of the war, approximately a half billion dollars had been spent on each of these techniques,[45] yet the result produced barely enough uranium 235 to make the one bomb dropped on Hiroshima. (As it turned out, during the war, electromagnetic separation, while wasteful, was the most effective. Just after the war, gaseous diffusion proved to be far superior and replaced it. And then slowly, over the next fifteen years, gas centrifuge emerged as the technique of choice.)

Groves's philosophy also dictated that MED would build at Hanford not one full-scale reactor, but three, simultaneously, and without any "pilot plant" or "semiworks" for guidance. Rather than one plutonium separation plant, three would be built, with one to be held in reserve if the others failed. Including the money spent on the production of heavy water, which also was held in reserve should graphite prove an unsuitable moderator for the reactors ($15 million), the cost for building and operating Hanford through the end of the war was more than $400 million.[46]

The final design for the production reactors called for them to be cooled by water from the Columbia River, and it was not known what effects raw river water would have on the efficiency of the reactors. While the weight of opinion suggested that this should present no problem, the designers of the reactors were concerned, and so Groves was concerned. With his unlimited access to funds, he decided that, just in case, at least one reactor should use deionized water. Groves was discussing this problem with G. M. Read, Du Pont's assistant chief engineer, one day when Chicago physicist Norman Hilberry came into the room. Asked for his opinion, Hilberry responded that deionized water probably would not be needed, but if it were then the reactor could not operate without it. Groves immediately turned to Read and said: "Go ahead and build it." Hilberry then asked what it would cost and Groves told him between six and ten million dollars. Hilberry replied, "I'm glad I didn't know that when I gave my opinion."[47] Deionized water turned out not to be necessary and the plant was never used.

But Groves was not being flamboyant and irresponsible with his money. As deputy chief of construction for the Corps, he had acquired a reputation for being very careful to minimize costs. In that regard, as head of the Manhattan Project, within the parameters dictated by not following the normal procedures for scaling up, he was just as ruthless. Evidence of unnecessary expenditures by contractors or Corps personnel led him to take swift action. But to build the bomb in the shortest time possible, rapid and full development of all likely processes became the order of the day.

Only the chemistry for separating plutonium from uranium went through the full pilot plant and semiworks steps. There were several reasons for this caution. Before 1944, the only samples of plutonium metal were produced using a cyclotron. With only microgram quantities of the material available, it seemed foolhardy to build industrial procedures on such tiny amounts. It was also expected that after being irradiated within the reactor for some time, the uranium slugs from which the plutonium was to be extracted would also contain dangerous levels of radioactive nuclear fission by-products. Scaling up seemed to be the only way to ensure that the process was both sure and safe. The semiworks for testing the necessary chemistry was built at Oak Ridge, adjacent to the experimental reactor designated as X-10. That reactor went critical near the end of 1943 and in the first months of 1944; milligram (and then larger) samples of plutonium were successfully separated from the uranium slugs irradiated in the reactor. The information gleaned from this work had profound effects on the final design of the separation plants at Hanford and still more profound effects on the design of the plutonium bomb.[48]

Matériel and Manpower Priorities

The fact that the Manhattan Project had unlimited buying power is one measure of the initial commitment that had been made by the president and the War Department to have an atomic bomb before Germany did. After it was clear that Germany would not build a bomb, I interpret the continued insistence of the Roosevelt and Truman administrations on giving the Manhattan Project top priority as reflecting a hope that the bomb would play a role in ending the war. But having unlimited funds would have done no good if Manhattan Project requirements for raw materials, finished goods, and manpower could not be satisfied. For this reason, one of Groves's first acts as head of the project was to get a commitment from Donald Nelson, director of the War Production Board (WPB), to delegate to him the authority to use AAA priority in those cases where unavailability of materials would result in an unacceptable delay in progress. The WPB, however, was locked into a complex structure of administrative agencies with overlapping authority.[49] Groves's detailed understanding of that structure not only allowed him to exploit, effectively, the authorization he had obtained from Nelson but also to manipulate the system. First, he applied constant pressure at the right points in the system in an attempt to raise the Manhattan Project's blanket priority rating from AA-3 to AA-1. Second, he worked behind the scenes to gain exceptions from particular priority restrictions. By March 1943, he had his AA-2X rating (a special priorities rating midway between AA-2 and AA-3), and after repeated attempts, by July 1, 1944, that was raised to AA-1, the highest blanket rating available.[50]

Still, there were difficulties. A number of the most vital war-related projects had authority to issue requisitions with AAA priority. In order to allocate resources among various claimants, a Priorities Critical List (sometimes called Priorities Urgency List) was created even before the war began. Periodically, this list was updated. In spite of the fact that, beginning in April 1943, Manhattan Project construction was in the number one position (i.e., was rated the most urgent of the urgent) on all such lists, not everyone on the WPB and its related organizations saw it quite that way.[51] A reason for not accepting at face value authoritative statements of the Manhattan Project's importance was the project's ultra-secret nature. Those who were told that the project was so important could not be told what the project was about. Even after being told by Groves, by Patterson, and by Stimson, and even after being presented with a statement from President Roosevelt that the Manhattan Project was the most important project of the war, on July 15, 1943, the War Production Board distributed a circular letter that said: "Please be advised that the Manhattan Project has the same relative urgency as Synthetic Rubber, High Octane, and Destroyer Escort Vessel programs."[52]

Typically, that statement galvanized Groves into action. His usual appeal was to Patterson, who would immediately turn Groves's memos on the subject into stern warnings to the chair and vice-chair at WPB. Groves's prodding was particularly intense during the first half of 1944 when construction at Hanford and Oak Ridge was at its peak. Periodically, Groves bolstered the Patterson-signed memos by inserting statements he would extract from Secretary of War Stimson and President Roosevelt. In the face of this solid chorus that the Manhattan Project was the "most important undertaking of the war" and that its "preferred position"—Groves's favorite characterization—relative to all other projects must be maintained at all costs, the WPB could do little else but grudgingly honor MED requisitions before those of the Landing Craft program, the Hi Octane and Rubber Factory Construction programs, all aircraft construction programs, all ammunition programs, all tank construction programs, all earth-moving and truck construction programs, and any other programs on the Priorities Critical List.[53] That, and nothing short of that, is what Groves meant by the "preferred position." Some idea of the extent to which his superiors backed this idea can be gleaned from a Groves-written memo that Patterson sent, in February 1944, to J. A. Krug, who oversaw the WPB Office of War Utilities. Through Patterson, Groves pointed out that power to run the Hanford Engineer Works would come from the Bonneville Power Administration system. It is absolutely vital, the memo continued, that steps be taken to ensure that during emergencies in the power transmission system, Hanford receive an "adequate supply of power." Moreover,

Even a short interruption of power could have serious results and all practicable means should therefore be taken to prevent such interruptions both by installing of suitable equipment in the transmission system and by *instantly curtailing* the power supply to *any other* load in the area should an occasion arise necessitating such action.[54]

But the critical problem at Hanford was a shortage of men, not material resources or electricity. Hanford's chief competitors for skilled and unskilled labor were the Boeing Company in Seattle and Kaiser Aluminum in Vancouver.[55] A major difficulty for those responsible for building Hanford was the extraordinarily large turnover in employees. The region is semiarid desert. And it is isolated. Also, construction on such a massive scale shook free thousands of acres of sand, creating sandstorms—especially at those times of the year when the winds blew unvarying for days. Blowing sand reduced visibility to zero and forced its way through every crevice and window frame, making it an unavoidable ingredient in everyone's diet. Quickly named "termination winds," they guaranteed that great numbers of workers would terminate their contracts rather than suffer living with the sand. At peak construction, the Hanford camp, with 50,000 skilled and unskilled workers, was the largest such construction settlement ever assembled in the United States. But almost three times that number passed through the camp.[56]

The War Manpower Commission (WMC) used the same priority criteria as its parent, the War Production Board. The WMC was organized by region, but for those projects with the biggest demand—such as airplane production, aluminum manufacture, or the Manhattan Project—the search for manpower was nationwide. In order to keep secret that the large construction project in the Northwest (Hanford) had something to do with the large construction project in eastern Tennessee (Oak Ridge), there was no labor recruitment for Hanford in Tennessee and vice versa.

Groves subjected Paul V. McNutt, head of the WMC, to the same kind of pressure he used on Donald Nelson. Again, his primary spokesman in this effort was Patterson. In April 1944, at the peak of the push to complete Hanford, a Groves-written, Patterson-signed fusillade to McNutt announced:

> Several instances recently arose where your field U.S. Employment Service offices have granted construction projects, particularly on the West Coast, a more favorable priority for labor than that given to Hanford. Hanford has had no. 1 priority of both War and Navy departments in all of their construction activities. Military necessity is the reason. The Production Executive Committee of WPB has just granted the top priority for referrals of labor to this project.
>
> I ask that you use every means at your disposal to keep your people in the field constantly aware of the importance of this project and the fact that it must be kept fully manned.[57]

Less than two weeks later a Patterson-signed memo informed Lawrence A. Appley, the WMC's executive director, that the Manhattan District's projects at Hanford and Oak Ridge were "the most urgent and important projects in the country." They had the "highest priority." "Nothing must interfere" with making sure that these two projects not be delayed because of unsolved labor problems.[58]

Even though Groves and Patterson always seemed desperate to obtain more workers for Hanford, there were some offers they turned down. At Hanford and Oak Ridge, the labor force was strictly segregated by sex (for single employees) and by race. This meant quadruple living facilities and dual facilities for social functions, such as church. Early in 1944, McNutt proposed sending to Hanford a large contingent of Mexican American laborers who were then working in Texas. Groves objected on the grounds that "Spanish labor is not particularly adaptable" to the work that remained to be done at Hanford. That was the phrase he used in drafting an appeal to President Roosevelt which was dispatched over Patterson's signature. The letter went on to say that what had been a serious labor situation at Hanford was now a critical one because "the War Manpower Commission is insisting that we use Spanish-American labor from Texas on the project in compliance with the Executive order on non-discrimination." It was felt that to comply would seriously delay the work: "Compliance would necessitate the construction of new separate housing for male and female Spanish Americans with the necessary facilities."[59] Few Mexican Americans were ever sent, but one wonders if Groves, Patterson, McNutt, or FDR appreciated the irony of invoking the Presidential Order on discrimination in this manner.

Other forces were less amenable to such pressure. One was slowdowns caused by jurisdictional disputes between unions and between categories of jobs. For example, in the face of specific labor shortages at Hanford, Du Pont asked some members of the International Association of Machinists to do millwright work. This brought an immediate protest from the United Brotherhood of Carpenters and Joiners (UBCJ), which had jurisdiction over millwright jobs. Though Matthias proved extraordinarily skillful at solving most union issues threatening to slow down the pace of Hanford construction, such disputes went well beyond his sphere of influence; in this case Patterson had to negotiate an agreement directly with the union presidents. Later, in the summer of 1944, he could point to that model in his appeal to Martin Durkin, president of the United Association of Steamfitters and Plumbers, to put aside, in the interests of winning the war, jurisdictional claims at Hanford, on the grounds that "this is the country's most vital construction project."

Groves himself had already importuned Durkin, in the hopes that Durkin could help fill a shortfall at Hanford of 1,000 fitters, plumbers, and welders and that he would issue instructions to release jurisdictional claims. "As you know," Groves told Durkin, "this is the no. 1 construction job in the United States. It is vital to the war effort."[60]

Another threat to both Oak Ridge and Hanford was the work of the Senate Committee to Investigate the National Defense Program, the so-called Truman Committee, formed in March 1941 to make sure that contractors were not "fleecing the government" and that the War and Navy departments were not giving unfair and even illegal preference to certain contractors at the expense of others. Groves and Somervell believed that the real basis of Truman's motivation was his anger that certain arsenals had not been located, as he had wished, in Missouri.[61]

Politics aside, the Truman Committee proved to be extremely powerful. Contracts and administrative agencies learned to fear the results of its investigations and hearings. General Somervell and the committee were almost always at loggerheads.[62] Usually it took only one or two letters from disgruntled employees to bring committee investigators running to the company files to determine if full-scale hearings would be justified. In the case of Oak Ridge and Hanford, the files bulged. (The Truman Committee did not learn until after the war ended that the huge construction project at Hanford had anything to do with the huge project at Oak Ridge.) Worth quoting in detail is the following letter from C. M. Schmitthausler, who described himself to Truman as originally from St. Louis and not yet a voter but a concerned citizen:

> The primary object Mr. Trueman [sic] of this letter is not to bore you with my political viewpoints, but to expose to you the scandalous, treacherous, intrigue which makes the Hanford Engineering Works the most mysterious place in the world and to which the attentions of the Federal Bureau of Investigation and a Senate investigating committee should be directed.
>
> This humble person would never attempt to estimate how many millions of dollars are squandered here within a week, nor would he pretend to know for what it is being wasted.
>
> He does not attempt to evaluate the immense quantities of idle equipment, of unsalvaged materials which accumulate day after day, week on week. . . .

I cannot and will not be convinced that any project, so vital to our war effort as we are asked to believe, would not better thrive with the support of an enlightened and enthusiastic public.

There can be no reason for secrecy about this vast enterprise except evil wrongdoing on the part of officials delegated to give America the industry she needs to fight this war to a successful conclusion. . . .

I demand on behalf of 130,000,000 Americans, to know why, and in detail, it is necessary to maintain such secrecy about a project which has been six months under way, and is so huge that it is not even well started.

My grateful thanks for your patience in reading this. . . .[63]

By the time this letter was received, Truman had already been warned off investigating Hanford or Oak Ridge—by Secretary of War Stimson himself. He assured Truman: (1) the work was top secret and absolutely vital; (2) it would be a major breach of security to throw national public light on the existence of these projects; (3) he had personally verified that all expenditures were justifiable; and (4) when the cloak of secrecy could be lifted, Truman's committee, and indeed the country, would be told the whole story.[64]

As constituent letters continued to mount, and as congressmen and senators from the states of Washington and Tennessee continued to press for information, Truman felt compelled to begin an investigation. But his committee was held at bay by Stimson, who politely—but firmly—declined to cooperate, invoking the authority of President Roosevelt.[65]

THE SPEEDUP

As Hanford neared completion, Groves turned his attention to pressuring Du Pont to speed up the production schedule. On October 18, 1944, Du Pont suggested that production of plutonium would be built up gradually over the course of 1945, beginning with 0.2 kilogram in February and climbing to 6.0 kilos a month by December.[66] Each of the first plutonium bombs—those used for the Trinity test and on Nagasaki—employed 6.1 kilos of plutonium. By Du Pont's schedule, it would be August before the first 6 kilos were accumulated. Groves was furious. W. O. Simon, manager of the Hanford Works, carefully explained on

October 29, 1944, that plutonium production was dictated by construction delays caused by the War Manpower Commission's inability to meet Du Pont's labor needs. On November 16, an annoyed Groves responded to Simon's letter in two ways. First he dispatched a letter to Du Pont's chief engineer, E. G. Ackart, describing Simon's approach as "super-cautious" and noting, "Apparently Mr. Simon had not been informed of my definite refusal to accept . . . [the] 'scheduled' completion dates." Groves informed Ackart that he was "unwilling to accept such a setback and, on the contrary, am expecting that an organization as competent and experienced as yours will beat the August date by an appreciable number of weeks." At the same time Groves sent the following teletype to Nichols: "I am at loss to understand the super cautiousness of the [Du Pont] schedule [for Hanford] from start to finish. . . . I want to see someone in Washington on Saturday who is able to explain differences between [this] . . . and previous information on which we have been proceeding. . . . When did Simon get into the picture[?] Who is he[?] What is his past[?]"[67]

From the tenor of these communiqués it is clear that just as Groves had been unwilling to accept Du Pont's initial refusal to become enmeshed in the business of manufacturing plutonium, and just as he had refused to allow the resource priority system or any other impediment to seriously delay the completion of Hanford (and all other MED facilities), he was determined that nothing would prevent the accumulation of significant amounts of plutonium "an appreciable number of weeks" before the end of August.

Roger Williams, the manager of Du Pont's TNX division, and Groves jousted over the production schedule for plutonium until March 1945. In November 1944, Du Pont projected that 5.7 kilograms of plutonium would be accumulated at the end of June 1945, 8.8 kilos by the end of July, and 12.1 kilos by the end of August.[68] Still Groves was not satisfied. He asked Williams for a series of production projections using different procedures of operation. Those comparisons were not completed until Saturday, December 23, 1944. When Groves called Williams in Wilmington, Delaware, on Wednesday, December 27, the projections had not yet arrived. Groves told Williams he wanted to see them as soon as possible. What Groves did not tell Williams was that he was, even then, preparing his year-end report to Chief of Staff General George C. Marshall and Secretary of War Stimson, a report which Groves and Stimson would review, personally, with FDR on December 30.[69] It began by stating that it is "reasonably certain" that a uranium 235 bomb should be ready by about August 1, 1945. Groves reported that confidence in its operation was so high that no test was deemed necessary. He estimated that it would produce an explosion equivalent to ten thousand tons of TNT. There would not be enough uranium 235, the report continued, to construct another such bomb until the end of 1945. After that, production of uranium 235 would be at a level sufficient to produce a bomb a month.

Groves now turned to the plutonium bomb:

> Our previous hopes that . . . [a plutonium] implosion (compression) type of bomb might be developed *in the late spring* have now been dissipated by scientific difficulties which we have not as yet been able to solve. The present effects of these difficulties are that more material will be required and that the material will be less efficiently used. *We should have sufficient material of the first implosion type bomb* sometime in the latter part of July. This bomb would have an effect which would be equivalent to about 500 tons of TNT.[70]

Groves estimated that as the difficulties were overcome, the destructive effects of the plutonium bomb would become the same as those of the uranium bomb. He also estimated that between August and December 1945, enough plutonium would be produced to construct seventeen additional bombs. Clearly, he knew something that Du Pont apparently did not know. In any event, given the pessimism of Williams and his sources, Groves was climbing out on a rather fragile limb. It was one of many such gambles that he took during the course of the war.

In his conversation with Williams on December 27, Groves was emphatic that he wanted the first 5 kilograms (about 11 pounds) of plutonium as soon as possible. He thought this could be accomplished by the first of May and that a second 5-kilo lot could be accumulated by month's end. (Five kilos was Los Alamos's best estimate then for the amount of plutonium that would be required for the bomb.)[71] Groves realized that such an acceleration of the process would come at a price. Williams was less optimistic than Groves. If possible, it would be at "a considerable price." There were three ways to affect the rate of production of plutonium: pushing slugs out of the reactor more frequently,[72] reducing the time the slugs remained under water, or reducing the time for processing.

There were two prices to be paid. If uranium was pushed out of the reactor at an accelerated rate, the lower concentrations of plutonium per slug could be compensated for by ejecting more slugs per push. The price would be in wasted uranium metal, a relatively expensive commodity. The second obvious way of speeding up the process was shortening the period between pushing and processing, from the recommended ninety days to forty or even twenty-five days. This would advance the date when the plutonium in each push would be extracted. The cost here was less immediate—a significant increase in the contamination of the surrounding countryside.[73] Groves estimated that the cost would be approximately 40 tons of uranium metal.[74] Based on the projections Groves had requested, Williams informed Groves that Du Pont agreed to deliver 5 kilos of plutonium by the end of June and another 5 kilos by the end of July 1945. Williams asked Groves to sign and return the letter to signify acceptance of that schedule. Rather than sign, Groves responded: "Your understanding is correct except the dates set by you in the letter, the end of June and the end of July, must of course be improved if it is possible to do so."[75]

The dialogue between Groves and Du Pont officials continued into March 1945. On March 9, Nichols informed Groves that Matthias had confirmed plutonium shipment dates in 1-kilo lots accumulating to 5 kilos by June 14 and to 10 kilos by July 12. Penciled at the bottom in Groves's hand was the notation: "This schedule was not satisfactory and was revised at my meeting with [R. Monte] Evans [plutonium plant operations director] of Du Pont on 22 March." Groves wrote Los Alamos Laboratory director J. Robert Oppenheimer on that day as follows: "I have just reviewed the production situation of the HEW with the responsible Du Pont officials. I can now give you a firm date as to the time when you should be ready for the first 5 kilos of material. . . . 1 June (this now seems a very firm date)." Groves further informed Oppenheimer that the second 5 kilos would be ready by July 5. In case a little more than 5 kilos of plutonium would be needed for each bomb, "the next two kilos would be shipped at a rate of one per week."[76]

As it turned out, plutonium shipments from Hanford to Los Alamos kept to this schedule. Hanford accomplished this acceleration by pushing more slugs more frequently and by shortening to twenty-five days the time the slugs cooled off before processing.[77]

Each bomb required about 1.1 kilos more than the 5 kilos originally allotted. According to Matthias, on the morning of July 10, 1945: "Six cans left . . . for Y [Los Alamos]. I called Oppy and he expressed himself as being very pleased with the shipment made and the extra effort made to obtain the 15 [extra] cans [total] before 12 July. The Du Pont Company employees really worked hard on this shipment." The first completed plutonium bomb core left Los Alamos by car for the Trinity test site, some 200 miles to the south, on July 11.[78]

THE MEANING OF HANFORD

Ground was broken for the first Hanford reactor (designated 100-B) on August 27, 1943. Barely a year later (September 13, 1944) it was being charged with uranium slugs, while two other reactors, 100-D and 100-F, were also nearing completion. The first of the separation plants was finished in December 1944, and the first batch of plutonium was shipped to Los Alamos on February 2, 1945.[79] The contributions of the scientists and engineers who *designed* these facilities were crucial. But without Groves's zeal and the unremitting pressure he was able to bring to bear on the WPB, the WMC, and their parent organization, the Office of War Mobilization (OWM), such a rapid *completion* of the facilities would have been impossible. Groves understood the wartime resources distribution system and what made it tick.[80] The Manhattan Project scientists and engineers did not.[81]

The moral of the story, however, is not simply that it was Leslie Groves's insights and administrative abilities which were essential to the timely completion of Hanford and other MED facilities. His initiatives, while effective, came at a price. Because of the decision to keep knowledge of the Manhattan Project from almost everyone in the administration, Groves, Stimson, Patterson, or the president could not tell the directors of OWM, the WPB, or the WMC the nature of the secret work. They could say things like "It is the most important project of the war," yet there was no visible evidence that the Manhattan Project had produced anything. At Oak Ridge, employees who were in the dark concerning the larger context of their immediate tasks often described it as a place "where everything comes in and nothing goes out," or "where they assemble the front ends of horses and then ship them to Washington for final assembly."[82] Meanwhile it did not go without notice that the Manhattan Project was a voracious consumer. Other projects were not pleased to see their requisitions for raw materials, intermediate goods, and manpower shunted aside to satisfy the demands of Groves's organization—whatever might be its unrevealed purpose. And as the war went on, skepticism grew. In 1943, OWM Director James F. Byrnes was worried enough to warn Secretary of War Stimson as follows:

> I have recently discussed with my staff the secret Army construction comprised under Manhattan. . . . [T]his enterprize has grown until it involved an expenditure of ½ a billion dollars by a date early this year . . . [and] at least nine separate projects in several locations from Florida to Puget Sound involve further expenditures roughly estimated at five hundred million dollars during the current year. . . . In the recent applications for allocation of steel under the CMP procedure [Controlled Materials Program] in the War Production Board, 75,000 tons of carbon steel was allocated to Manhattan for the 4th quarter. This compares with only 8,500 tons in all other industrial construction and with 53,000 tons for all Army construction (excluding Manhattan) including command construction, industrial construction, rivers and harbors, and "passive protection." It would appear probable from these figures that more than half of Army military construction will fall in the Manhattan category.
>
> I know that the War Department may have some enterprise so important and so secret that it might be unwilling to divulge the purpose or details even to the Office of War Mobilization. However, you and I should assure ourselves that projects in Manhattan are of such character and that zealous officials do not use the convenience of the high priorities and secrecy for the purpose of securing material for unrelated projects. If not, then this project will sooner or later reach a point where such huge expenditures of public funds and use of high priority material and labor will have to be justified.
>
> I would greatly appreciate it if you would inquire into this situation and convince yourself there is justification for these great expenditures and that the procedure being followed is a correct one.[83]

A memo attached to this letter in Stimson's hand noted that he had satisfied Byrnes that he, Stimson, had indeed looked into the matter and was confident that Manhattan Project requests were all legitimate.

By 1945, hostile attitudes toward the Manhattan Project had increased within portions of the administration, the military, and the Congress. On February 24, 1945, Fred Searls, Jr., a consultant to the O W M, now renamed the Office of War Mobilization and Reconversion (O W M R), wrote a detailed memo to O W M R's departing chairman, James Byrnes, warning about the consequences from the likely congressional backlash when what Searls considered excessive military expenditures become known. Four concerns reflected four seemingly independent approaches to winning the Pacific war: the Navy's insistence, even now, on building more and more ships and planes; undiminished appetite of the Army, Army Air Forces, and Army Service Forces for more and more forces; enormous increase in post-VE Day lend-lease grants to England and the Soviet Union; and the Manhattan Project. About the latter he wrote: "The enormous Manhattan Project . . . has for three years . . . burdened all of our war programs like an old man of the sea; with over-riding priority, it has come first of all, for man-hours, steel, transportation, and everything else. Its cost of nearly two billion dollars is not a measure of its real cost to our war-effort, which will never be appreciated by the professors who dream that by this fourth method the Japanese and subsequent wars can be brought to a speedy and successful termination."

Searls's ultimate fear was stark and prescient: "We have sent our young men to fight in Europe and in Asia, and while they were away we have made of America a different place than the one for which they think they are fighting."[84]

This memo's political implications were not lost on Byrnes. A little more than a week later he wrote FDR that he understood that Manhattan Project expenditures were approaching two billion dollars without any "definite assurance yet of production." He admitted that it might be possible to continue stonewalling the Congress for the rest of the war, but the price might be very high indeed. In blunt terms calculated to capture Roosevelt' s attention, Brynes warned the president: "If the project proves to be a failure, it will then be the subject of relentless investigation and criticism. I know little of the project except that it is supported by eminent scientists. Even eminent scientists may continue a project rather than concede its failure. Also, it may be reasonable to continue the experiment on a reduced scale."[85] Byrnes urged Roosevelt to appoint a small independent committee of scientists to evaluate the project. Even if such a panel recommended continuation, the administration would escape political liability. FDR passed this memo on to Stimson with a note saying they should discuss it.

It is doubtful that Groves ever saw or knew about the Searls memo,[86] but on March 6 or 7, 1945, Stimson did discuss Byrnes's note with Groves, and while Groves thought a review by scientists *inside* the project might be possible, Stimson absolutely opposed any kind of review and said so to Roosevelt.[87] Although Roosevelt's death a month later made the Byrnes initiative moot, such a review would have been too late to affect the drama already unfolding at Hanford—in Matthias's words of April 20, "the speed up."[88]

On April 25, 1945, two weeks after he became president, Truman had his first briefing on the Manhattan Project by Stimson and Groves. Despite earlier efforts with the Truman Committee, it was only now that he learned about the nature and size of the project; only now that he learned that several atomic bombs would soon be ready.[89]

The day before Stimson and Groves briefed the president, Vannevar Bush raised the question with Harvey Bundy of when it would be best to inform the Soviet Union and other nations about American progress in fission technologies. He was motivated by a visit from the physicist Niels Bohr, who had for over a year been attempting to convince U.S. and British leaders to work for international control of atomic energy before events overtook an unprepared world. Bush also included a revision of a paper that Bohr had written a year before when preparing for a meeting with FDR. At the time, Bush and Conant were strong advocates of international control of nuclear energy as the only way to avoid a postwar disastrous arms race.[90]

Stimson's special assistants for atomic energy, Harvey Bundy and George Harrison, had been urging Stimson to appoint an advisory committee to serve as a temporary bridge between wartime military control and postwar civilian control of atomic energy. On May 1, Harrison handed Stimson a memo urging him to appoint such a committee: "In view of the possibly short time available before the actual military use and the relaxations of secrecy, it seems to me . . . that it is becoming more and more important to organize such a committee as quickly as possible. It should serve temporarily until Congress can appoint a permanent Post War Commission."[91] Harrison argued that it was essential to explain to the public the nature of the devices and the history of their development, the implications for military and civilian use, and the dangers posed by this new and relatively untried technology.

When he created it the very next day, Stimson named it "The Interim Committee." He wanted broad representation from the Roosevelt-Truman administration but did not want the committee to be too large for effective discussion and interchange. In order to ensure that the president was kept abreast of the proceedings and to bring the president's own perspectives on the issues, Stimson asked Truman to designate a personal representative. With no visible hesitation, Truman named former OWM chairman and soon-to-be secretary of state, James F. Byrnes.[92]

Stimson had not charged the Interim Committee with consideration of the atomic bomb's use against Japan. Though not part of the agenda, the question was discussed briefly.[93] Byrnes was a vocal and active voice favoring dropping the bomb on Japan without any warning. He was also part of the majority recommending that, for the time being at any rate, no technical information bearing on atomic energy be shared with the Soviets. That these were Byrnes's positions is part of the record.[94] It is much more difficult to divine his motives.

According to Messer, "Byrnes embraced the bomb with all the zeal of a newly converted believer." But Messer goes on to suggest that whereas Truman saw the atomic bomb as a way of gaining a net savings in lives, Byrnes saw it not only as a way of ending a costly war quickly but as giving the United States an edge in postwar diplomatic jousting, especially with the Soviet Union. To another observer, Byrnes's chief motivations were to use the bomb as a warning to the Soviets with regard to postwar adventurism and to end the war as quickly as possible to forestall the imminent Soviet declaration of war against Japan, or at the very least, to limit the impact of that invasion.[95]

Byrnes's rhetoric reflected such concerns, but, as we have seen, before he knew anything about the Manhattan Project his concern was that if the war ended without the project's "product" having produced results, it would create a huge political liability to the Roosevelt-Truman administration. I believe that there is a strong case for the importance of politics in Byrnes's calculations concerning the possible use of the bomb. The Manhattan Project had spent two billion dollars building the atomic bomb without consulting Congress about the effort. Furthermore, Stimson and Groves had effectively quashed all attempts on the part of individual congressmen and congressional committees to learn anything about the project's size, nature, or purpose. This kind of issue Byrnes would have discussed only with Truman when they were alone and isolated from the rest of the world.[96]

Assistant Secretary of State Robert Patterson found himself in a special jam. As the person responsible for procurement in the War Department, by the beginning of 1945, he had put his signature on Manhattan Project authorizations approaching two billion dollars. He was, of course, not solely responsible. Back in 1941, when Bush and Conant had decided to undertake a crash program to build the bomb, the best estimate they had for the total cost of the project was $133 million. When expenditures had already surpassed $500 million by December 1942, Conant was shaken, but still determined to go ahead. Most likely Bush and Conant may have been subconsciously as anxious as Byrnes to see the bomb used in order to justify the decision to proceed.[97]

Patterson's role in making sure that the Manhattan Project remained "the most important single project of the war" had been a well-known puzzle to many contractors and many supply officers frustrated at their inability to obtain badly needed resources. The muscle Patterson applied on behalf of Hanford was replicated for Oak Ridge, and for every other phase of the project that Groves deemed to be crucial. One can only imagine the whirlwind he would have faced had the war ended without the bomb being used. There is no doubt that he worried about this very thing. In December 1944 he dispatched Jack Madigan to visit major Manhattan Project sites and examine their books.[98] According to Groves, Patterson had asked him if Madigan might not look into the rumors which had come back to Patterson concerning the adequacy of the project's management. Madigan was gone on this trip for several weeks. Before giving a full oral report to a harried and busy Patterson, Madigan provided him with a thirty-second summary: "If the project succeeds, there won't be any investigation. If it doesn't they won't investigate anything else."[99]

Later that day, Madigan assured Patterson that the books were in order. Still, Patterson must have been worried. Shortly after Madigan returned, Patterson wrote General Styer: "At the beginning of the [Manhattan] project I told Groves that the greatest care should be taken in keeping thorough records, with detailed entries of decisions made, of conferences with persons concerned, of all programs. . . . The import of keeping full, accurate and intelligible records is so great that I want you personally to examine . . . the matter and to let me have your conclusions. I want you to take any corrective measures, to make sure that a complete, current history of the project is being set down on paper by competent personnel."[100] Clearly, Patterson was not yet completely sanguine.

Two of Groves's initial motivations for getting the atomic bomb built speedily were a fear that the Germans might be developing their own bomb and a desire to win the war as quickly as possible. But as the war in Europe wound down, it became clear that there would be no German bomb, and even Groves admitted that by the time the bomb was used, the war with Japan had already been won.[101] Curiously, at the time Germany surrendered, the pace of activities intensified in the Manhattan Project, especially at Los Alamos, where the bombs were being designed.[102] Years later, some of the scientists who had worked at Los Alamos no longer understood how they could have allowed that to happen.[103] For some scientists there never were any regrets. Japan was an enemy that had been committed to destroying American democracy; making and using the bomb had been, in the eyes of these scientists, a response to a real threat.[104] In any event, it is often noted, the casualties resulting from the systematic destruction of Japanese cities by fire bombing had produced far more deaths and gruesome injuries.[105] The dynamic that drove the other scientists at Los Alamos is understandable: they had become totally involved in the challenging technical puzzles. As if in a dream, that concentration was broken when they saw and felt the surging half-mile fireball at the Trinity test and, later, by reports about the bomb's effects on Hiroshima and Nagasaki.

If Leslie Groves ever had any doubts or qualms about using the atomic bomb, he never revealed them, before or after August 1945. On the contrary, as this Hanford saga has revealed, he exerted unremitting pressure on all fronts, first to ensure that Hanford was completed quickly and then to make sure that sufficient plutonium was produced as rapidly as possible. And Hanford was no special case. He had applied the same pressures at Oak Ridge and all other Manhattan Project facilities.

The pressure that Groves exerted on Hanford and Oak Ridge paled compared to the force he brought to bear on Los Alamos between August 1944 and August 1945. Recall that in the summer of 1944 it became clear that a plutonium bomb could not be detonated by the same process as the uranium bomb. Whether the alternative, implosion, would work was still an open question, but many of the experts were skeptical. Groves had not only authorized the building of Hanford, he had catapulted it into the "the most important project of the war." And now it looked as if the material Hanford produced might be totally useless. Not only would the expenditure of $400 million have to be explained, Groves would also have to answer to having preempted resources desperately needed for other war-related projects. Rather than halt the Hanford program in the summer of 1944, he immediately authorized Oppenheimer to oversee an enormous expansion and a reorganization of Los Alamos focused on solving the puzzle of the assembly of a plutonium bomb.

In one sense, Groves had completed his mission once the two types of atomic bomb had been built. His orders called for him only to oversee the construction of the laboratories and to assist the scientists in every way possible. So, having delivered the bombs to the forward base at Tinian at the end of July, he could have withdrawn, safe in the knowledge that he had discharged his responsibilities. In fact, he had voluntarily taken on much more responsibility. At the end of December 1944, as part of his report to General Marshall and Secretary Stimson, he had recommended bringing the Army's Operations Department (OPD) into the picture to begin planning the strategic use of the new weapons. General Marshall's response had been to ask Groves why he couldn't undertake that job himself. Groves was surprised but delighted. According to him, those were the only orders he ever received on the matter.[106] It was his staff that worked closely with the Army Air Forces in preparing for operations at Tinian, the island in the Marianas from which the atomic bombs would be flown to Japan. A special unit, the 509th Composite Air Group, had been training for over a year to drop the new weapons.

Tinian was, by then, a major base for the 20th Air Force's assault on the Japanese homeland. Following his usual modus operandi, Groves delegated to Lieutenant Colonel E. E. Kirkpatrick the job of building, on Tinian, the special facilities required for the 509th. He had long since tested Kirkpatrick's competence, and he knew he could trust him to make sure the mysterious 509th's needs were satisfied regardless of competition from other squadrons based on Tinian. It was Hanford, Oak Ridge, or any other Manhattan Engineer District operation all over again. Resentment grew against this air group that seemed only to practice, never to fly combat missions.[107]

The orders for dispatching the bombs to Japan were issued by General Thomas Handy, head of OPD and acting chief of staff in General Marshall's absence. They were formally addressed to General Carl Spaatz, commander of Strategic Air Forces. But they were actually drafted by Groves himself, and so carefully worded they left considerable discretion to the field commander for the date, time of attack, and choice of target. That gave General Spaatz a free hand. The particulars would depend on local conditions.[108] In a separate, Groves-drafted memo approved by Marshall, the chain of command for authorizing the dropping of each atomic bomb was established to be from Groves to Groves's representatives on Tinian, to Spaatz to Le May, to the commander of the 509th Air Group, Colonel Paul Tibbets.[109]

Bad weather delayed the dropping of the first bomb, the uranium bomb used on Hiroshima, several days. But as early as July 19, 1945, Groves was urging his minions on the island to speed up the schedule, or at the very least to do nothing to put off the use of the bombs then being prepared on Tinian. On that day, when Oppenheimer suggested delaying the first drop in favor of substituting an improved design which used a composite uranium-plutonium core, Groves fired off an immediate answer to Oppenheimer saying that he had discussed the proposal "with some of our Washington associates":

> Factors beyond our control prevent us from considering any course other than to proceed according to existing schedules for the time being.
>
> It is necessary to drop the first Little Boy [the uranium bomb] and the first Fat Man [the plutonium bomb] and probably a second one in accordance with our original plan.[110]

At the same time, Groves kept pushing the Los Alamos group that had gone to Tinian to speed up the process so as to drop the bombs as soon as possible. On July 24, Groves sent word to Tinian that some of the tests planned for the Fat Man detonation system should be curtailed in order to shorten the interval between the first and second drops. A worried group of scientists and technicians on Tinian uneasily complied and altered the schedule. Still, they projected August 11 as the earliest the second bomb could be used.[111] In the meantime, on August 1, Groves send a coded message to Tinian:

IS THERE ANYTHING LEFT UNDONE EITHER HERE OR THERE WHICH
IS DELAYING INITIATION OF FIRST TABLE FIVE LINE TWENTY
EIGHT [Little Boy] OPERATION. QUESTION ALSO WHAT ARE PROS-
PECTS ON TABLE FIVE LINE TWENTY NINE [Fat Man] OPERATION[112]

The day after the bombing of Hiroshima, General Farrell cabled Groves
that because of "good technical progress" it was likely that Fat Man
could be dropped on August 9. The next day, August 8, Farrell confirmed
that barring bad weather, Fat Man would be on its way that day.[113] And
so it came to pass.

Having successfully tested one type of bomb and having delivered
both types to the Army Air Forces, Groves seemed in unusual haste.
Why, having successfully used the uranium bomb on Hiroshima, was it
so important that the plutonium bomb be used as soon as possible? I
believe the answer can be gleaned from an event just after the plutonium bomb was successfully tested. When congratulating Groves, General Farrell said, "The war is over." Groves replied, "Yes, after we drop
two bombs on Japan."[114] Interestingly enough, earlier, before the Yalta
Conference, Groves had made the same prediction. He later explained
that his choice of the number two, rather than any other number, had
come from a conversation with Admiral William R. Purnell, the Navy
liaison to the Manhattan Project, "who knew more about the Japanese"
than he did:

> It was his conviction and it was mine too, that the Japanese
> wanted an excuse to get out. We did not know how much the
> Emperor had lost control of the people and the leaders. There were
> a lot of things we did not know about the Japanese character or
> what would happen. This was the reasoning back of the philoso-
> phy of my report to the President before Mr. Roosevelt went to
> Yalta that two bombs would end the war.[115]

But a much more straightforward explanation is at hand. The bomb
dropped on Hiroshima, a uranium bomb, justified the more than $1
billion investment in isotope separation at Oak Ridge. The bomb
dropped on Nagasaki justified the more than $400 million spent on
Hanford. It seems clear today that the rush to produce the active material and to drop the bombs on Japan as soon as possible was driven

largely by a fear that the war might end before both types of fission bombs could be used.

Groves had not been a member of the Interim Committee but as an invited guest sat in on every meeting, including those in which the question of using the bomb on the Japanese had been debated. As Groves later wrote to General Styer: "I had to do some good hard talking at times. One thing is certain—we will never have the greatest congressional investigation of all times."[116]

Once again, Leslie Groves's instincts proved right. There never was "the greatest congressional investigation of all time." There wasn't even a small investigation on the tactics that had made it possible for the bomb to be used prior to the end of the war or on the effects those tactics had on other military programs. If there had been such an investigation, the overall cost of the Manhattan Project might have been judged much higher than the money spent to bring it all about.

NOTES

I am indebted to Susan G. Goldberg, Nancy Taylor, and William E. Lanouette for comments on an early draft of this manuscript. I am especially indebted to Mara Benjamin for her work sorting out the complexities of the World War II manpower and matériel priority system in the United States.

1. See Stanley Goldberg, "Racing to the Finish: The Decision to Bomb Hiroshima and Nagasaki," *Journal of American–East Asian Relations* 4 (Summer 1995): 117–29. That paper is based on a talk given at the American Historical Association meeting, Chicago, January 6, 1995.

2. Traditionally, the Army Corps of Engineers has been organized by geographic divisions, corresponding approximately to nine major U.S. watersheds. Each District, with a name more or less descriptive of the geographic region for which it had responsibility, reported to the corresponding Division. When, as sometimes happened, a District's boundaries crossed Division lines, the District reported to only one of the affected Divisions. Examples of Engineer Districts include the Albuquerque Engineer District, the Baltimore Engineer District, and the New Orleans Engineer District. The name "Manhattan Engineer District" was suggested by Groves in the summer of 1942, just before he took charge of the atomic bomb project. He was then deputy chief of construction for the Corps of Engineers, and as such was being consulted about potential construction by the first Corps of Engineer officer in charge of the project, Colonel James C. Marshall.

Among other things, Marshall was looking for a name for the project. Groves suggested Manhattan Engineer District, because Marshall intended to locate his office in the New York City borough of Manhattan. To Groves that kind of name, having no signification for the nature of the project, was ideal. The Manhattan Engineer District was the only Corps district whose responsibilities were not defined in terms of geographic boundaries. For the organization of the Corps of Engineers and its evolution, see John D. Millett, *The Organization and Role of the Army Service Forces* (Washington, D.C.: Office of the Chief of Military History, Department of the Army, 1954), passim; Lenore Fine and Jesse A. Remington, *The Corps of Engineers: Construction in the United States* (Washington, D.C.: Office of the Chief of Military History, Department of the Army, 1972), 491–99; for an account of the naming of the Manhattan Engineer District, see p. 659.

3. On the use of the bomb to warn the Soviets, see Gar Alperovitz, *Atomic Diplomacy: Hiroshima and Potsdam: The Uses of the Atomic Bomb and the American Confrontation with Soviet Power* (New York: Simon and Schuster, 1965; 2d ed., 1985). Alperovitz has recently supplemented the argument with new evidence in "Why the United States Dropped the Bomb," *Technology Review* 93, no. 6 (1990): 22–34. Documentary and oral evidence support at least five reasons for using the bomb: *momentum* (a $2 billion, three-year secret nationwide enterprise had been created, and no one had said "stop!"); *personal reputations* (scientific and military leaders who all through the war had pushed the project to the top of military priorities faced an outraged Congress and an irate public if the bomb was not used); *personal ambitions* (individual scientific leaders and military commanders saw the project as a route for swift personal advancement); *an instrument in international diplomacy* (the atomic bomb would shorten the war and thereby minimize Soviet involvement in the Pacific settlement, at the same time serving notice to the Soviets with regard to their designs on Western Europe); and *humaneness* (it would shorten the war and effect a net savings of lives).

Although most scholars agree on the evidence, there is serious disagreement about the relative importance of these motivations. My own view is that one can find individuals who participated in the decision to use the bomb who evinced at least one or several of these motivations. In this article, my purpose is to show the extent to which the military and civilian leadership of the project was concerned about the effect on the Congress and the American public should the considerable investment in the atomic bomb not result in a weapon that played an active role in ending the war.

4. For details, see Stanley Goldberg, "Groves Takes the Reins [about the incident at Stagg Field]," *Bulletin of the Atomic Scientists* 48 (December 1992): 32–39. Cf. Fine and Remington, *Corps of Engineers,* 244 ff.

5. Fred B. Rhodes, interview by the author, Anderson, South Carolina, Octo-

ber 19, 1991; the physicist in question was Rossi Lominitz, a student of J. Robert Oppenheimer's. See Lominitz's description of this process in his letters to Oppenheimer in the J. Robert Oppenheimer Papers, Library of Congress Manuscript Collection, folder "Lominitz, Rossi."

6. Groves's office was staffed by a handful of people. For details of the organizational structure of the Manhattan Project, see Fine and Remington, *Corps of Engineers,* 678. Cf. Goldberg, *Fighting to Build the Bomb.* It should be noted that Groves's office does not even appear on the organizational chart.

7. See Alfred Goldberg, *The Pentagon: The First Fifty Years* (Washington, D.C.: Historical Office of the Secretary of Defense, 1992). Fine and Remington, *Corps of Engineers,* passim.

8. Leslie R. Groves, *Now It Can Be Told: The Story of the Manhattan Project* (New York: Harper and Row, 1962; New York: Da Capo, 1983), 3. Goldberg, "Groves Takes the Reins."

9. Stanley Goldberg, "Inventing a Climate of Opinion: Vannevar Bush and the Decision to Build the Bomb," *Isis* 83 (1992): 429–52.

10. For details see ibid.

11. For details see Goldberg, "Groves Takes the Reins."

12. Groves, *Now It Can Be Told,* 22–23. Manhattan District History, book I, vol. 9, app. A, docs. 3 and 4. A microfilm copy of this history is available in Washington, D.C., at the National Archives and Records Administration (hereafter NARA), Microform Reading Room, A1218, reel 3. Cf. Vincent C. Jones, *Manhattan: The Army and the Atomic Bomb* (Washington, D.C.: Center for Military History, U.S. Army, 1985), 81–82.

13. Nelson to Groves, September 19, 1942, NARA, Record Group (hereafter RG) 407, Army Adjutant General Classified Decimal File, 1946–1947, box 3451, folder 221.3, General Styer's Manhattan Engineer District File (hereafter Styer's MED File). For Groves's description of his encounter (the first of many) with Nelson, see Groves, *Now It Can Be Told,* 22–23. Cf. Stephane Groueff, *Manhattan Project: The Untold Story of the Making of the Atomic Bomb* (Boston and Toronto: Little, Brown, 1967), 24–25. It should be noted that Groves's account is at odds with the one given by K. D. Nichols in "The Chronology of District X," a diary that Marshall and Nichols kept during the early days of the Manhattan Project. According to that account (entry for September 17): "I prepared a draft of a letter for Col. Groves which is to be signed, addressed to Donald Nelson, and signed by Gen. [George C.] Marshall. This procedure was subsequently modified to be a letter from Nelson to Col. Groves. . . ." The entry for September 19 notes that "Groves presented a brief letter on the subject of AAA priorities which Gen. Somervell was to get signed by Donald Nelson." "The Chronology of District X," NARA, RG 77, Papers of the Corps of Engineers, Files of the Manhattan Project,

Entry 1, General Groves Top Secret Files (hereafter General Groves's Secret Files), subseries II, folder 6, "Miscellaneous." Cf. K. D. Nichols, *The Road to Trinity: A Personal Account of How America's Nuclear Policies Were Made* (New York: Morrow, 1987), 49–50.

14. Groueff, *Manhattan Project,* 15–16. See especially the footnote, p. 15.

15. Unless there are specific references to the contrary, the discussion of the decision of where to locate the plutonium production facilities is derived from the following sources: Groves, *Now It Can Be Told,* 38–59; Richard G. Hewlett and Oscar E. Anderson, Jr., *A History of the United States Atomic Energy Commission,* vol. 1, *The New World, 1939/1946* (University Park: Pennsylvania State University Press, 1962), 105–15; Arthur H. Compton, *Atomic Quest* (New York: Oxford University Press, 1956), 80 ff.; and a group interview, conducted by Stanley Goldberg, "Administration of Plutonium Production Facilities in Hanford, Washington, Interview with Oswald H. Greager, Richard F. Foster, Leonard F. Perkins, Sr., Frederic W. Albaugh, and Franklin T. Matthias, January 14, 1987, Hanford Washington" (hereafter Hanford Administration Interview). The videotape of this interview, session 3 of an 18-session series, is held by the Smithsonian Institution Archives. A transcript of the interview, and a description of the entire Manhattan Project interview series, can be obtained from the Smithsonian Institution Archives, Arts and Industry Building, Smithsonian Institution, Washington, D.C. 20560.

16. For an assessment of Conant's role in the decision to build the bomb, see Goldberg, "Inventing a Climate of Opinion." Cf. Hewlett and Anderson, *The New World,* 104–5; James G. Hershberg, *James B. Conant: Harvard to Hiroshima and the Making of the Nuclear Age* (New York: Knopf, 1994), 135–63; S. Goldberg, "Conant Conundrums," *Bulletin of the Atomic Scientists* 51 (March–April 1995): 63–65.

Initially, scientists had thought that the rare uranium isotope, uranium 235, was the only substance they could use to make a fission bomb. By the middle of 1941, however, Glenn Seaborg and his associates had verified that element 94, named "plutonium," was also fissionable. When uranium 238, the most common isotope of uranium, absorbs a neutron, it is transformed, via two beta-decays, into element 94, atomic weight 239—plutonium 239. This means that plutonium should be produced in any environment that is rich in free neutrons. A nuclear reactor is such an environment. Therefore, using uranium 238 to manufacture plutonium became an alternative to isotope separation for the production of fissionable material. Once the plutonium is produced in a reactor, it has to be chemically isolated and separated from the uranium in which it is manufactured.

17. It is no accident that Conant chose Du Pont. During his tenure in the Chemistry Department at Harvard, he was a consultant to the company. It proved to be a lucrative arrangement for him. The relationship ended in 1932, when he became president of Harvard. See Hershberg, *James B. Conant,* 56.

18. For details of Groves's itinerary, see his diary (hereafter Groves Diary) for October 1942, NARA, RG 200, Leslie Groves Papers, Entry 7. Groves, *Now It Can Be Told,* 4.

19. See, for example, the remarks of Franklin T. Matthias, in Hanford Administration Interview (p. 13 of the transcript corresponding to time marker 01:30:07:00 of the tape).

20. Richard Rhodes, *The Making of the Atomic Bomb* (New York: Simon and Schuster, 1986), 431 ff.; Groueff, *Manhattan Project,* 35 ff.; William Lanouette, *Genius in the Shadows: A Biography of Leo Szilard, the Man Behind the Bomb* (New York: Scribner's, 1993), 237 ff.; William Lawren, *The General and the Bomb: A Biography of General Leslie R. Groves, Director of the Manhattan Project* (New York: Dodd, Mead, 1988), 76 ff.; Compton, *Atomic Quest,* 114 ff.

21. This explains, I think, his habit of publicly humiliating, with some regularity, the District Engineer, Colonel Kenneth D. Nichols. According to physicist Robert Serber, "General Groves . . . turned up in Berkeley in October [1942]. That was the first time I met him. I was in the office with Oppy [J. Robert Oppenheimer] when Groves came in with a colonel in tow, probably Ken Nichols. Groves walked in, unbuttoned his tunic, took it off, handed it to Nichols and said, 'take this and find a dry cleaner and get it cleaned.' Treating a colonel like an errand boy. That was Groves's way." Robert Serber, *The Los Alamos Primer: The First Lectures on How to Build an Atomic Bomb* (Berkeley: University of California Press, 1992), xxxii. It should be pointed out that Nichols was one of the few members of the Corps of Engineers who held a Ph.D.

22. Lawren, *The General and the Bomb,* 78.

23. The issue of compartmentalization within the Manhattan Project is explored in Stanley Goldberg, "Groves and the Scientists: Compartmentalization and the Struggle to Build the Bomb," *Physics Today* 48 (August 1995): 38–43.

24. Hewlett and Anderson, *The New World,* 104–6. According to Groves's diary, the Met Lab director, Arthur Compton, and associate director, Norman Hillberry, were present at the October 2 meeting at which this first MED contract with Du Pont was negotiated. It is likely therefore that when Groves arrived in Chicago on October 5, the Met Lab scientists already knew that Du Pont was going to design and operate the separation plants.

25. See Conant to Groves, December 9, 1942, NARA, RG 227, S-1, Bush-Conant Files, folder 86. At the end of 1941, the best estimate of the cost of the bomb project available to Conant put the price at $133 million. This memo was in response to a summary of expenses *to date* that Groves had provided to Conant, which totaled $500 million. A shocked Conant responded that if he were not convinced that we were in a race with the Germans, he would recommend immediate cancellation of the project.

26. During his first contacts with the Chicago scientists on October 5 and October 15, 1942, several of them tried to convince Groves that if he would assign to them some fifty to one hundred junior engineers and draftsmen they could quickly complete the construction of the industrial reactors and separation plants. When it is realized that in order to build Hanford, the largest construction camp ever assembled (some forty-five to fifty thousand people) was required and that the effort stretched the limits of the Du Pont corporation, it should not be surprising that Groves never put much stock in the advice of the scientists on matters of engineering and construction.

27. These negotiations are best described by Hewlett and Anderson, *The New World,* 103–14, and by Groueff, *Manhattan Project,* 63–84.

28. Groueff, *Manhattan Project,* 67. Of course one dollar was not the sum total of Du Pont's profits from their work on the Manhattan Project. The expertise they acquired during the war was an investment that has since paid for itself many times over. See David A. Hounshell and John Kenly Smith, Jr., *Science and Corporate Strategy: Du Pont R&D, 1902–1980* (Cambridge and New York: Cambridge University Press, 1988), 332–33.

29. Hewlett and Anderson, *The New World,* 110–12, 186.

30. See, for example, the letter of complaint, dated August 13, 1943, from Eugene Wigner, the Met Lab physicist largely responsible for the design of the production reactors, to Met Lab director A. H. Compton, NARA, RG 77, Records of the Army Corps of Engineers, Files of the Manhattan Engineer District, Entry 5, The Decimal File (hereafter Decimal File), folder .080 ("Laboratories"). Even long after the war, Wigner still referred to the fact that Du Pont "stole my reactor"; personal communication to the author from Professor Wigner, March 3, 1987. Cf. Andrew Szanton, ed., *The Recollections of Eugene P. Wigner* (New York: Plenum Press, 1992), 231–35.

31. Quoted in Fine and Remington, *Corps of Engineers,* 666. (Nichols became district engineer, succeeding Colonel Marshall, in summer 1943; he commanded the headquarters at Oak Ridge, under Groves in D.C.) At one point, after the reactors were up and running, Fermi suggested to one of the Du Pont reactor engineers that if Du Pont had not been so conservative about making sure the reactor was well shielded, it could have been completed in much less time. When the engineer asked Fermi how he would have coped with the problem of ionizing radiation, Fermi replied that he would have placed the reactor on an island and operated and serviced it by remote control from a submarine. Personal communication to the author from Ralph K. Wahlen, January 13, 1987.

32. For something of the flavor of the situation see Lawren, *The General and the Bomb,* 116–17.

33. See, e.g., L. R. Groves, "Memo to File," February 16, 1968, NARA, RG 200,

Groves Papers, Entry 10, Interviews, comments, etc. (hereafter Groves Papers, Entry 10), folder "Seaborg, Glenn."

34. Hanford Administration Interview, pp. 12–14 of the transcript corresponding to the portion of the videotape after time marker 01:28:21:00.

35. Groves, *Now It Can Be Told,* 71.

36. Hanford Administration Interview, pp. 17–18, after time marker 01:37:21:00 on the tape.

37. Cf. Robert E. Johnstone, *Pilot Plants, Models and Scale-up Methods* (New York: McGraw-Hill, 1957); Glenn Murphy, *Similitude in Engineering* (New York: Ronald Press, 1950).

38. Hounshell and Smith, *Science and Corporate Strategy,* 257–74.

39. Minutes of the Military Policy Committee (MPC), November 12, 1942, General Groves's Secret Files, folder 23, tab A. The MPC had been created by Vannevar Bush, with the president's approval, to oversee Manhattan Project decisions. It was a three-man committee. Bush served as chair and was flanked by a representative from the Army, General Styer, and one from the Navy, Admiral Purnell. Groves served as recording secretary, and once Bush and the others realized how well Groves could manage things, the committee became largely a rubber stamp for his decisions. Ironically, its original purpose was to allow Bush to make sure that control of the direction of the project did not simply accrue to the Army and result in no input from civilian scientists. See Goldberg, "Groves Takes the Reins."

40. The phrase "in time" can and later did take on several other meanings. It might mean in time to prevent the Soviets from getting a firm toehold in the Pacific theater; or it might mean in time to obviate the need for an invasion of the Japanese homeland.

41. Groves did have help in understanding technical issues of nuclear physics, chemistry, and chemical engineering. Early in his tenure as head of the Project, he received informal advice from both Conant and Tolman. In June 1943, he formalized these arrangements. See Groves to Tolman, June 11, 1943, Decimal File, folder 201, "Tolman." Prior to his appointment as president of Harvard, Conant had made his reputation in organic chemistry and had extensive experience in chemical engineering. See Hershberg, *Conant,* 35–84. Tolman had come to Washington from the California Institute of Technology in 1940. He had been dean of the Graduate School at Cal Tech, but had volunteered his services to Vannevar Bush, then head of the NDRC. He remained in Washington for the duration of the war. Tolman was considered America's leading proponent of the special and general theories of relativity. He was trained, originally, as a physical chemist. See Stanley Goldberg, *Understanding Relativity: The Origin and Impact of a Scientific Theory* (Boston: Birkhauser, 1984), 267 ff.

42. Somervell to Chief of Engineers, September 17, 1942, Styer's MED File.

43. See, for example the memo from James Marshall to Groves, November 9, 1942, Decimal File, folder 110 ("Appropriations").

44. See, for example, Groves to F. C. Alexander, June 6, 1961, Groves Papers, Entry 2, Correspondence, 1941–1970, folder Ac-Az.; and undated speech (1946?), Groves Papers, Entry 1, General Correspondence, 1941–1970, folder "Public Relations Articles, Misc (by L. R. Groves)"; Groves to Maxwell Stamp, January 7, 1947, Groves Papers, Entry 3, Personal Correspondence, 1906–1970, folder "Groves, L.R.—Letters to Friends."

45. Hewlett and Anderson, *The New World,* 723.

46. Ibid.

47. Groves, *Now It Can Be Told,* p. 81.

48. Hewlett and Anderson, *The New World,* 204–12. The experimental reactor, X-10, at Oak Ridge, was not a semiworks for the Hanford reactors. X-10 was air cooled; the Hanford reactors were water cooled. Reactor-produced plutonium differed from plutonium produced in a cyclotron. The former contained a significant fraction of an isotope, plutonium 240, which fissions spontaneously at a rate high enough to preclude using the same method of assembly for the plutonium weapon as is used for assembly of the uranium bomb. The confirmation of this fact in the summer of 1944 resulted in a major reorganization of the bomb design laboratory at Los Alamos so as to emphasize research on a different form of bomb assembly. See Lillian Hoddeson et al., *Critical Assembly* (Cambridge and New York: Cambridge University Press, 1993), 228 ff.

49. See Civilian Production Administration, *Industrial Mobilization for War,* vol. 1, *Program and Administration* (New York: Greenwood Press, 1969); Millet, *Organization and Role of the Army Service Forces;* Donald Nelson, *Arsenal of Democracy: The Story of American War Production* (New York: DeCapo Press, 1973); Elberton R. Smith, *The Army and Economic Mobilization* (Washington, D.C.: Government Printing Office, 1959). I am indebted to Mara Benjamin for background material on the relationship between the wartime priority system bureaucracy and the Manhattan Project.

50. NARA, RG 225, Records of the Army-Navy Munitions Board File, folder 400.174/216.2; Tehron Weaver to Groves, Decimal File, folder 322.011. (Brig. Gen. Weaver was deputy director of the Resources and Production Division of Army Service Forces.) Col. F. R. Denton to Chief Engineer, Decimal File, folder 400.1301. (Denton was Tehron Weaver's assistant.)

51. Smith, *The Army and Economic Mobilization,* 509–53, passim. For examples, see the correspondence between Groves and Assistant Secretary of War Robert P. Patterson as well as the correspondence between Patterson and Donald Nelson, Patterson and Nelson's assistant J. A. Krug, and Patterson and Paul McNutt, head

of the War Manpower Commission, in NARA, RG 77, Papers of the Army Corps of Engineers, Files of the Manhattan Engineer District, Entry 2, Harrison-Bundy Files, folders 51 and 80. It should be noted that Groves drafted most of Patterson's letters to Nelson, Krug, and McNutt.

52. The circular letter was signed by H. D. Batcheller, Vice Chair, Operations, WPB. See Harrison-Bundy Files, folder 51.

53. Ibid., folders 51 and 80.

54. Patterson to Krug, February 22, 1944, ibid., folder 51. Emphasis added.

55. Interview with Charles W. Campbell, NARA, RG 319, Office of the Chief of Military History, Manhattan Files, folder "Manhattan Interviews—Los Alamos, Berkeley, and Hanford, 1964." (Campbell was with the War Manpower Commission during the war and assisted in the recruitment of manpower for Hanford in 1944.) Cf. Collins to Patterson, NARA, RG 107, Records of the Secretary of War, Robert Patterson Files, box 142, folder "Hanford." (Lt. Col. John K. Collins was chief of the Labor and Manpower Branch, Resources Division, Office of the Assistant Chief of Air Staff.)

56. S. L. Sanger, *Hanford and the Bomb: An Oral History of World War II* (Seattle: Living History Press, 1989), 45 ff. Cf. Smithsonian Video History Program, Manhattan Project, Division I, Hanford, especially sessions 1 and 2, "Operations of Plutonium Production Facilities," passim.

57. Patterson to McNutt, April 21, 1944, Harrison-Bundy Files, folder 51.

58. Patterson to Appley, May 2, 1944, Harrison-Bundy Files, folder 80. The same memo was sent to Major Ira B. Cross, Industrial Personnel Division, Armed Forces Services.

59. Patterson to Roosevelt, February 24, 1944, Harrison-Bundy Files, folder 51.

60. See Franklin Matthias, "Notes and Diary," Department of Energy Public Reading Room, Richland, Washington (hereafter Matthias Diary), passim. Patterson to Hutcheson, May 11, 1944, and Hutcheson to Patterson, May 12, 1944, Harrison-Bundy Files, folder 51. (William L. Hutcheson was general president of the UBCJ.) Patterson to Durkin, August 29, 1944, Harrison-Bundy Files, folder 51. Groves to Durkin, July 20, 1944, ibid.; cf. Anonymous (Madigan?) to Patterson, August 28, 1944. (Jack Madigan was a longtime civilian troubleshooter consultant to the Army Corps of Engineers Construction Division.)

61. See an undated set of notes by Groves on this subject in the Groves Papers, Entry 10, folder "Pogue."

62. Remington and Fine, *Corps of Engineers*, 387–92, 427–30.

63. Schmitthausler to Truman, October 4, 1943, NARA, RG 46, Records of the Senate, Sen 79A-F30 National Defense Committee OP-19 Ordnance Plants (hereafter Truman Committee Files), folder "Hanford Ordnance."

64. Bundy to Stimson, June 11, 1943, Harrison-Bundy Files, folder 62; Amberg

to Fulton, June 24, 1943, Truman Committee Files. (Julius H. Amberg had been president of the Michigan Bar Association and was now an assistant to Secretary of War Stimson; Hugh A. Fulton was the Truman Committee's chief counsel.)

65. See, for example, the Matthias Diary entry for December 7, 1943; Amberg to Groves, February 22, 1944; Patterson to Stimson, March 11, 1943, Harrison-Bundy Files, folder 62; Truman to Cooper, March 13, 1944, Truman Committee Files. Stimson to Truman, March 13, 1944, Harrison-Bundy Files, folder 62.

66. Tilley to Sapper, October 18, 1944, *Seaman v. Du Pont,* Exhibits accompanying deposition of Kenneth David Nichols, August 20, 1991 (hereafter Nichols Deposition), defendant exhibit 23. (J. N. Tilley was assistant manager of Du Pont's TNX division, the special explosives division devoted to plutonium production. Major W. L. Sapper was MED Wilmington [Delaware] area engineer.)

67. Groves to Ackart, November 16, 1943, Nichols Deposition, exhibit 24. Teletype, Groves to Nichols, November 16, 1944, Nichols Deposition, exhibit 24. (All Manhattan Project area offices, the district office at Oak Ridge, and Groves's office were connected to a secure teletype system independent of other War Department teletype networks.) A note was penciled on the teletype: "tt [teletype] sent to Maj. Sapper. req. he be in LRG's [Groves's] office on Sat."

68. Otto and Simon to Tilley, November 21, 1944, Nichols Deposition, exhibit 25. (F. A. Otto was Du Pont's production superintendent at Hanford.)

69. Groves Diary, November 29, 1944. Simon to Tilley, December 23, 1944, Nichols Deposition, exhibit 26. Groves Diary, December 27, 1944. Groves to Marshall, December 30, 1944, General Groves's Secret Files, folder 24, tab C. On the last page of the document Marshall has written: "To: S/W. I think the foregoing proposal should be approved with your concurrence. GCM." Groves has written, "The Sec of War and the President both read this paper and approved it.—12/30/44 LRG."

70. Groves to Marshall, December 30, 1944. A note attached to the memo, in Groves's hand, states that the penciled underlining was done by Secretary Stimson in preparation for the meeting with the president.

71. On the uncertainties about the amount of plutonium required for the early bomb designs being mainly a function of how rushed Los Alamos was to complete the bomb "in time," see Hoddeson et al., *Critical Assembly,* 311–45.

72. The slugs of uranium, jacketed in aluminum "cans," were approximately 8 inches (20.5 cm) long. They were inserted into the reactor in long aluminum tubes that ran from the front to the rear of the reactor. They were discharged by being pushed out of the rear of the reactor, thereby falling into a chute that carried them down to the "swimming pool" storage area. They would then be allowed to "cool" under water while the short-lived fission product iodine 131 (half-life between 8 and 9 days) dissipated. During the design of the process, it was decided that the standard cooling-off period should be 90 days—a little more

than eleven half-lives. At that point the billets, still highly radioactive, were to be shipped, in large lead casks, on rail tracks, over to the separation plants. The first step in the separation process was to dissolve the aluminum jacket, at which point any residual iodine (a gas at these temperatures) would be swept up the stack and exhausted to the atmosphere.

73. See the discussion in note 72 above. The effects on the environment are similar to those that occurred during the "green run" experiments we now know were conducted at Hanford in December 1949. The Department of Energy declassified reports of those experiments in 1990. See, e.g., W. Singlevich, "Health Instrument Environs Report for the Month of December 1949." This HEW report was dated January 9, 1950, Department of Energy Reading Room, Richland, Washington.

74. Groves to Williams, January 13, 1945, General Groves's Secret Files, folder 5, tab H. Later (Groves to Williams, February 15, 1945, folder 5, tab I), when enough data had been gathered, this estimate was increased to a waste of 50 tons of uranium metal. It is difficult to estimate the cost of uranium metal. During the war, the United States was paying approximately $2.00 per pound for relatively rich ore from the Belgian Congo (now Zaire). The cost of refining and smelting is quite high. Shortly after the war, Canada was buying uranium metal from the United States at about $11.00 per pound. See Robert Bothwell, *Eldorado: Canada's National Uranium Company* (Toronto: University of Toronto Press, 1984), 268. If one uses a nominal figure of $10.00 per pound (1940s dollars), the cost of 50 tons is $1 million, not much money on the scale of the cost of the entire project. However, uranium metal was a precious and rare commodity in 1945. See, e.g., Jonathan E. Helmreich, *Gathering Rare Ores: The Diplomacy of Uranium Acquisition, 1943–1954* (Princeton: Princeton University Press, 1986).

75. Williams to Groves, February 14, 1945, and Groves to Williams, February 15, 1945, General Groves's Secret Files, folder 5, tab I.

76. See, e.g., Matthias Diary, entries for February 20, 21, and 26, 1945 (the February 21 entry refers to the "super acceleration"); Groves Diary, February 27, 1945: "JO'L [Jean O'Leary, Groves's administrative assistant] called Mr. Tilley" and "Tilley advised that . . . [they are discharging on an accelerated basis] but the degree of acceleration is still to be determined." Nichols to Groves, March 9, 1945, General Groves's Secret Files, folder 5, tab I. Groves to Oppenheimer, March 22, 1945, folder 5, tab L. Cf. Groves to Williams, March 22, 1945, folder 5, tab J.

77. See Williams to Groves, February 14, 1945; Matthias Diary, May 9, 1945.

78. Matthias Diary, July 10, 1945. Barbara Storms and John Savage, "Reach to the Unknown," a special issue of *The Atom* 2, no. 8 (July 16, 1965). *The Atom* is a publication of the Los Alamos National Laboratories.

79. F. G. Gosling, *The Manhattan Project: Science in the Second World War* (Washington, D.C.: U.S. Department of Energy, 1990), 62 ff.

80. Groves later reported that shortly after the war General Lucius Clay admitted knowing, once he learned of Groves's appointment to head the Manhattan Engineer District, that when it came to claims on vital resources, it would be impossible for him to control Groves the way he had controlled and throttled Groves's predecessor, Colonel James Marshall. Undated memo to file, Groves Papers, Entry 10, folder "Marshall, James C."

81. Groves, *Now It Can Be Told,* 155.

82. For a sense of the flavor of life in Oak Ridge during the war, see Stanley Goldberg, Smithsonian Video History Interviews, session 5, "Life in Oak Ridge, Tennessee, Interview with Connie Bolling, Colleen Black, Audrey Livingston and Jane Larson, 3 March 1987, Oak Ridge Tennessee." The quotations were personal comments to the author by Connie Bolling and Colleen Black. Cf. James Overholt, ed., *These Are Our Voices: The Story of Oak Ridge, 1942–1970* (Oak Ridge: Children's Museum of Oak Ridge, 1987).

83. Brynes to Stimson, September 11, 1943, Harrison-Bundy Files, folder 8.

84. Searls to Byrnes, February 24, 1945, included in Vinson to Searls, April 20, 1945. NARA, RG 250, Papers of the Office of War Mobilization and Reconversion, Files of the Director's Office, box 161, folder "Memorandum—Fred Searls." Fred M. Vinson was Byrnes's successor as director. Subsequently, in June 1946, his appointment as chief justice of the Supreme Court was confirmed by the Senate. I am indebted to David M. Hart for calling this document to my attention and for providing me with a copy. (For a brief account of Searls's career, see his obituary, *New York Times,* October 23, 1968, 47:2.)

85. Byrnes to Roosevelt, March 3, 1945, Harrison-Bundy Files, folder 8.

86. After the war, Searls served as consultant to the United States's UN Atomic Energy Committee delegation, as did Groves. If Groves had known of Searls's 1945 position on the Manhattan Project, it is likely that he would have confronted him, and they probably would not have worked together as well as they did. See, e.g., Searls to Baruch, March 31, 1946, folder 20.11, "Baruch, Bernard," and Hancock to Searls, October 9, 1946, folder 20.119, "Searls, Fred," in NARA, RG 59, Records of the Department of State, Files of the Special Assistant to the Secretary of State for Atomic Energy Matters, 1944–52 (Lot 57D688).

87. Groves, Memo to file, April 7, 1945, General Groves's Secret Files, folder 20, tab L. For Stimson's reaction to the memo, see his account of his discussion of the matter with FDR in Henry L. Stimson and McGeorge Bundy, *On Active Service in Peace and War* (New York: Octagon Books, 1971), 615–16.

88. Matthias Diary, April 20, 1945.

89. The twenty-five page report that Groves prepared for Truman is dated April 23, 1945, and is in the form of a memo from Groves to Stimson. See General Groves's Secret Files, folder 25, tab M. Cf. Groves, Memo to file, April 25, 1945, Groves Papers, Entry 10, folder "Truman, Harry S."

90. Bush to Bundy, April 24, 1945, Harrison-Bundy Files, folder 19. Cf. Rhodes, *Making of the Atomic Bomb,* 523–38; Martin Sherwin, *A World Destroyed: The Atomic Bomb and the Grand Alliance* (New York: Knopf, 1975; Vintage, 1977), 105–9; Hewlett and Anderson, *The New World,* 344. Bush and Conant to MED Post War Policy Committee, Harrison-Bundy Files, folder 76. This Groves-appointed committee, chaired by R. C. Tolman, was considering postwar alternatives for nuclear technologies. See Hewlett and Anderson, *The New World,* 322 ff. On the development of Bush and Conant's attitudes toward international control of atomic energy, see Hershberg, *Conant,* 194 ff.

91. Bundy to Stimson, December 9, 1944, Harrison-Bundy Files, folder 108; December 16, 1944, folder 69; December 30, 1945, folder 5. Harrison to Stimson, May 1, 1945, folder 69.

92. The name given the committee was meant to assure Congress of its temporary nature and that it was not an attempt to undermine congressional authority for legislation in the area of nuclear energy. For a detailed account of the composition of the committee and its workings, see Sherwin, *A World Destroyed,* 167–70, 202 ff., and appendixes K–O; cf. Hewlett and Anderson, *The New World,* 344–45, 353 ff.; Rhodes, *Making of the Atomic Bomb,* 641–49. On Byrnes, see Robert L. Messer, *The End of an Alliance: James F. Byrnes, Roosevelt, Truman and the Origins of the Cold War* (Chapel Hill: University of North Carolina Press, 1982), 84–86; cf. Harry S. Truman, *Memoirs,* vol. 1, *Year of Decisions* (Garden City, N.Y.: Doubleday, 1955), 419.

93. Hershberg, *Conant,* 224.

94. See the references cited in note 92 above.

95. Messer, *End of an Alliance,* 86, 114 ff. Alperovitz, *Atomic Diplomacy,* passim. Alperovitz's central thesis is that the atomic bomb was used as a tool in the service of the American confrontation of Soviet power.

96. See, e.g., the photograph of Byrnes and Truman, at the bow of the cruiser *Augusta,* on their way to the Potsdam Conference in Messer, *End of an Alliance,* 85.

97. See note 25 above. Conant's concerns have been discussed in Hershberg, *Conant,* 78 and 808, note 19.

98. Patterson to Madigan, Harrison-Bundy Files, folder 51.

99. Groves, *Now It Can Be Told,* 360.

100. Patterson to Styer, February 15, 1945, Styer's MED File. This may account for Groves's insistence on producing an elaborate history of the entire project, the so-called Manhattan District History. See note 12 above.

101. In fact there never was a race with Germany. Between the fall of 1940 and the summer of 1941, German authorities had decided that an atomic bomb could never be finished in time to play a role in the war. See Mark Walker, *German National Socialism and the Quest for Nuclear Power* (Cambridge and New York: Cambridge University Press, 1989). Groves's view on ending the war with Japan

was one of the themes that recurred in the many speeches he delivered between the end of the war and his death. Many of these speeches are preserved in the Groves Papers, Entry 9. See, for example, the end of his speech at West Point, November 12, 1945.

102. Hoddeson et al., *Critical Assembly,* 315 ff.; Hewlett and Anderson, *The New World,* 347 ff.

103. See, e.g., Richard P. Feynman, *Surely You're Joking, Mr. Feynman: Adventures of a Curious Character* (New York: Norton, 1985; Bantam, 1986), 118; Luis W. Alvarez, *Alvarez: Adventures of a Physicist* (New York: Basic Books, 1987), 147–52.

104. Remarks of Robert Serber in Smithsonian Manhattan Project Video History, Division 3, Cambridge, session 12, "Interview with Robert Serber, Philip Morrison, Bernard Feld, Cyril Smith"; Alvarez, *Alvarez,* 147–52.

105. Michael Sherry, *The Rise of American Air Power: The Creation of Armageddon* (New Haven: Yale University Press, 1987), 219–356, esp. 273 ff.; Leon V. Sigal, *Fighting to a Finish: The Politics of War Termination in the United States and Japan, 1945* (Ithaca: Cornell University Press, 1988), 158–223; Ronald Schaffer, *Wings of Judgment: American Bombing in World War II* (New York: Oxford University Press, 1985), 106–89; Rhodes, *Making of the Atomic Bomb,* 584–600. But see John Dower, *War Without Mercy: Race and Power in the Pacific War* (New York: Pantheon Books, 1986). Dower points out (p. 298) that if one excludes the March 15, 1945, raid on Tokyo in which 100,000 Japanese lost their lives, more deaths resulted from the raids on Hiroshima and Nagasaki than from the combined total resulting from the sixty-three other fire bombings of Japanese cities.

106. Groves to General Marshall, December 30, 1944; Groves, *Now It Can Be Told,* 266–68.

107. No secondary source does justice to how quickly Kirkpatrick was able to establish the 509th's required facilities on Tinian. See The Files of the Manhattan Engineer District, Entry 3, Tinian Files. The best, albeit brief, accounts of the ambiance surrounding the 509th's work on Tinian are in Lawren, *The General and the Bomb,* 229–31; Alvarez, *Alvarez,* 144–46.

108. Marshall to Handy, July 22, 1945, and Handy to Marshall, July 24, 1945, Harrison-Bundy Files, folder 64. The orders, drafted by Groves, have been widely reprinted. See, e.g., Groves, *Now It Can Be Told,* 308–9; Rhodes, *Making of the Atomic Bomb,* 691. Cf. Fletcher Knebel and Charles W. Bailey, *No High Ground* (Westport: Greenwood Press, 1985), 95–96; Sigal, *Fighting to a Finish,* 212.

109. Groves, *Now It Can Be Told,* 309–11.

110. Groves to Oppenheimer, July 19, 1945; teletype, Oppenheimer to Groves, July 19, 1945, John Manley Papers, Los Alamos National Laboratory Archives, folder "Third Bomb Documents."

111. Minutes of the Meetings of the Special Project Technical Committee [on Tinian] for July 24, July 28, and August 1, 1945, Tinian Files, envelope A.

112. Teletype, Groves to Kirkpatrick and Farrell, August 1, 1945, Tinian Files, envelope I. (General Thomas Farrell was Groves's second in command. He had been appointed to that job in December 1944.)

113. Farrell to O'Leary, August 7 and 8, 1945, Tinian Files, envelope G.

114. Groves, *Now It Can Be Told,* 298.

115. Groves Papers, Entry 9, Speeches, 1941–1964, folder "Industrial Preparedness: A speech before the Industrial College of the Armed Forces."

116. Groves to Styer, October 12, 1945, Groves Papers, Entry 2, folder "Stu-SZ."

Building the Atomic Cities

Richland, Los Alamos, and the
American Planning Language

Carl Abbott

Los Alamos and Richland—the atomic cities that the Manhattan Engineer District built in New Mexico and Washington in 1943—were isolated by intent. Los Alamos met the seemingly contradictory requirements of defensible landscape, isolation from concentrated populations, a location at least 200 miles from the Pacific coast and international borders, and reasonable convenience to rail transportation and a commercial airport. It was also J. Robert Oppenheimer's strong preference once the search for a site narrowed to New Mexico.[1] Seclusion was easily maintained with a single washboarded access road that crossed the Rio Grande, clawed its way up the steep face of the Pajarito Plateau, passed through a fence and checkpoint, and continued for three more dusty miles along a finger of the plateau before reaching the laboratories and their supporting community.[2]

Richland was doubly isolated. The 620-square-mile Hanford Site in central Washington was chosen for its remoteness and its sparse local population as well as its access to fresh water, electric power, and sand and gravel deposits for construction aggregate. As Du Pont manager Walter Simon remembered, "Only after the design work was started did someone raise the question of where the workers were going to live." The small townsite of Richland, with a population of about 200, was picked for the "operating village" because its location 25 miles from the plutonium production facilities well exceeded the 10-mile minimum set by project scientists. It was also 20 miles from the huge construction camp that engulfed the even smaller town of Hanford.[3] At the same time, Richland had the advantage of being a preexisting town with road access, a handful of buildings, and rudimentary utility systems.[4]

In these two towns, as in a number of predecessor communities in the intermountain West, the early descriptions and later recollections of residents placed less emphasis on the towns themselves than on the hardships and attractions of their settings—vistas, sunrises, and high skies counterbalanced by heat, cold, dirt, and "dust pneumonia." Many residents understood and later represented their experiences in the hectic years of 1943 and 1944 as pioneer life on a western frontier—a choice between "adventure or disaster, depending on how you wanted to look at it." So did Manhattan Project head General Leslie R. Groves, who reportedly told Colonel J. C. Marshall that the scientists at Los Alamos "will like anything you build for them. Put up some barracks. They will think they are pioneers out here in the Far West."[5]

The frontier imagery would take on new meanings as the towns evolved. Both communities were obviously participants in the scientific frontier of the mid-twentieth century. "We were pioneers—we were pushing back the frontiers of knowledge," recalled one Hanford worker about the 1950s.[6] In a contrary vein, residents sometimes argued that the new "frontier" cities were hardship posts whose improvised facilities should be compensated by financial breaks from the federal landlord. A third restatement of the pioneer theme was an effort to construct a public identity that connected the "special" towns with the traditional West. Richland's Atomic Frontier Days, first celebrated under that name in 1948, was a consciously constructed civic festival identifying the instant city with the innumerable western towns that staged dusty rodeos and other invocations of the Anglo-American frontier.

Just as often, however, observers described the postwar cities as ideal communities rather than frontier towns. No longer were they prefab slums surrounded by wintertime mire or choked with wind-driven grit. Instead, said their residents and corporate managers, they were ideally built, ordered, and governed examples of "modern and normal" American communities. Neither the "Shangri-La of the Atom" nor the "Model City" of Richland suffered the stresses of slums, crime, poverty, and local taxes.[7] Richland, proclaimed a General Electric pamphlet, was "recognized as one of the best planned cities in the nation." It was a "shiny new village," wrote a San Francisco reporter, "isolated, self-contained . . . happy."[8] Newcomers, said a brochure from the Los Alamos Scientific Laboratory, would find a sophisticated community with great climate, nice housing, and "exceptionally able" teachers.[9] Scientists and engineers could now set off for Los Alamos without embarking on an unwelcome adventure.

Implied in these changing representations is a rapid transformation of the two towns as physical and social environments. My intent in this article is to explore these transformations through the lens of city planning history. What were the precedents on which the Army Corps of Engineers, University of California scientists, and Du Pont managers drew in 1943–46? What models informed planning decisions by the Atomic Energy Commission, its contractors, and their consultants after 1947? What sorts of communities did residents inherit when Richland and Los Alamos became privately owned and self-governing communities in the late 1950s and early 1960s? In turn, how did physical design shape or reflect the social evolution of the two communities?

In addressing these questions, I use the analogy of language to distinguish between the *vocabulary* and the *rhetoric* of city planning. Planning vocabulary consists of a set of design elements and styles that can be expressed in single construction decisions about specific land parcels and buildings. It involves a range of particular options for siting civic buildings, locating commercial districts, running streets, placing playgrounds, and handling traffic. Residential blocks, for example, can be rectilinear or curved; they can be large or small; they can offer builders equal-size or unequal building lots; they can have central alleys or central green spaces or abutting rear lot lines.

Planning rhetoric is the way in which these various elements are combined into a coherent design and community vision. Town plans can be organized around a central point or a dominant axis, as we can see in the extreme contrast between the circles and epicycles of Ebenezer Howard's garden city and the *ciudad lineal* of Arturo Soria y Mata. They can repeat a multitude of small components, like the street grid of Manhattan Island, or a handful of large components, like the neighborhood units of late twentieth-century new towns. They can privilege public or private space. They can integrate or segregate work place and home space. The railroad towns of the northern plains, with their single axis connecting railroad depot and hinterland, are a simple example of an American planning rhetoric. The era of "City Beautiful" planning in the United States from the 1890s to the 1910s was an effort to impose a new and more elaborate rhetoric on functional but unimaginative communities. Current interest in "neotraditional" urban planning attempts to revisit the planning rhetoric of the streetcar era.

The structure of my argument is simple. Los Alamos and Richland were designed and built in 1943 and 1944. They were replanned and substantially rebuilt between 1946 and 1960. The Atomic Energy Commission's model cities of the 1950s, it turns out, were not so much the wartime towns grown up as they were permanent replacements built on the foundations of the emergency settlements. The community imagery changed so markedly from the 1940s to the 1950s because there were new communities to describe.

The "first" and "second" communities, moreover, expressed two different planning rhetorics. The jerry-built towns of the wartime emergency were pale reflections of a self-conscious tradition of idealized community-making with the assistance of the federal government. The more substantial cities of the Truman and Eisenhower eras, in contrast, enthusiastically adopted the commonplace approaches to housing preferred by a newly prosperous nation. In consequence, these "second towns" give the historian a window into American communities and values during the great boom of 1946–74.

THE FIRST CITIES: 1943–45

Richland and Los Alamos rose in 1943 as adjuncts to the real jobs of nuclear weapons research and production. It is a telling commentary that officially sponsored histories of the Corps of Engineers and the Atomic Energy Commission treat the towns themselves as distractions from the main tasks, or even as jokes played on obstreperous scientists.[10] The practical result was to pass the detailed decisions on town design from the Army to the prime contractor and thence to architecture-engineering and construction subcontractors.

Planning in both cases also faced the problems of uncertain futures and unanticipated needs. Projections for the number of scientific staff needed at Los Alamos began with Oppenheimer's improbable estimate that a handful of scientists (cited variously as six, thirty, and one hundred) could design an atomic bomb with the help of a few hundred technical and support staff and family members. Before planning started for the town, the estimate for total population grew from 265 to

450 and then to 600. The planning target was upped twice in 1943 as the decision to pursue the implosion technique for bomb detonation required staff expansion. Actual population by the end of the war was between 6,000 and 7,000. "It always grew much faster than anyone could anticipate," David Hawkins told a visiting journalist in 1946. "It doubled, tripled, quadrupled before anyone could figure out what was happening."[11]

The combined uncertainties about both the success of the enterprise and the postwar future of the Los Alamos site gave strong reasons to build a minimal town to minimum standards. In addition, community facilities and housing were one of the few places where General Groves could dare to cut costs, insisting, for example, on green lumber and on coal or wood stoves. In effect, wartime Los Alamos was a collaboration of four different sets of planners and builders. Willard C. Kruger and Associates of Santa Fe were in charge of overall site planning and development. The primary construction contractor was M. M. Sundt of Tucson. Robert E. McKee of El Paso did general contracting and manufactured prefabricated housing. Bernis E. Brazier was a Denver architect who became a de facto community planner while working for Oppenheimer as his manager of facility development from May 1943 to January 1944.[12]

Kruger developed the site plan from preliminary work done by Stone and Webster, the engineering firm that was also playing a central role in the development of Oak Ridge, Tennessee. The University of California approved the Kruger plans in its role as prime contractor at the end of 1942. The general plan used the Los Alamos Ranch School buildings (previously occupied by a boys' school) as a nucleus, with the technical area to the south and residential community to northeast.[13] Living space came as "barracks, garages, and crackerboxes" in the opinion of one early resident. The buildings and locations also reflected the social hierarchy of Los Alamos. A handful of top scientists and managers lived in "bathtub row," the old Ranch School houses that boasted full plumbing. The first "generation" of 332 Sundt apartments, with convenient location and hardwood floors, took second rank and accommodated scientists such as Edward Teller, Hans Bethe, and Enrico Fermi. Brazier's last job for the project was to prepare sketches for new duplexes, built by J. E. Morgan and Sons of El Paso. Other junior scientists and latecomers were assigned to the McKeeville grid of 100 flat-roofed single-family houses. The community also got just over 100 "Pasco" houses built to the pattern of prefabs used for Richland. At the bottom of the list were trailers and uninsulated quonset huts for construction and maintenance staff, and barracks for the military police and for the Special Engineering Department—GIs with scientific or technical training who had been drafted and assigned to the Manhattan Engineer District.[14]

The visible touches of good planning, like many other positive aspects of Los Alamos, have been attributed in retrospect to Oppenheimer. He was credited with street layouts that occasionally respected the contours of the mesa or at least looped in long curves rather than following the straight lines of an army cantonment. He and architect Brazier also received credit for the beautifully situated and perhaps overbuilt school that faced north to the Jemez Mountains through a wall of glass. In fact, the school design responded to the suggestions of Walter Cook, a University of Minnesota education professor hired as consultant by a six-member school committee appointed jointly by Oppenheimer and the post commander.[15]

The planning of Richland faced similar problems, although pressures from Du Pont helped to secure housing and facilities that were a step up from those at Los Alamos. Staff from the Chief Engineer's office in Washington, D.C., prepared a master plan for the village in the winter of 1942–43, identifying land use patterns and locations for major buildings. Du Pont then engaged architect G. A. Pehrson of Spokane to design individual buildings and housing models and to supervise the construction process.[16] When Pehrson began work in March 1943, the Corps of Engineers was projecting a need for 980 family housing units plus dormitory space for 6,500 people. By the time the first of the new houses were occupied in July 1943, the population projections were already at 15,000. Before the war was over, the original projections had grown by nearly threefold to 17,500, and the number of houses on the ground totaled 4,300.[17]

At the core of the new village were hurriedly built wooden administrative buildings, a hospital, and a small commercial strip that incorporated *two* of the original main street buildings. Dormitories clustered west of the commercial and administrative core. The bare-bones administrative buildings and barracks gave the town an initial appearance of "an army post-type village," overbalancing the new shopping strip that faced a small grassy mall.[18] The "army" theme was carried through in the residential neighborhoods. South and northwest of the village center were frame duplexes. The "A" house was a three-bedroom, two-story duplex clad in clapboards. The "B" house was a smaller one-story, two-bedroom duplex covered with shingles. Colonel Franklin T. Matthias, the officer in charge at Hanford, directly negotiated a contract with Prefabricated Engineering Company of Portland, which produced 2,300 prefab houses on an 800-foot assembly line. Sited directly west of the village center, these all-plywood, flat-roofed boxes had the great advantage of electric rather than coal heat.[19]

General Groves begrudged the diversion of resources from plutonium plants to community development and operated within War Department guidelines that limited the cost of each type of housing, from $3,000 for a duplex unit to $7,500 for one of the rare four-bedroom houses. In particular, the master plan and the scarce resources combined to narrow many streets, to substitute a common open space in each block for individual yards, and to keep the nascent downtown to a minimum.[20] Commercial services were scaled to a population of 7,750—the anticipated size of the permanent town after removal of the prefabricated housing. They were also limited to single concessionaires for each service or retail category, for an eventual total of thirty-seven businesses.[21] Dormitory residents could eat in the government cafeteria in the center of town. "If you didn't want to eat there," remembered one worker, "you could go to Kennewick and eat at some cafe. Kennewick was still small. . . . People still kinda resented us."[22] Residents of Richland were also dependent on Kennewick and Pasco for all but the most basic goods.

Under the pressure of tight deadlines and scarce resources, managers and planners in these first three years of the Atomic West borrowed haphazardly from two "traditions" of federal town-making that had developed over the previous quarter century. Elements of the planning vocabulary came from cooperative communities. Rhetoric and decision processes imitated public works towns.[23]

From 1917 to the early 1940s, the federal government built or financed a series of specialized communities that expressed a coherent set of "communitarian" values.[24] The list includes World War I communities for shipyard workers built by the Emergency Fleet Corporation and the U.S. Housing Corporation, the Greenbelt towns of the Resettlement Administration in the 1930s, the Tennessee Valley Authority's construction and operating town of Norris, Tennessee, and several projects built by the Federal Works Administration in the early years of World War II.

All of these efforts drew directly or indirectly on the approach of a group of ideologically committed architects and planners who were trying to bring the "good planning" ideas of British garden city planners to the United States. Key participants in this transatlantic tradition were a self-conscious group of northeasterners who participated in or had close ties with the Regional Planning Association of America.[25]

Communitarian planners wanted to provide internally egalitarian and "protected" environments for the skilled working class and middle class. Protection meant spatial definition and isolation from surroundings by distinct street plans and limited access points. Project designers tried to balance low housing costs with variety in lot size, housing style, and siting. The projects also tried to provide a wide range of community services and public open spaces that might facilitate interaction among the residents. The preferred planning vocabulary included superblocks with interior open spaces; civic centers or village greens; pedestrian paths separated from automobile routes; and "naturally" curving streets.[26]

Specific elements of this interwar planning vocabulary appeared in each town. Los Alamos residents enjoyed a number of streets adapted to contours and views. Richland's small "downtown" fronted a strip of grass with parking behind the buildings.[27] Richland grouped housing by rudimentary neighborhood units, in part because of the necessity to divide building sites between two ridges of higher land relatively safe from flooding. "Inner-block" commons in some of the residential areas echoed design elements from Greenbelt, Maryland, and Radburn, New Jersey.

Early residents of Richland have remembered an egalitarian spirit, promoted by similar backgrounds and a sense of being operations personnel rather than construction workers. Indeed, construction workers were evicted when operations staff began to arrive early in 1944. Du Pont's project manager shared dormitory space along with other workers for his first three months in town. Other reminiscences indicate easy social mixing between dormitory dwellers and householders, who generally shared similar backgrounds and a common sense of "challenge" and "adventure." "After we moved from Hanford Camp to Richland," recalled Hope Sloan Amacker, "it was better because the married couples had houses and they entertained a lot." Single-family and duplex houses were mixed at a relatively fine grain, a pattern that Pehrson described as an explicit expression of a "democratic attitude." It is important to remember, however, that corporate bureaucracy soon outweighed architectural utopianism.

The new housing was assigned according to an eligibility list based on employee rank within the Du Pont Company's organization chart; single family houses were for engineers, the duplexes for technical and support staff.[28]

The same sort of community spirit was clearly limited at Los Alamos by class and gender. Memoirs of the male scientists are filled with the excitement of doing science for a great cause.[29] Those of their wives detail the ways that isolation, poor housing, and relative youth fostered a strong sense of unity.[30] Laura Fermi, for example, later talked about the "commune-nature" of life in wartime Los Alamos: "I was in Los Alamos only a year and a half or even less, and *still* it seems such a big portion of my life. . . . It was so different, it was such intense living." Jane Wilson agreed that the war years were marked by "neighborliness and warmth and esprit de corps."[31] Historian Hal Rothman has remarked that Los Alamos to young science families could seem like an exciting reprise of college days.[32] As postwar tensions would reveal, however, support staff and their families in barracks and quonsets felt little of the same frontier camaraderie.[33]

In the larger picture, the numerous and substantial constraints on the planning of one-industry Richland and Los Alamos were more like those in federal public works towns than in cooperative suburbs. Construction towns of the 1930s such as Coulee Dam, Washington, and Boulder City, Nevada, were designed to attract and house a stable construction labor force and later serve a smaller group of dam operators. With constant concern about overbuilding and cost overruns, Reclamation Service engineers simplified the original plans for Boulder City, straightened circular streets, and focused the plan on the administration building rather than a commercial center. Amenities such as trees to combat the fierce heat and basic facilities such as a school were doled out incrementally; the number of retail outlets was kept to a carefully controlled minimum. As a consequence, the government town itself was supplemented by nearby Las Vegas. In the same way, the town of Coulee Dam was incomplete without privately built mushroom towns on the other bank of the Columbia River.[34]

It is hardly surprising that the army engineers who helped to develop and manage the atomic towns drew on the rhetoric of other public works towns for their own communities. Franklin Matthias, for example, had visited Tennessee Valley Authority construction camps and was familiar with the Grand Coulee site.[35] Indeed, a number of elements in the makeup of Richland and Los Alamos reflected the hierarchy of purposes in a public works town. The centrality of the administration buildings in Richland was matched by the centrality of the Los Alamos labs and lab offices that lined both sides of the main road. Retail districts were essentially throw-ins, forcing use of adjacent cities for very ordinary goods and services.[36] Even the school was an add-on in Los Alamos.

THE SECOND CITIES: 1946–60

Los Alamos and Richland were ratified as permanent towns in 1946–47. At the beginning of 1946, General Groves wrote to Oppenheimer's successor, Norris Bradbury, that he expected Los Alamos to remain in use for several more years at the least. Bradbury began planning for the transition to permanency and quickly made Groves's commitment public at a meeting of the advisory Town Council. In November, he told the new Atomic Energy Commissioners that maintenance of Los Alamos had great advantages both for security and for attracting scientists who preferred the mountains to a big city. He then forced a shakeout of ambivalent residents by refusing to pay return transportation for anyone who left after September 1947.[37] The subsequent rebuilding of staff and program brought the population to 8,000 in 1948, 9,100 in 1949, 10,500 in 1950, and 12,600 in 1960.

Richland followed a similar trend. Population dropped from its wartime peak of 15,400 to 13,000 in the winter and spring of 1946. Trucks hauled away hundreds of prefab houses to accommodate veterans at university campuses throughout the Northwest, the first steps in the dismantling of temporary and dormitory housing over the next decade.[38] When General Electric took over from Du Pont on September 1, 1946 (a few months before the Atomic Energy Commission began operations in January 1947), the company found a "nervous, wondering community" whose residents were not sure whether they would be expected to stay or go. Within a year, however, AEC's decision to undertake a major expansion required comprehensive rebuilding. The waiting list for housing at Richland had 1,300 names at the start of 1948, when population had already climbed back to 17,000.[39] The population grew to 21,800 in 1950 and 25,000 in 1955. GE's arrival and promise of a stable operation and employment base even inspired local adaptations of popular songs that simultaneously recognized the attractions of steady work and the ironies of dependence on a company town:

> G.E. loves me, this I know,
> Mr. Milton told me so,
> Du Pont's left me high and dry
> But I won't worry, I won't cry.
> Yes. G.E. loves me,
> Sure G.E. loves me,
> I know G.E. loves me,
> Mr. Milton told me so.[40]

The purpose of postwar replanning was to create communities that could attract educated but not necessarily sophisticated staff. General Electric at Richland and the University of California at Los Alamos had to compete with academic and industrial employers by offering a high quality of everyday life. As their managers and planners sought to appeal to postwar Americans, the second towns of the late 1940s and early 1950s turned out to be archetypically "suburban" in overall design. Rather than borrow from earlier federal planning, they utilized and helped to develop both the vocabulary and the rhetoric of postwar suburbia. The clear goals of the new planning discourse were expressed in neighborhoods focused and organized around schools; densities and designs that assumed and forced use of automobiles; large-grain separation of activities; and use of space to protect class distinctions.

Richland was replanned in 1948 by J. Gordon Turnbull, Inc. and Graham, Anderson, Probst and White, Inc., architectural and engineering firms from Cleveland and Chicago.[41] An interim land use map in 1947 provided a systematic framework for the wave of new growth that was already under way. Plan recommendations geared to an anticipated population of 25,000 and possible increases to 30,000 and 35,000 were made public in July 1948.[42] The systematic master plan dealt with schools, parks, public facilities, streets and traffic, flood control, utilities, and the allocation of residential, commercial, and industrial land. The master plan formed the basis of actions by General Electric and the AEC into the mid-1950s.[43]

Expansion of housing stock was already under way. In September 1947, a contract was let for 450 pre-cut "Hudson houses" to be built on lots from which the wartime prefabs had recently been removed, economizing by using existing utility hookups. More than 300 two- to four-bedroom concrete block "A-J houses" were simultaneously built on the northeast side of town by Atkinson-Jones Company. The 1948–49 building program provided 1,000 three-bedroom ranch-style houses on the west side.[44] The AEC opened the way for 1,000 units of private housing west of George Washington Way and north of McMurray Avenue in April 1952. One-story ranch houses were occupied as soon as they were finished, but boxy modernistic two-story apartments held less interest for the city's plant operators and production engineers.[45]

The new Richland also boasted a prototype for the shopping mall. The first "downtown" had been tucked between administrative and public buildings and the main highway along the Columbia River; it had room for only a quarter of the retail stores found in cities of a comparable size. The master plan projected an increase from 38 to 132 retailers in neighborhood and central shopping, using standard market analysis that allocated disposable income to different goods according to national patterns and derived appropriate square footage of retail space.[46] The site of the supplemental "uptown" district was developed at government expense, with private investors erecting the commercial buildings on a long-term ground lease. Its first stores in 1949 sold men's clothing and sporting goods; then came a furniture store, a service station, a women's apparel shop, a shoe store, a bakery, a theater, a barbershop, and a lunchroom.[47]

Far more interesting than the standard list of community-scale retail outlets was the project's location and design. Although described as the "Central Commercial Area," the new shopping mall lay a mile north of the old town core and substantially off-center for the existing housing. The site was sandwiched between parallel north-south arterials that served large parking lots (3,000 spaces) on the east and west sides of the site. Between the parking lots were two parallel rows of shops lining a central service court and encompassed by a circumferential drive. The relationship between highways, parking, and retail buildings was fully "modern." What the Richland shopping center did not do was take the final step in creating a modern mall by upgrading the central court into the primary axis of circulation.[48]

By 1952, about half of the city's retail and service businesses were operating in the uptown center and many of the rest in new neighborhood shopping clusters. As identified in the 1948 plan and described in 1949, the "up-to-date" layout of neighborhood shopping areas included small greenbelts as well as ample parking.[49] Westgate Shopping Center at Van Giesen and Wright, for example, opened February 1956 with grocery, sporting goods, hardware, and jewelry stores, barber and beauty shops, and a real estate office.[50]

Taken together, the commercial, residential, and transportation elements of the master plan amounted to a deliberately automobile-friendly and automobile-dependent city. The full range of adult activities and the major new recreational space along the Columbia River would be separated by long distances within the city. In addition, most workers faced a 25-mile commute from town to the Hanford work sites. The city would offer plenty of parking lots, improved arterial roads, and few parking meters.[51]

The other underlying principles of the 1948 master plan were a large-scale separation of land uses and a focus on individual household space. The plan defined its fundamental goal as the development of Richland as a "home community." It proposed that expansion occur within neighborhood units of 5,000 residents served by an elementary school and buffered by distance from industrial and employment areas. Public open space outside the school yards was to be kept to a minimum to reduce maintenance costs. The same motivation led to the recommendation that no more publicly maintained areas be built in the middle of residential blocks.[52]

The town itself was developing as a middle-class island in the larger Tri-Cities area. Residence was limited to Hanford employees and direct support workers. In 1948, for example, 90 percent of the paychecks came from General Electric, 4 percent from the Atomic Energy Commission, 2 percent from subcontractors, and 3 percent from local businesses.[53] The city had no truly poor residents, and its limited social range was defined by union craftsmen and GE managers. Comparison of GE and AEC salaries in 1950 with the national distribution of family income found no Richland households in the bottom quartile of the national distribution and only 13 percent in the top quintile.[54] There were, however, fine postwar social distinctions that mirrored the assignment of housing during the war years. With expansion in the 1940s and 1950s, there developed a social gradation from south to north, with the best housing in the newer "Gold Coast" northward along the Columbia River.

Social homogeneity was preserved by planning out incompatible residents. Parking of trailers within Richland was banned in April 1945.[55] Construction workers for the Cold War expansion program were channeled six miles north of town to the temporary settlement of North Richland. When North Richland was phased out in 1954–55, many of its families moved to trailer parks in West Richland. As a working class "suburb" separated from the "central city" by two miles of sagebrush, West Richland counted 1,300 residents in seven trailer parks by 1958.[56] Two decades later, during the Washington Public Power Supply System construction boom of the 1970s, a new generation of construction workers filled motel style apartments in Kennewick.

Census data allow Richland of the 1950s and 1960s to be compared with Benton County as a whole. They showed virtually identical ethnic profiles in the 1950s and 1960s, although Richland would be bypassed by a growing Hispanic population in the 1970s. In 1950, Richlanders were substantially better educated, with 12.5 years of schooling for persons twenty-five or older compared to 11.9 years for Benton County as a whole. By the 1960s and until 1970, however, the educational edge narrowed as Hanford personnel spread through the entire Tri-Cities. Richland's difference was maintained most consistently in median family income, which ran 10 to 15 percent higher than in Benton County in 1950, 1960, and 1970.[57]

The comforts of isolation and economic security fed trepidation about the transition from a publicly owned to a privately owned city. A Census Bureau survey in 1953 found that 50 percent of residents thought they would be worse off in a privatized city and only 8 percent thought they would be better off. A March 1955 vote was 2,414 to 1,914 against self-government and 3,315 to 1,213 against disposal of property to private owners. Residents feared additional costs, "unfair" prices on their homes, and the stress of opening the comfortable town to outsiders. Nevertheless, Congress in August 1955 adopted a law mandating that Richland (and Oak Ridge) be incorporated within five years and assume all municipal functions. The first houses were sold in 1957 and the last in May 1960: $6,000 for a 1948 ranch house, $7,300 for both units of a two-story duplex, $9,000 for the newest houses.[58] General Electric transferred municipal functions to the City of Richland during the course of 1959.[59]

Los Alamos, of course, had literal gates to complement the symbolic gatekeeping of suburban planning. The increasingly complacent town of the 1950s had been completely replanned in 1946–47 by Lawrence B. Sheridan of Salt Lake City, who had a twenty-five-year career as a comprehensive planner and consultant to Depression-era state planning boards in the Ohio Valley. Sheridan developed and refined a master plan between February and June 1946. In 1947–48, W. C. Kruger expanded the plan to accommodate 13,000 rather than 8,000 residents by including the north mesa.[60] The Sheridan plan and its follow-ups were essentially plans for a new permanent city on top of the old camp.[61] They imposed a new orderliness by sorting out the original jumble of uses into distinct residential, commercial, and technical districts. They guided massive reinvestment to upgrade or replace the city's infrastructure and buildings, including the demolition between 1948 and 1955 of 306 wartime and 490 immediate postwar housing units.[62]

As in Richland, the normalization of Los Alamos utilized and contributed to the evolving vocabulary and rhetoric of suburban planning. The first new housing began to go up in the summer of 1946 at the west end of the mesa, on the hard-packed ground of a rudimentary golf course. A long horseshoe arterial road entered from the east. Most of the two- and three-bedroom houses were inside the loop on crescents and cul de sacs in full suburban style. The curving street pattern was cloned for the apartment units of North Mesa in 1949–52 and the single family houses of the eastern area in 1954–57.[63] It was imitated as well on Barranca Mesa, where the first private housing construction began in 1958.[64] Gradually lost over the decade was the southwestern style of the first postwar houses, which had wide windows, flat roofs, and exposed beam ceilings.[65] By the 1960s, the city was filling in with contemporary ranch and split-level styles from the Sunday real estate section of any American newspaper.

Visiting reporters had nothing but good words for the $4 million spent on the "model, 20th century business center."[66] This "modern nexus" of stores, theater, and community facilities looked both backward and forward. Civic and commercial buildings in New Mexican territorial style were grouped around a cruciform green space that was reminiscent of the 1930s. But two of the four arms opened onto surrounding parking lots, and the centerpiece was a gleaming supermarket far larger than most prewar grocery stores. The shopping center was essentially unaltered in the early 1990s, but the peripheral parking lots with access from the city's main traffic arteries were much more lively than the green core.

The rhetoric of suburban planning supported the social distance that was valued as highly by the scientific middle class of Los Alamos as by their engineering counterparts at Richland. The town of 1944–45 had been deeply segregated by economic class. The best housing was allocated to scientists to keep them as happy as possible, and even the best-appointed dormitories for single men were carefully assigned to scientific personnel rather than support workers.[67] The same pattern carried into the postwar community. While machinists, maintenance men, and construction workers lived in a confusion of quonset huts at the east end of the mesa, General Groves insisted that the first new housing in 1946 be aimed at the scientific and technical elite. Two years later, AEC field manager Carroll Tyler commented, "We have no railroad, but right now you'd think we had railroad tracks running through the town, with the eastern area on the wrong side."[68]

The solution offered by the Sheridan plan was replacement and displacement. As described above, Los Alamos would replace the flimsiest and most affordable housing with homes and apartments built to increasingly high standards. At the foot of the mesa, White Rock was built as a separate housing project for construction workers in 1949. At peak occupancy in 1950–51, it was a smaller twin of North Richland; its small one-story houses kept workers and their families ten miles away and several thousand feet lower than Los Alamos. The construction camp closed in 1957; redevelopment of the site with private market housing to supplement Los Alamos itself began in 1961. Beyond White Rock, the towns and farms of Sandoval and Santa Fe Counties housed the Native Americans and Hispanics who provided much of the labor force for support and maintenance work.[69]

Census data confirm that Los Alamos in the 1950s and 1960s was richer, whiter, and better educated than the other towns of Rio Arriba. Los Alamos County, established as a rudimentary government coterminous with the Manhattan Project boundaries in 1949, was 89 percent Anglo in 1960 and 90 percent in 1970. Median income for families and unrelated individuals in 1960 was more than four times that of Sandoval County and nearly twice that of Santa Fe County. A decade later, only 2 percent of Los Alamos residents fell below the poverty line, a remarkable figure compared to the 18 and 38 percent figures for Santa Fe and

Sandoval Counties. Los Alamos residents twenty-five or older had completed a median 12.7 years in school in 1950, compared with 9.5 years for Santa Fe County and 6.1 years for Sandoval County. The educational gap narrowed by 1970, but the figure of 13.9 years in Los Alamos County was still far higher than the 12.3 years in Santa Fe and 10.3 in Sandoval.

Local resistance to dropping the barricades around the city sprang from the same comfort with class and ethnic homogeneity. A telephone survey in 1955 found residents overwhelmingly in favor of gates and guards. The reasons given in public were "privacy" and "safety," and the surprise announcement that the barriers would disappear on February 15, 1957, precipitated a run on the local gun shop.[70] Since the only invaders in the mid-1950s were likely to be handfuls of tourists and local New Mexicans, it is hard not to read these terms as code words for class and ethnic prejudice—attitudes as deeply embedded in the country's sci-tech elite as among any other Americans of the 1950s.

CONCLUSION

It was the second cities that fully represented the atomic era in the American West. The first cities of 1943–44 (to the extent they were planned at all) looked backward to a federal planning tradition of the 1920s and 1930s. In the first decade of the "second cities," residents of Richland and Los Alamos still had to take the housing and facilities that the government and its contractors offered. They could agitate for planning and design improvements, but they had few alternatives in limited markets.[71] In this way, their situation paralleled that of suburbanites in the tight postwar housing market of the late 1940s. Richland's planning decisions in the early 1950s were made by a "town planning board" that was in fact a joint GE-AEC committee. It included a member of the elected town advisory council but did not hold open meetings. Planning updates for Los Alamos were done by AEC staff. Self-determination in land use planning would depend on two developments. One was the rise of a private housing market with the development of Barranca Mesa (1958) and White Rock (1961) and the privatization of federal housing in Richland (1957–60) and Los Alamos (1962–67). The other change was the transfer of planning responsibility to the newly created City of Richland in 1959 and the new Los Alamos County Planning Commission in 1962.[72]

Despite their halting political evolution, the second cities of the Truman and Eisenhower years epitomized an increasingly prosperous America, with social and spatial patterns that reflected the desires of the "American generation" ushered in by V-J Day. Los Alamos, said the first issue of the *Los Alamos Times* in 1946, was beginning its transformation into "a typical American community." Richland, wrote reporters in 1948 and 1949, was fast assuming "all the characteristics of a normal American city" with "neatly curving rows of comfortable frame houses." The Atomic Energy Commission agreed with the need to promote "normal life" in its atomic towns, in part by ensuring that orderly "suburbanized" development replaced the chaos and uncertainty of 1943–46.[73]

"Normal" also meant white, middle-class, and family oriented. Both communities nurtured the full middle-class lifestyle of the 1950s. Richlanders in 1950 supported 25 churches, attended by 57 percent of adult residents (twice the state average). In Richland, 250 organizations helped new residents construct a sense of community through action and activity.[74] Civic activities deliberately fostered a sense of community, especially the Richland Days of 1945, 1946, and 1947, which evolved into Atomic Frontier Days in 1948. Visitors marveled and local officials beamed about similar statistics for Los Alamos and its "suburbanized horde of civic organizations." Reporters counted 146 voluntary associations at the start of the 1960s and 250 by the 1980s. Like that in many new suburbs, the age structure of Los Alamos in 1960 showed disproportionate numbers of children (ages 5–14) and young adults (ages 25–44) and a corresponding lack of the middle-aged and elderly. Debra Rosenthal's snide characterization was "Anytown, U.S.A." with shopping center and bored housewives ("there are two cars in the driveway of the comfy house with the neatly trimmed lawn. Dad is a professional. Mom may work; she helps out at the church").[75]

In many accounts of the postwar decade, "normal" was traded back and forth with "model." Seven out of eight Richlanders in 1953 believed that their town was "a model place to live." A decade later, community leaders agreed that Los Alamos was a "self-conscious model town."[76] The overlap of the two terms suggested the depth of the postwar drive to enjoy the fruits of prosperity. Although "model" implies above average in quality or outstanding as an example, the two cities were in fact built out of the common planning language of the 1950s. These ideal cities of the Cold War decade were neither communitarian nor utopian. They were middle American and middle of the road—mainstream settlements floating in sparsely settled landscapes.

What the 1950s called model towns, in short, we can now see as prototypical "suburban" environments erected in physical isolation but deeply embedded in middle-class American culture. The old hands of Richland, wrote journalist Paul Loeb in 1982, were frozen in 1961, the year that the National Municipal League and *Look* magazine named it an All-American city.[77] Exploring Los Alamos with a similar mission to understand the worldview of atomic professionals, Rosenthal came to virtually the same conclusion, that she had found "a mundane version of the 1950s suburban dream."[78] The last gasp of federal town planning gave us neither desert utopias nor vanguards of social harmony. We built instead a Palos Verdes for Ph.D.s, a Park Forest for plutonium producers.

NOTES

1. John H. Dudley, "Ranch School to Secret City," in *Reminiscences of Los Alamos, 1943–1945*, ed. Lawrence Badash, Joseph O. Hirschfelder, and Herbert P. Broida (Boston: D. Reidel, 1980), 3–5.

2. The entry to Los Alamos is described by Bernice Brode, "Tales of Los Alamos," in *Reminiscences of Los Alamos*, 134–35.

3. Walter Simon, letter to author, April 8, 1992; F. T. Matthias, "Building the Hanford Plutonium Plant," *Engineering News-Record* 135 (December 13, 1945): 118–24; Vincent C. Jones, *Manhattan: The Army and the Atomic Bomb* (Washington, D.C.: Center for Military History, U.S. Army, 1985), 450–51.

4. Jones, *Manhattan*, 456. The entire Hanford project site had a population of approximately 1,500 (1,000 on farms and 500 in the towns of Hanford, White Bluffs, and Richland).

5. Phyllis Fisher, *Los Alamos Experience* (New York: Japan Publications, 1985), 59; Lenore Fine and Jesse A. Remington, *The Corps of Engineers: Construction in the United States* (Washington, D.C.: Office of the Chief of Military History, U.S. Army, 1972), 695; Marie Kinzel, "The Town of Beginning Again," *Survey Graphic* 35 (October 1946): 354, describes Los Alamos residents of 1943 as "pioneers on a new frontier."

6. Hanford worker quoted by Patricia Nelson Limerick in "What Have We Done to the Columbia," address at Great River of the West Conference, Vancouver, Washington, May 3, 1992.

7. "The Atom: Model City," *Time*, December 12, 1949, p. 21; "Richland,

Wash., Plans for Growth," *The American City,* May 1949, pp. 118–20; Eleanor Snyder and Thomas Lanahan, Jr., "Family Income and Expenditures: Los Alamos, 1948," *Monthly Labor Review* 49 (September 1949): 247.

8. *Richland: The Atomic City* (Richland, Wash.: General Electric Community Operations, 1958); Michele Stenehjem Gerber, *On the Home Front: The Cold War Legacy of the Hanford Nuclear Site* (Lincoln: University of Nebraska Press, 1992), 61.

9. *Living in Los Alamos, New Mexico* (Los Alamos: Personnel Department, Los Alamos Scientific Laboratory, undated, ca. 1963–64).

10. Richard G. Hewlett and Oscar E. Anderson, Jr., *A History of the United States Atomic Energy Commission,* vol. 1, *The New World, 1939/1946* (University Park: Pennsylvania State University Press, 1962); Fine and Remington, *Corps of Engineers.*

11. Hawkins quoted in Alden Stevens, "Small-Town America: v. Los Alamos, New Mexico," *The Nation* 163 (August 3, 1946): 127. Population estimates include 5,700 in early 1945 (Jones, *Manhattan,* 468); 5,000 in September 1945 (Norris Bradbury, "Los Alamos: The First Twenty-Five Years," in *Reminiscences of Los Alamos,* ed. Badash, Hirschfelder, and Broida, 162); 6,500 in late 1945 (Ferenc Morton Szasz, *The Day the Sun Rose Twice: The Story of the Trinity Site Nuclear Explosion, July 16, 1945* [Albuquerque: University of New Mexico Press, 1984], 17); 7,000 in August 1946 (Stevens, "Small-Town America," 127). An official census in May 1946 found 6,524 (*Los Alamos Times,* May 24, 1946).

12. Fine and Remington, *Corps of Engineers,* 696; Marjorie Bell Chambers, "Technically Sweet Los Alamos: The Development of a Federally Sponsored Scientific Community" (Ph.D. diss., University of New Mexico, 1974), 107–8.

13. James W. Kunetka, *City of Fire: Los Alamos and the Birth of the Atomic Age, 1943–1945* (Englewood Cliffs, N.J.: Prentice-Hall, 1978), 93; Chambers, "Technically Sweet Los Alamos," 109–14.

14. Fisher, *Los Alamos Experience,* 30, 42–44; Kunetka, *City of Fire,* 94. As of 1946, the nonbarracks housing inventory of Los Alamos was as follows: 332 Sundt and McKee apartments; 56 Morgan Construction apartments; 100 McKee Prefabs; 107 Hanford Units; 47 standard trailers; 35 expansible trailers; 51 winterized hutments; 56 Pacific huts; 62 other units. From *The Housing Manual for Laboratory Employees and Supervisors* (Los Alamos: Los Alamos Scientific Laboratory, Personnel Department, 1965).

15. Brode, "Tales of Los Alamos," 137; Fisher, *Los Alamos Experience,* 64, 179; Kunetka, *City of Fire,* 94, 96; Chambers, "Technically Sweet Los Alamos," 97–106.

16. Franklin Matthias, telephone interview by author, April 9, 1992. Pehrson was picked over several other candidates because of his local base and his broad experience designing office buildings, residential projects, and hotels. Walter Simon, letter to author, April 8, 1992, confirms the importance of proximity in the choice.

17. There were forty-five dormitories in addition to the site-built and prefabri-

cated houses. Matthias, "Building the Hanford Plutonium Plant," 123; Jones, *Manhattan,* 457–58.

18. George Prout, General Electric Company general manager, December 28, 1951, quoted in Paul John Deutschmann, "Federal City: A Study of the Administration of Richland, Washington, Atomic Energy Commission Community" (master's thesis, University of Oregon, 1952), 16. Walter Simon's characterization is "an austere place with a temporary aspect" (letter to author, April 8, 1992).

19. Jones, *Manhattan,* 460; Matthias, interview.

20. Deutschmann, "Federal City," 22, 122; Jones, *Manhattan,* 457. Colonel Matthias has commented that Richland's housing in fact came in under budget.

21. J. Gordon Turnbull, Inc. and Graham, Anderson, Probst and White, Inc., *Master Plan for Richland, Washington* (Richland: General Electric Company Nucleonics Department and U.S. Atomic Energy Commission, 1948), 8; Deutschmann, "Federal City," 18.

22. Jerry Saucier, quoted in S. L. Sanger, with Robert W. Mull, *Hanford and the Bomb: An Oral History of World War II* (Seattle: Living History Press, 1989), 96.

23. The full range of planned communities built in the first decades of the twentieth century is summarized in the thirty short case studies in Arthur C. Comey and Max S. Wehrly, "Planned Communities," part I of *Urban Planning and Land Policies: Vol. II of the Supplementary Report of the Urbanism Committee to the National Resources Committee* (Washington, D.C.: Government Printing Office, 1939).

24. The very extensive literature on communitarian housing reformers and planners includes: Kristin S. Bailey, "The Federal Government and the Cooperative Housing Movement, 1917–1955" (Ph.D. diss., Carnegie-Mellon University, 1988); John F. Bauman, *Public Housing, Race, and Renewal: Urban Planning in Philadelphia, 1920–1974* (Philadelphia: Temple University Press, 1987); Stanley Buder, *Visionaries and Planners: The Garden City Movement and the Modern Community* (New York: Oxford University Press, 1990); Daniel Schaffer, *Garden Cities for America: The Radburn Experience* (Philadelphia: Temple University Press, 1982); Paul K. Conkin, *Tomorrow a New World: The New Deal Community Program* (Ithaca: Cornell University Press, 1959); Joseph L. Arnold, *The New Deal in the Suburbs: A History of the Greenbelt Town Program, 1935–1954* (Columbus: Ohio State University Press, 1971); Roy Lubove, *Community Planning in the 1920s: The Contribution of the Regional Planning Association of America* (Pittsburgh: University of Pittsburgh Press, 1963); Clarence S. Stein, *Toward New Towns for America* (New York: Reinhold, 1957); Diane Ghirardo, *Building New Communities: New Deal America and Fascist Italy* (Princeton: Princeton University Press, 1989); Christian Topalov, "Scientific Urban Planning and the Ordering of Daily Life: The First 'War Housing' Experiment in the United States, 1917–19," *Journal of Urban History* 17 (November 1990): 14–45; K. C. Parsons, "Clarence Stein and the Greenbelt Towns: Settling for Less," *Journal of the American Planning Association* 56 (Spring 1990): 161–83; Marion Clawson, "Resettle-

ment Experience on Nine Selected Resettlement Projects," *Agricultural History* 52 (January 1978): 1–92 (reprint of 1943 report); W. J. O'Toole, "A Prototype of Public Housing Policy: The United States Housing Corporation," *Journal of the American Institute of Planners* 34 (May 1968): 140–52; Michael H. Lang, "Yorkship Garden Village: Radical Expression of the Progressive Housing and Planning Reform Movement," paper delivered at the Fourth National Conference on American Planning History, Richmond, Virginia, November 1991.

25. Key figures from the 1910s to the 1930s were Frederick Ackerman, Clarence Stein, Henry Wright, and Frederick Law Olmsted, Jr. World War II housing projects that incorporated elements of the communitarian rhetoric were designed by such architects as Oscar Stonorov, Walter Gropius, Marcel Breuer, and Richard Neutra. Norris was designed by Earle Draper and Tracy Augur.

26. Greenbelt, Maryland, and Norris, Tennessee, are well-preserved examples that define the "semi-urban" and "bucolic" styles within the communitarian rhetoric.

27. The park area is now a paved street with angle parking. Only the theater at one end retains the shingled surface which shouts "1940s."

28. Sanger and Mull, *Hanford and the Bomb,* 107; Michele Stenehjem Gerber, "Government Richland," paper delivered at the Conference on "Columbia's Communities," Kennewick, Washington, September 9, 1994; Walter Simon, letter to author, April 8, 1992; John Findlay, letter to author, April 21, 1993.

29. "It was their great moment," I. I. Rabi would later comment (quoted in Szasz, *Day the Sun Rose Twice,* 17).

30. A well-thumbed but still useful model for the experience of Los Alamos's elite women is found in Stanley Elkins and Eric McKitrick, "A Meaning for Turner's Frontier: Part I: Democracy in the Old Northwest," *Political Science Quarterly* 69 (September 1954): 321–53. They interpret "frontier" democracy as the product of shared efforts to respond to common problems in the formative years of a community, drawing their model from studies of a World War II housing project for shipyard workers. For Los Alamos evidence, see Kathleen E. B. Manley, "Women of Los Alamos during World War II: Some of Their Views," *New Mexico Historical Review* 65 (April 1990): 251–66; Eleanor Jette, *Inside Box 1663* (Los Alamos: Los Alamos Historical Society, 1977); Jane Wilson and Charlotte Serber, eds., *Standing By and Making Do: Women of Wartime Los Alamos* (Los Alamos: Los Alamos Historical Society, 1988).

31. Laura Fermi, "The Fermis' Path to Los Alamos," in *Reminiscences of Los Alamos,* ed. Badash, Hirschfelder, and Broida, 102. Also see Brode, "Tales of Los Alamos," 138; Jane Wilson, "The Atom and Eve," manuscript at Los Alamos Historical Society, quoted by Manley, "Women of Los Alamos," 266.

32. Hal Rothman, *On Rims and Ridges: The Los Alamos Area since 1880* (Lincoln: University of Nebraska Press, 1992), 225.

33. Chambers, "Technically Sweet Los Alamos," 137–39, 271–75.

34. Paul Kleinsorge, *The Boulder Canyon Project: Historical and Economic Aspects* (Stanford: Stanford University Press, 1941), 219–26; Joseph E. Stevens, *Hoover Dam: An American Adventure* (Norman: University of Oklahoma Press, 1988), 117–58; Murray Morgan, *The Dam* (New York: Viking Press, 1954); L. Vaughn Downs, *The Mightiest of Them All: Memories of Grand Coulee Dam* (Fairfield, Wash.: Ye Galleon Press, 1986).

35. Matthias, interview.

36. Leslie R. Groves, *Now It Can Be Told: The Story of the Manhattan Project* (New York: Harper and Row, 1962), 165–67.

37. Bradbury, "Los Alamos," 165; Chambers, "Technically Sweet Los Alamos," 162–63, 173, 186.

38. Howard R. Ennor, "Richland—Washington's Atomic City," *Western City*, June 1949, pp. 20–25.

39. Paul Laartz,"Full-time Workers' Problem Grim in Finding Housing at Richland," *The Oregonian*, January 11, 1948, sec. 1, p. 18; Gerber, *On the Home Front*, 61–62. Quotation from editor of *Richland Reporter*, in "Richland Day, Sept. 2, 1946," quoted in Deutschmann, "Federal City," 20.

40. Poem quoted in Nelson W. Hope, *Atomic Town* (New York: Comet Books, 1954), 107. Also quoted was an adaptation of the Twenty-third Psalm: "Milton is my shepherd, I shall not question. He maketh me to lie down in Richland, he leadeth me beside the Columbia, he restoreth my job. Yes, though I walk through the valley of Wilmington, thou art with me, thy insurance and thy housing comfort me, thou preparest a pension for me in the presence of my creditors, thou anointest me with soft soap, my service runneth over. Surely raises and bonuses shall follow me all the days of my life, and I shall dwell in the house of G.E. forever."

41. Graham, Anderson was the successor firm to the famous architectural partnership of Burnham and Root.

42. *The Long Road to Self-Government: The History of Richland, Washington, 1943–1968* (Richland: City of Richland, 1968), 16, states that the plan was "made public" on July 26, 1948. The completed document was printed in November 1948 as *Master Plan for Richland, Washington*. Access to the limited number of copies was apparently carefully controlled. As late as 1949, reporters complained that GE and the AEC refused to make the plan available, although a copy was leaked to Senator Bourke Hickenlooper of the Joint Committee on Atomic Energy in that same year. In the early 1950s, two copies were on deposit in the public library (see Deutschmann, "Federal City," 114–19).

43. Planning decisions in the early 1950s were made by a "town planning board" that was in fact a joint GE-AEC committee that included a member of the

elected town advisory council but that did not hold open meetings. A member of the joint committee in a 1951 interview described the master plan as "a good one" (Deutschmann, "'Federal City," 119).

44. Ennor, "Richland," 21; Ted Van Arsdol, *Boomers on Wheels: The Story of Trailers in the Development of the Tri-Cities of Pasco, Richland, and Kennewick, Washington, 1943 to 1958* (Vancouver, Wash., 1970), 31; *Pacific Northwest Industries: The Hanford Works* (Seattle: Seattle-First National Bank, 1948), 6.

45. "Richland, City of Atoms, Biggest 'Company Town' Still Grows," *The Oregonian*, November 1, 1953, sec. 1, p. 32.

46. *Pacific Northwest Industries*, 7.

47. Ennor, "Richland," 22.

48. *Master Plan for Richland, Washington*, 28, 46–48; Meredith Clausen, "Northgate Regional Shopping Center: Paradigm for the Provinces," *Journal of the Society of Architectural Historians* 43 (May 1984): 144–61; Howard Gillette, Jr., "The Evolution of the Planned Shopping Center in Suburb and City," *Journal of the American Planning Association* 51 (Autumn 1985): 449–60.

49. "Richland Plans for Growth," 120 (see note 7 above); *Master Plan for Richland, Washington*, 48.

50. Thirty-six years later, the Westgate Center had followed the trajectory of many similar L-shaped shopping centers of the 1950s, with physical deterioration and a mix of businesses a notch below its original tenants.

51. At the start of the 1950s, General Electric did operate limited bus service using thirteen vehicles. *A Commercial and Industrial Survey of Richland, Benton County, Washington, Atomic Energy City of the Tri-Cities Area* (Richland: Greater Richland Chamber of Commerce, 1951), 21.

52. *Master Plan for Richland, Washington*, 2, 14–16, 20, 36.

53. Ibid., 5. The pattern was essentially the same in 1953, when 8,700 GE employees lived in Richland, 420 AEC employees, 450 school district employees, and 1,600 proprietors or employees of Richland businesses (*Long Road to Self-Government*, 28).

54. Deutschmann, "Federal City," table 8.

1950 Income	Richland	U.S.
Under $2,000	—	26%
$2,000–2,999	17% ⎫	
	⎬	53%
$3,000–4,999	70% ⎭	
$5,000+	13%	21%

55. *Long Road to Self-Government,* 9.

56. Van Arsdol, *Boomers on Wheels,* 37.

57. There were also fewer poor families in Richland than in Benton County in 1970 (4.5 percent versus 7.3 percent) and 1980 (3.7 percent versus 5.6 percent).

58. Leverett Richards, "AEC Pushes Bill to Sell Houses in Government-Owned Richland," *The Oregonian,* November 1, 1953, sec. 1, p. 33; Paul Loeb, *Nuclear Culture: Living and Working in the World's Largest Atomic Complex* (New York: Coward, McCann and Geoghegan, 1982), 53–54.

59. *Long Road to Self-Government,* 29, 37. Benton County adopted the Richland zoning ordinance in March 1958.

60. Chambers, "Technically Sweet Los Alamos," 190–203.

61. The essence of the transition from temporary to permanent community is well summarized in Hanson Baldwin, "Los Alamos—Capital of the Atomic Age," *New York Times Magazine,* April 24, 1949, 12–13, 62–65, and in Daniel Lang, "A Reporter in New Mexico: Los Alamos," *New Yorker* 24 (April 17, 1948): 68–77.

62. *Housing Manual for Laboratory Employees and Supervisors,* 20.

63. Ibid.

64. Barranca Mesa was planned by the architectural firm of Stanley and Wright, and street names were selected by a Homeowner's Association consisting of persons most interested in acquiring lots. Private housing allowed household-ers who were no longer affiliated with the laboratory, such as widows and retirees, to remain in the community.

65. The first issue of the *Los Alamos Times,* March 15, 1946, announced plans for 300 to 500 new houses in "Spanish Mission" style, a substantial exaggeration of the architectural truth.

66. "Atomic Cities' Boom," *Business Week,* December 18, 1948, p. 69; Carey McWilliams, "Shangri-La of the Atom," *The Nation,* December 31, 1949, p. 639; Baldwin, "Los Alamos," 64; Chambers, "Technically Sweet Los Alamos," 200.

67. Chambers, "Technically Sweet Los Alamos," 128, 137–40.

68. Lang, "Reporter in New Mexico," 71; Chambers, "Technically Sweet Los Alamos," 196.

69. Rothman, *On Rims and Ridges,* 239.

70. Daniel Lang, "A Reporter at Large: Evolution of a Mesa," *New Yorker* 34 (June 7, 1958): 39–40; *Albuquerque Journal,* February 15 and 17, 1957; "Love That Fence," *Fortune* 50 (August 1954): 69.

71. Rothman, *On Rims and Ridges,* 242, describes the efforts of Los Alamos women to argue for housing amenities.

72. *Long Road to Self-Government,* 36; Chambers, "Technically Sweet Los Ala-mos," 367–77; *Los Alamos, New Mexico: A Comprehensive Plan Report* (Los Alamos: Leo A. Daly: Planners—Architects—Engineers, 1965).

73. Chambers, "Technically Sweet Los Alamos," 192; Laartz, "Housing at Rich-

land," 18; "Model City," *Time,* 21; Atomic Energy Commission, Fourth Semiannual Report to Congress, 1948, quoted in *Master Plan for Richland, Washington,* 2. The creation of a normal or ordinary community is the theme of Hal Rothman's brief treatment of postwar Los Alamos in *On Rims and Ridges.*

74. Loeb, *Nuclear Culture,* 42, 69. General Electric in 1958 identified 28 churches, 24 business and professional clubs, 28 civic and welfare groups, 17 fraternal societies, 63 recreational and social clubs, 20 labor unions, 7 veterans organizations, 20 youth groups, 18 baseball or bowling leagues, 8 musical groups, and 5 political organizations in *Richland: The Atomic City.*

75. "New Mexico: Atomic-Age Fiefdom," *Time,* February 3, 1961; Debra Rosenthal, *At the Heart of the Bomb: The Dangerous Allure of Weapons Work* (Reading, Mass.: Addison-Wesley, 1990), 27–37. Hal Rothman's characterization as "Anywhere, U.S.A." is based on the town's "suburban and bland" architecture (*On Rims and Ridges,* 275).

76. Leverett Richards, "Richland Becoming a Home City Despite an Air of Impermanence," *The Oregonian,* November 2, 1953, sec. 1, p. 12; "New Mexico: The Suburb without the Urb," *Time,* October 1, 1965, p. 31.

77. Loeb, *Nuclear Culture,* 139.

78. Rosenthal, *Heart of the Bomb,* 30. The phrase "frozen in time" is also applied to Los Alamos by Tad Bartemus and Scott McCartney, *Trinity's Children* (New York: Harcourt Brace, 1991), 92.

II. THE ATOMIC ENERGY COMMISSION AT WORK

The University of California, the Federal Weapons Labs, and the Founding of the Atomic West

Gregg Herken

Those interested in building and testing bombs have always found in the West the same allure that once drew the pioneer and now attracts the tourist, for sparse population and wide-open spaces are conducive to secrecy as well as to solitude.[1] Although the Manhattan Project initially considered remote places in eastern states like South Carolina and Virginia for a secret site to build the atomic bomb, ultimately both of the government's nuclear weapon design laboratories would find their home in the West.[2]

The choice of a western site for the first nuclear weapons laboratory was somewhat serendipitous, the decision owing not a little to the fact that three of those whom Manhattan Project director Leslie Groves consulted about the location—Robert Oppenheimer, Ernest Orlando Lawrence, and Edwin McMillan—were physicists at the University of California.[3] According to legend, Oppenheimer was instrumental in picking Los Alamos, New Mexico, as the site for the first atomic lab. Not only did this location allow him to combine his two loves—physics and the desert— but both he and his brother Frank had fond memories of summers spent nearby at the ranch they called "Perro Caliente" ("Hot Dog").[4]

Yet, if geography and convenience made the West the obvious choice, these attributes do not explain why this relationship not only continued after the war but grew and flourished—when isolation and solitude were no longer prerequisites for designing nuclear weapons. For that, one must look to another motive, also long associated with the West: the dream of Empire.

While Groves and Oppenheimer played key roles in the choice of Los Alamos for wartime atomic research, it was Oppenheimer's University of

119

California colleague—Lawrence—who deserves credit for sustaining and nurturing the tie that bound the West to nuclear weapons and the federal government: first by persuading the university to continue its stewardship of Los Alamos after the war; and, later, by his efforts to establish under the university's auspices a second weapons laboratory at Livermore, California, which now also bears his name. Lawrence's success in building an empire is all the more impressive for having been carried out by a professor at a public university.

The inventor of the cyclotron, for which he received the Nobel Prize in 1939, Lawrence was no less famous among colleagues for his unparalleled skills as an entrepreneur and promoter of "big science."[5] Born in South Dakota, he abandoned a prestigious teaching post at Yale University in favor of greater opportunity out west. As the chairman of Berkeley's physics department never failed to point out, Lawrence was the rara avis among scientists—a Nobel laureate from a state-supported university.[6]

In the Radiation Laboratory, Lawrence by the outbreak of war had built a scientific mecca on the hill above the Berkeley campus. Characteristically operating behind the scenes rather than in the limelight—a personal trait that well predated wartime secrecy—Lawrence played a major role in mobilizing scientific brainpower for the Manhattan Project.[7] Most notably, the "Calutrons" of Lawrence's design were used to separate the uranium for the atomic bomb dropped on Hiroshima in 1945.

By war's end, he was launched upon the creation of an even more grandiose "paradise of physics" under his personal direction.[8] With a degree of success that probably even he found surprising, Lawrence would accomplish that goal—first by salvaging the tie between weapons work and the West at the conclusion of the war, and then by making that bond enduring in the wary peace that followed.

That the University of California would be chosen to steward the military atom from the Manhattan Project to the end of the Cold War was far from obvious at the time of Japan's surrender. As scientific director of wartime Los Alamos, Oppenheimer had continually chafed at the bureaucratic restrictions imposed by the university, which administered the lab on behalf of the Army. In order to circumvent delays and avoid endless questions from prying UC administrators, Oppenheimer successfully kept the purpose of the Los Alamos project a secret even from the regents' secretary-treasurer, Robert Underhill, who was responsible for overseeing the Army contract. (It was Lawrence who later let Underhill in on the secret.)[9]

The relationship between the University of California and the Army was, to be sure, one that both patron and client often found frustrating. Groves, for his part, complained that Los Alamos held the record for the greatest number of prima donnas ever assembled in one place. As early as March 1944, more than a year before the first bomb was ready to test, the university's president, Robert Gordon Sproul, instructed Oppenheimer and Underhill to begin planning for a "tapering off" of the institution's involvement with Los Alamos.[10]

Its wartime arrangement with the university evidently seemed an unnatural alliance to the Army, too. On August 20, 1945—less than a week after the Japanese surrender—Groves's aide, Colonel Kenneth Nichols, confirmed to Underhill that the Army and the University of California would sever their ties by the beginning of March 1946.[11] President Sproul was likewise eager upon the cessation of hostilities to liquidate this wartime partnership, and to "get rid of bomb making, plutonium, and New Mexico," he told the regents.[12]

Nonetheless, by early 1946, when efforts to create a mostly civilian successor to the Army's Manhattan Project bogged down in Congress, even Groves had begun to drag his feet in fleeing the groves of academe. Memories of Lawrence's skills at organizing scientists probably contributed to the general's change of heart. Sproul, too, had evidently begun to have second thoughts. At the very meeting where the university's president vowed to rid himself of Los Alamos, he had also professed a desire to keep Lawrence "close to atomic energy." Facing stiff competition from the University of Chicago in what promised to be the lucrative arena of postwar atomic energy research, Sproul had assured Lawrence during a September 1945 meeting in the president's office that he was "unwilling to yield this field, in which we are now preeminent, to any other institution."[13]

Sproul's motivation for a postwar alliance with the Army went beyond mere regional pride or academic parochialism. As Lawrence was no doubt quick to point out, the new field of atomic energy seemed an area not only ripe for new discoveries but full of opportunities for the institutions that sponsored the research. While the financial aspect was probably not a major inducement for extending the relationship, Underhill, for one, was aware that the university's charge for overhead meant that not only glory, but money, would continue to flow from such an alliance.[14]

Lawrence himself was undoubtedly the most eager to foster a tie that permanently bound the university and the Army in the matter of the atom. Before the war, he had found it necessary to turn to private philanthropies like the Rockefeller Foundation to fund the cyclotrons that were ever growing in size and expense, basing his appeal on speculative hopes that, in addition to treating diseases like leukemia, the radioisotopes produced by the machines might even, one day, cure cancer.[15] Now, in the afterglow of victory, the prospect of a never-ending struggle for private grants was supplanted by the vision of an inexhaustible cornucopia of government funding, readily at hand.

Within weeks of the war's end, Lawrence had submitted to Groves a detailed plan for federal support of a burgeoning postwar Rad Lab.[16] During subsequent months, Lawrence and members of his Rad Lab urged Underhill and Sproul to postpone termination of the contract with the Army to run Los Alamos.[17]

The potential connection between the Army's continuing dependence on the university and his own ambitious plans for the future Rad Lab certainly did not escape Lawrence. When Oppenheimer threatened to leave Berkeley and Cal Tech, Lawrence cited "Oppie's" close ties to Groves and government funding as a reason Sproul should try to persuade the temperamental physicist to stay. "How much we pay Professor Oppenheimer really means nothing because the Government will place such large sums at our disposal if Oppenheimer is here, that his salary will be insignificant," Lawrence told Sproul. (The latter demurred, however, that "this should not be the basis of our arrangements with Oppenheimer.")[18]

At an April 1946 meeting which Sproul, according to his office diary, originally intended to be "a roundup and showdown on the New Mexico project," the president not only again delayed ending the contract for Los Alamos but approved new Army funding for Lawrence's lab. A week later, Sproul extended the University's contract to administer Los Alamos for another four months.[19]

Ultimately, Lawrence's legendary persuasiveness succeeded in changing the minds of the university's president, its head regent, and the regents' treasurer concerning the wisdom of continuing the wartime partnership with the government. In return, Lawrence received a virtually guaranteed source of continued funding for his burgeoning empire of the atom on the West Coast.

Partly in recognition of Lawrence's role in maintaining the link between the bomb and the University of California, in January 1947 the newly created Atomic Energy Commission agreed that it would regard the installation on the slopes of UC's Charter Hill as "somewhat of a national lab."[20] Following a six-day meeting of the AEC at the exclusive Bohemian Grove that August—a gathering arranged by Lawrence and underwritten by his friend and benefactor, Alfred Loomis—the director of the Commission's Research Division, James Fisk, reversed an earlier decision and cleared the way for government funding of a new kind of particle accelerator at the Rad Lab.[21]

Before his rivals at the University of Chicago or Columbia University could rally their forces, Lawrence had pulled off a fait accompli, assuring for the University of California a dominant position in federally funded postwar atomic research. In the face of Lawrence's persistent and skillful lobbying, even the AEC's own General Advisory Committee (GAC) proved unable, or unwilling, to break what one of its members, Columbia physicist I. I. Rabi, would come to call—with perhaps equal measures of envy and rue—the "University of California atomic trust."[22]

At Los Alamos itself, meanwhile, Oppenheimer's successor—Stanford University physicist Norris Bradbury—although appointed by Groves rather than by the university, soon made peace with Sproul and Underhill, and learned to exploit the fact that neither his masters in Washington nor those in California were close enough to check up on the daily operations of the laboratory.[23] Lawrence, too, discovered that there were benefits to having an absentee landlord, and similarly took advantage of his lab's geographic separation from Washington.[24]

At a climactic meeting between Sproul and the AEC on January 9, 1948, Lawrence persuaded the president to finally cement the university's relationship with the AEC by agreement on separate and renewable contracts, under which the university would continue to administer Los Alamos and the AEC would continue to fund research at the Rad Lab. Not coincidentally, AEC General Manager Carroll Wilson also promised Sproul at this meeting that Lawrence, as the university's representative for Los Alamos, would have "a free run of the place."[25]

After January 1948, neither the university's president nor the AEC's general manager was any longer under the illusion that the bond between them was tenuous or temporary. Wrote Sproul in his office diary of the meeting on January 9: "My final word was 'We are now engaged, but the banns are not to be published, until each party has had an opportunity to investigate the background and intentions of the other more thoroughly.' "[26]

Sproul's disclaimer notwithstanding, it was still, for both sides, a union of convenience. For the government, the university connection allowed Los Alamos to attract and hold talented scholars who might otherwise have balked at working for the military directly. In return, the lab's scientists received top-notch facilities, and the university a guarantee of additional funding through the yearly management fee charged to the AEC.

The seemingly unlikely marriage of the University of California and the Atomic Energy Commission was consummated shortly thereafter—with the regents' approval of two renewable agreements: Contract 36, for the administration of Los Alamos, and Contract 48, for AEC-related work at Lawrence's Rad Lab.[27]

Although Lawrence would continue to be at the center of the relationship between the university and the AEC, another increasingly important role in the postwar years was played by San Francisco attorney John Neylan, chairman of the board of regents and also of the regents' Special Committee on the Los Alamos Project. Wealthy, conservative, and well connected in California politics, Neylan—who counted William Randolph Hearst among his legal clients—was, like Lawrence, a transplant from the East who had come West to better his prospects. Neylan became both a social mentor and unofficial political adviser to Lawrence.[28]

Just as Sproul was endeavoring to untangle the university from Los Alamos, Neylan in August 1945 had created the Special Committee, a move whose effect would perpetuate the tie binding the university to the government and the atom.[29] Evidently overcoming his own earlier doubts about such a marriage, Neylan appears to have been motivated by his personal friendship with, and unwavering faith in, Ernest Lawrence, as well as by the vision he and Lawrence shared of an expanding laboratory funded with federal money.[30]

If the union of a public university and a secret laboratory was unusual, then Neylan's Special Committee, charged with responsibility for overseeing the running of Los Alamos, was surely unique. From the outset, Neylan and the three other members of the committee—Sproul and Regents Harrison and Rowell—agreed to accept the AEC's assurance that the requests it forwarded to them for approval, although shrouded in secrecy and sometimes obscured by technical esoterica, were made in good faith and in the nation's best interests. As a result, those who served on the Special Committee routinely, and deliberately, operated in a state of ignorance concerning the substance of the AEC business they were asked to sanction on behalf of the university.

While Neylan and the Special Committee were given "Q" clearances by the AEC, it is evident from the minutes of their meetings that the committee's members did not feel they had the technical competence— or, perhaps, the right—to question the AEC's actions during the height of the Cold War.[31] Instead, they chose to defer to those whose opinion they trusted most. As Neylan later acknowledged to Lawrence and Bradbury: "As you gentlemen know, the Committee, with full knowledge of the Regents, has at all times relied very heavily on your judgment. . . . In fact, there has been little else they could do."[32]

Under these circumstances, when the Special Committee received, in mid-December 1951, an "exceedingly urgent" but typically vague AEC request "for special equipment and material necessary in connection with the primary purposes of Project 36," its members agreed—without substantial debate, or even much discussion—to administer three subcontracts on behalf of the AEC, totaling $11 million. By this seemingly innocuous act, the president and regents of the University of California unanimously—and evidently unknowingly—approved funding for the construction of the world's first hydrogen bomb. Eleven months later, the device was successfully tested in the Pacific.[33]

Just as Oppenheimer established the tie between the West and the bomb, and Lawrence cemented and defended that relationship, a third University of California physicist—Edward Teller—deserves credit for providing the impetus that would extend the UC-AEC bond to include establishment of a second weapons lab.

A figure from the dawn of the atomic age, Teller subsequently boasted that he entered the drama as a chauffeur, driving Leo Szilard to Einstein's house on Long Island in 1939, where the two men wrote the fateful letter to Roosevelt that eventually resulted in the Manhattan

Project.[34] A decade later, Teller was a committed advocate of proceeding with the next, more powerful generation of nuclear explosives—the "super" (hydrogen) bomb, which was then under development at Los Alamos.

Teller's argument that competition would mean more rapid progress toward a hydrogen bomb proved irresistible in the political climate of the time. The case for the second lab made by Teller and other members of the so-called H-bomb lobby—a politically conservative coalition of forces which included the Air Force, the Joint Congressional Committee on Atomic Energy (JCAE), AEC Commissioner Lewis Strauss, and Ernest Lawrence—thus eventually overrode opposition from the director of Los Alamos, the GAC, and a majority of AEC commissioners.[35]

In a compromise worked out between advocates of the superbomb, the AEC, and the university regents in June 1952, it was agreed that, in addition to helping Los Alamos with "diagnostic and measurement work" on the H-bomb, Lawrence's Rad Lab would "eventually suggest broader programs of thermonuclear research to be carried out by the U.C.R.L. or elsewhere." Three weeks later, on July 1, the regents of the University of California approved the creation of the second weapons lab "with the advice of E. O. Lawrence."[36]

Although Teller provided the final impetus, it was the organizing skill and reputation of Lawrence that made the second lab possible. The previous February, Lawrence and Teller together had picked Livermore— where the Rad Lab was building a mammoth new accelerator—as the site for the second lab.[37]

Despite the creation of the Livermore laboratory under conditions of near-wartime urgency, America's first hydrogen bomb was in fact designed by scientists at Los Alamos. As outlined in the AEC's June 1952 letter to the regents, Livermore's sole contribution to the "Mike" test the following November was a series of diagnostic experiments that would confirm the prototype weapon's success.

However, misleading popular accounts of the development of the superbomb—abetted by allies of the H-bomb lobby—mistakenly assigned to Livermore the credit that should have gone to Los Alamos.[38] Neither public protests from the director and staff of Los Alamos, nor subsequent disclaimers by Teller and Lawrence, were able to defuse the animosity between scientists at the two labs.[39] Moreover, adding a bitter personal dimension to this feud was the fact that Teller and Lawrence were known to have sided with those in the AEC and JCAE who, in the spring of 1954, provoked a security investigation of Oppenheimer on the charge of disloyalty.

In spectacular Wild West fashion, the rivalry between Los Alamos and Livermore was played out in the tests of competing weapons prototypes at proving grounds in Nevada and the Pacific during the early to mid-1950s.[40] Abiding by its unwritten charter that it would not duplicate work being done at Los Alamos, Livermore agreed early on to tackle novel approaches to weapons design, and to explore avenues that had been tried previously but abandoned as unpromising by Los Alamos.[41]

The first two fission bombs designed at Livermore utilized just such an unorthodox approach; it was one that, not coincidentally, had been favored by Teller at wartime Los Alamos and afterward. Since both bombs were highly experimental, the failure of the Nevada "Ruth" and "Ray" tests to produce satisfactory results in the spring of 1953 was not entirely unexpected.[42] However, the fact that the bomb tested in "Ruth" failed to demolish even the tower on which it stood provoked merriment among Los Alamos weaponeers—one of whom reportedly observed, sotto voce, that in future tests Livermore should use either a bigger bomb or a smaller tower.[43]

A year later, the first Livermore-designed fusion bombs—devices code-named "Morgenstern" and "Ramrod"—yielded similarly disappointing results in the Pacific. In the "Koon" test, the thermonuclear component of the Morgenstern device failed to ignite, producing an explosion only a fraction of the million-ton force expected.[44] Reluctantly, but wisely, embarrassed Livermore scientists decided not to proceed with the test of Ramrod, which was similar to Morgenstern in design.[45]

By the spring of 1955, however, the tide had begun to turn for the second lab. With the explosion that March of two Livermore-designed fission devices in Nevada tests code-named "Turk" and "Tesla," the lab that Lawrence and Teller built finally achieved its first successes in the weapons field.[46] Two tests—code-named "Zuni" and "Tewa"—of H-bomb prototypes the following year in the Pacific proved that Livermore was now able to build multimegaton hydrogen bombs as well.[47] Within weeks of the successful Tewa test, in fact, Teller was sufficiently confident of the lab's ability to promise the Navy that Livermore would deliver within five years a one-megaton warhead small enough to fit on a submarine-launched ballistic missile—a feat reportedly dismissed as impossible by some Los Alamos scientists.[48]

The successful test of the W-47 Polaris warhead, in the July 1958 "Hardtack" series, marked the true coming-of-age of the Livermore lab—putting it on a par with, or even slightly ahead of, Los Alamos. But ironically Livermore's long-delayed respectability as a nuclear lab occurred just as both labs were confronting the prospect of fundamental change. Only a month after Livermore's triumph with Polaris, the lab's patron, Lawrence, was dead of ulcerative colitis. Lawrence had been stricken while representing the AEC in negotiations at Geneva aimed at bringing an end to nuclear testing. Barely a fortnight after his death, the United States and the Soviet Union agreed to a moratorium on nuclear tests.

Even before the moratorium began in the fall of 1958, realization was dawning at the labs that the "boom" brought about by federal support might some day go "bust." The possibility that both nuclear weapons and nuclear testing might be entering a rococo phase had occurred to Los Alamos director Bradbury as early as the fall of 1955. In a response to an AEC inquiry about long-range planning at Los Alamos, Bradbury candidly observed that the future looked "somewhat unrewarding."[49] In terms of technical challenges, there no longer appeared "to be any unscaled peak on the horizon," he mused. The time seemed to be approaching when "[e]veryone will ultimately have all the weapons in all the variety wanted," in which case the bomb itself might "gradually cease to have a dominant role in international relations." He concluded, somewhat plaintively: "In short, what should Los Alamos then be in a position to do?"

Increasingly, public concern with the fallout from nuclear testing—spurred by the accidental irradiation of a Japanese fishing boat in the March 1954 "Bravo" test, and manifested during the 1956 presidential campaign by support for pro-ban candidate Adlai Stevenson—also cast a pall of uncertainty over the future of the labs.[50]

Despite an imaginative holding action in the spring of 1957, when Teller, Lawrence, and a third Livermore colleague briefly persuaded the Eisenhower administration of the potential merits to be found in a virtually fallout-free "clean" bomb, the moratorium ultimately overwhelmed test-ban opponents with the force of an idea whose time had come.[51]

Indeed, Lawrence's role as a putative arms controller at Geneva that summer suggests that even he had by then lost some of the faith of his original conviction that the country needed bigger and better bombs.[52]

The prospect of a permanent end to nuclear testing, implicit in the moratorium, provoked not only anxiety but also a change in focus at the weapons labs. At Los Alamos, work was initiated on an atomic-powered rocket aimed at carrying American astronauts to Mars, and possibly beyond. At Livermore, development began on a nuclear-powered ramjet— the precursor of today's cruise missile—which would carry to targets in Russia the bombs that the lab was no longer able to test in Nevada and the Pacific.[53]

Perhaps because of the test moratorium, Bradbury was more pessimistic than ever about the future of Los Alamos in a September 1959 letter to the AEC. The following year, Teller resigned as director of Livermore, in part so that he might more effectively lobby for a resumption of nuclear testing and promote an antimissile defense for the country.[54]

As events developed, Bradbury and Teller need not have worried that a temporary end to nuclear testing was the harbinger of a permanent peace. The sudden, unexpected resumption of Soviet nuclear testing in September 1961, and the consequent revival and acceleration of both the arms race and the Cold War, removed for the next thirty years the danger that the weapons labs would have nothing left to do.

During that time, Los Alamos and Livermore produced new weapons, including the so-called neutron bomb, as well as further refinements of old ones—like the miniaturized warheads which made possible MIRVed missiles and in turn led to the almost explosive growth of nuclear weapons in the U.S. stockpile. In what was perhaps the culmination of this trend, the advent of directed-energy weapons such as the nuclear bomb-pumped X-ray laser, invented at Livermore, opened the doors in the early 1980s both to a new "third generation" of nuclear weaponry and to the Strategic Defense Initiative ("Star Wars").[55]

The end of the Cold War would raise anew the question that worried the director of Los Alamos in 1955, and then came to haunt both labs three years later, during the moratorium: What are the weapons labs to do when nuclear weapons have ceased to have a dominant role in international relations?

Beginning in the early 1970s, and repeatedly since then, faculty and students at the University of California, disaffected with that institution's role as overseer of the nuclear labs, have actively lobbied the university to sever its ties with Los Alamos and Livermore. In a sign emblematic of this change in outlook, Ernest Lawrence's widow, Molly, petitioned Congress to have her husband's name removed from the Livermore lab.[56]

For the university itself, neither patriotic appeal nor the financial incentive of the annual management fee has succeeded in dispelling the growing belief that what was once an asset has become a liability.[57] Meanwhile, for the first time in its own history, even the Department of Energy, the AEC's successor, is reportedly willing to entertain the possibility that there may no longer be a case for maintaining two nuclear design labs.[58]

In the absence of a strong advocate like Lawrence or a convincing reason-for-being based on national security, the sun has seemingly begun to set on the dream of Empire that first gave rise to the Atomic West. Indeed, the laboratory that Lawrence and Teller built has had its foundations undermined by the end of the conflict that originally nurtured and sustained it.

For both sides, the wisdom of maintaining the bond, now more than half a century old, between the federal atomic energy establishment and the University of California is being seriously questioned anew. In a world fundamentally different from the one that saw it come into being, the marriage between the weapons labs and the West is under increasing strain; the two partners have grown distant and quarrelsome, and there is talk of separation.

NOTES

The author would like to gratefully acknowledge the assistance of the MacArthur Foundation in the research for this essay.

1. Perhaps fittingly, Thomas Mann's *The Magic Mountain* turned out to be among the favorite books of those heading off from eastern universities to the mesa top in the land of enchantment in the spring of 1943. Robert Wilson, interview by author, April 14, 1983, Los Alamos, New Mexico.

2. A third nuclear weapons lab, Sandia, concerned with ordnance engineering

rather than design, would be created at the old Albuquerque airport near the end of the war. See Richard G. Hewlett and Oscar E. Anderson, Jr., *A History of the United States Atomic Energy Commission,* vol. 1, *The New World, 1939/1946* (University Park: Pennsylvania State University Press, 1962), 625, 632; and Necah Stewart Furman, *Sandia National Laboratories: The Postwar Decade* (Albuquerque: University of New Mexico Press, 1990).

3. Concerning the choice of Los Alamos, see John H. Dudley, "Ranch School to Secret City," in *Reminiscences of Los Alamos, 1943–1945,* ed. Lawrence Badash, Joseph O. Hirschfelder, and Herbert P. Broida (Boston: D. Reidel, 1980), 1–11.

4. The ranch, first leased by Robert Oppenheimer in 1928, reportedly got its name from his comment upon learning the property was available. See A. K. Smith and Charles Weiner, eds., *Robert Oppenheimer: Letters and Recollections* (Cambridge: Harvard University Press, 1980), 132.

5. Concerning the history of the prewar Radiation Laboratory, see J. L. Heilbron and Robert Seidel, *Lawrence and His Laboratory: A History of the Lawrence Berkeley Laboratory* (Berkeley: University of California Press, 1989).

6. Raymond T. Birge, "History of the Physics Department, University of California, Berkeley," vol. 3, pp. 1–23.

7. On Lawrence's role in the Manhattan Project, see Richard Rhodes, *The Making of the Atomic Bomb* (New York: Simon and Schuster, 1986), pp. 361–62; and Herbert Childs, *An American Genius: The Life of Ernest Orlando Lawrence, Father of the Cyclotron* (New York: Dutton, 1968), 324–38.

8. Childs, *An American Genius,* p. 371.

9. In November 1943, according to Underhill, Lawrence invited him into his office and, after locking the door, asked, "You know what they're doing down in Los Alamos?" "No, I don't know what they're doing down there," Underhill confessed. "As far as I'm concerned, Oppenheimer is running a scientific study in physics down there." Interview by Arthur Norberg, 1976, "Robert Underhill: Contract Negotiations for the University of California," 18, Robert M. Underhill Papers, Bancroft Library, University of California, Berkeley.

10. Robert Seidel, "The University of California and the Mobilization of Science for National Defense," LA-UR 92–53, Los Alamos National Laboratory (hereafter LANL), 26. The author would also like to thank Robert Seidel for comments on an earlier draft of this paper.

11. "Series 3, Correspondence, 1941–52," box 5, Robert M. Underhill Papers, Los Alamos National Laboratory Archives.

12. Sproul's comment was made at a September 1946 meeting of the regents' Finance Committee and is quoted on page 27 of Seidel's paper (see note 10 above).

13. September 27, 1945, entry, "1945 Memos," Robert Sproul Papers, Bancroft Library, University of California, Berkeley.

14. In the spring of 1942, the University of California lowered its overhead rate on federal contracts from 50 percent to 30 percent. Robert Seidel, "The DOE Weapons Laboratories," LA-UR-92–2571, 5, LANL.

15. Childs, *An American Genius*, 223–24.

16. On December 28, 1945, Groves informed Lawrence that his postwar plan for the lab had been approved. Groves to Lawrence, Record Group (RG) 77, Manhattan Engineer District, National Archives, Washington, D.C.

17. For example, in January 1947, Nichols wrote to a colleague that Ken Priestley, business manager of the Rad Lab, was keeping Underhill "calm" about the UC-Army relationship. Nichols to Kirkpatrick, January 10, 1947, U.S. Department of Energy Archives, Las Vegas, Nevada (hereafter USDOE Archives).

18. October 11, 1945 entry, "1945 Memos," Sproul Papers.

19. Entries of March 12, April 10, and April 17, 1946, "1946 Memos," Sproul Papers.

20. Oak Ridge to AEC, January 20, 1947, RG 326, Atomic Energy Commission (AEC), National Archives, Washington, D.C.

21. Documents on the August 1947 meeting at the Bohemian Grove are in "AEC Lab Directors Meetings, 1947–49," carton 30, folder 28, Ernest Orlando Lawrence Papers (hereafter EOL Papers), Bancroft Library, University of California, Berkeley.

22. Rabi is quoted in Robert Seidel, "Accelerating Science: The Postwar Transformation of the Lawrence Berkeley Laboratory," *Historical Studies in the Physical Sciences* 14, no. 2 (1983): 394. In his office diary, Sproul thought provincialism lay behind the GAC's efforts to put the new accelerator at the Brookhaven lab instead of Berkeley: "There is strong pressure from Conant, Robi [*sic*] of Columbia, and other eastern interests, to have [a new accelerator] put at Bookhaven [*sic*], Long Island. The chief argument is that new exploration in the field of science can be conducted better under private auspices than public. The real reason, of course, is a desire to concentrate on the Atlantic Seaboard the significant advances in this important field." Entry of December 31, 1947, "1947 Memos," Sproul Papers.

23. Norris Bradbury, interview by author, October 2, 1992, Los Alamos, New Mexico.

24. For example, attached to a Manhattan Engineer District memo of September 4, 1946, was this plaintive inquiry from one of the Army officers responsible for administering the Rad Lab contract: "We asked EOL on 5 August for a general statement re Lin[ear] Ac[celerator] plans. Similarly, we asked [Rad Lab Business Manager] Reynolds on 5 August for a general statement of Wilson Site Development plans. The attachment satisfies neither request, but postpones the whole matter for 30–60 days. . . . Should we wait or send a reminder in reply to EOL's letter?" Contract 48 Records, folder "Linear Accelerator Correspondence," Federal Records Center, San Bruno, California.

25. Entry of January 9, 1948, "1948 Memos," Sproul Papers. It was subsequently agreed that the contracts would be reviewed for renewal every four years; they are now reviewed every five years.

26. Ibid.

27. Regents of the University of California to General Manager of the AEC, June 15, 1948, USDOE Archives.

28. In 1950, Neylan would become the chief defender among the regents of the university's controversial loyalty oath, an issue that would split the UC faculty and the Rad Lab. On the oath and its consequences, see David P. Gardner, *The California Oath Controversy* (Berkeley: University of California Press, 1967); and George R. Stewart, *The Year of the Oath* (Garden City, N.Y.: Doubleday, 1950).

29. Neylan proposed creating the committee at an emergency regents meeting called to discuss the need for new dormitories to house students returning from the war. Minutes of special meeting of the regents, August 24, 1945, box 171, folder 1, John Francis Neylan Papers, Bancroft Library, University of California, Berkeley. The author would like to thank the University of California for granting him access to these restricted papers.

30. Neylan wrote of Lawrence in a July 1, 1946, letter to Bernard Baruch: "Ernest Lawrence is not only a great scientist, he is a wonderful human being. He is sane and level-headed and a genuinely modest man." Neylan Papers, box 171, folder 1.

31. The first renewal of the lab contracts, in 1952, coincided with the Korean War. Because of the national emergency, there was little consideration given to breaking the tie to Los Alamos.

32. Neylan to Lawrence, November 20, 1953, Neylan Papers, box 171, folder 3. Neylan's comment was in response to a suggestion by the two lab directors that they give the Special Committee an unclassified briefing on the projects to be funded two weeks prior to the meeting where permission for the subcontracts would be requested by the AEC. "In this way," they wrote, "classified documents will not have to be received by the Regents." Lawrence and Bradbury to Neylan, November 6, 1953, ibid.

33. Minutes, December 14, 1951, Neylan Papers, ibid.

34. Edward Teller, *Better a Shield Than a Sword: Perspectives on Defense and Technology* (New York: Free Press, 1987), 48.

35. Concerning the H-bomb debate and its role in the creation of the second lab, see Peter Galison and Barton Bernstein, "In Any Light: Scientists and the Decision to Build the Superbomb, 1942–1954," *Historical Studies in the Physical and Biological Sciences* 19, pt. 2 (1989); and Barton Bernstein, "The Struggle for the Creation of America's Second Weapons Laboratory: The Triumph of Teller and Lawrence," unpublished paper. The author would like to thank Professor Bernstein for a copy of his paper.

36. Gordon Dean to UC Regents, June 9, 1952, RG 330, Office of the Secretary of Defense, Series 199, File CD 471.6, 1952, National Archives, Washington, D.C.; Underhill to Dean, July 1, 1952, USDOE Archives.

37. Bernstein paper, 19.

38. These included an article in the April 12, 1954, issue of *Life* magazine, and a book by two anti-Oppenheimer journalists, James Shepley and Clair Blair, *The Hydrogen Bomb* (New York: David McKay, 1954).

39. Los Alamos press release, September 24, 1954, USDOE Archives. In response to the *Life* article, Teller wrote the editor from the Pacific Proving Ground: "What you would find here are people from two laboratories working together effectively and in friendship. . . . I should like to convey to you that the spirit on this island is a spirit of cooperation, modesty and awe in face of the forces of nature, which we are trying to explore for the defense of our Country to the best of our ability." Teller to "Dear Editor," April 11, 1954, Neylan Papers, box 171, folder 3.

40. According to the subsequent director of the test program, this rivalry was manifested, for example, in the treatment given Livermore's "upstarts" by Los Alamos "veterans," and in the preference accorded Los Alamos scientists in the matter of housing and transportation at both test sites. Gerald Johnson interview by author, June 10, 1988, La Jolla, California.

41. On the differences between the "cultures" of the two labs, see Herbert F. York, *Making Weapons, Talking Peace: A Physicist's Odyssey from Hiroshima to Geneva* (New York: Basic Books, 1987), 75. From Livermore's perspective, its scientists designed "race horses," and Los Alamos "work horses"; see Sybil Francis, "Race Horses vs. Work Horses: Competition Between the Nuclear Weapons Labs in the 1950s," paper given at the conference "The Decade of Innovation: Los Alamos, Livermore, and National Security Decision Making in the 1950s," February 19–21, 1992, Pleasanton, California.

42. Chuck Hansen, *U.S. Nuclear Weapons: The Secret History* (New York: Orion Books, 1988), 39 n.

43. Gerald Johnson, interview.

44. Hansen, "Announced U.S. Nuclear Detonations and Tests, 1945–1962," manuscript, 5. The author would like to thank Chuck Hansen for this listing and other papers prepared for a forthcoming updated edition of *U.S. Nuclear Weapons*.

45. Hansen, *U.S. Nuclear Weapons*, 67.

46. Hansen, "Announced U.S. Nuclear Detonations and Tests, 1945–1962," 7.

47. Ibid., 8–9.

48. Chuck Hansen, "W-47," manuscript, 3.

49. Bradbury to Johnson, November 21, 1955, "AEC General Correspondence, 1956," EOL Papers, carton 32, folder 12.

50. On the controversy over the test ban, see Robert A. Divine, *Blowing on the Wind: The Nuclear Test Ban Debate, 1954–1960* (New York: Oxford University Press, 1978), 84–112.

51. In a June 1957 meeting with President Dwight Eisenhower, Teller, Lawrence, and Livermore associate director Mark Mills held out the prospect of developing the "clean" bomb as an argument for continued testing. Concerning the clean bomb episode, see the author's *Cardinal Choices: Presidential Science Advising from the Atomic Bomb to SDI* (New York: Oxford University Press, 1992), 97–98.

52. The man whom Lawrence picked to be the first director of the Livermore lab, physicist Herbert York, recalls that his mentor seemed surprisingly committed to the goal of a test ban; at one point in the Geneva negotiations, Lawrence even pleaded with his Soviet counterpart, as a fellow physicist and Nobel laureate, to return to the bargaining table when the collapse of the talks seemed imminent. Herbert York, interview by author, July 9, 1992, La Jolla, California.

53. On Project Rover, see James Dewar, *To the End of the Solar System: The Nuclear Rocket Engine and President Kennedy's Vision of Manned Space Exploration* (Washington, D.C.: Smithsonian Institution Press, forthcoming). On Project Pluto, see Gregg Herken, "The Flying Crowbar," *Air and Space/Smithsonian,* April-May 1990, 28–34.

54. Bradbury to Starbird, September 14, 1959, USDOE Archives; Edward Teller with Allen Brown, *The Legacy of Hiroshima* (Garden City, N.Y.: Doubleday, 1962), 76.

55. On Teller's role in the origins of SDI, see William Broad, *Teller's War: The Top-Secret Story Behind the Star Wars Deception* (New York: Simon and Schuster, 1992).

56. Molly Lawrence, interview by author, August 11, 1992, Balboa Island, California.

57. In 1949, University of California faculty members concluded on the subject of contract research for the military and the AEC: "Gold is where you find it. It would be folly for the University to refuse to participate in a program of promotion of research because it does not approve of some features of its organization." Cited in Seidel, "The DOE Weapons Laboratories," 29. Concerning the arguments in the debate over whether to break the university's ties with the weapons labs, see, for example, *Forum on the Involvement of the University of California in Nuclear Testing at Lawrence Livermore and Los Alamos National Laboratories,* February 11, 1987, California Senate Committee on Health and Human Services, Sacramento.

58. "Weapons Labs: After the Cold War," *Science,* November 22, 1991, pp. 1100–1103; York, interview.

James L. Tuck

Scientific Polymath and Eternal Optimist
of the Atomic West

Ferenc M. Szasz

The name of James L. Tuck rings few bells with the American public. Even those who associate him with wartime Los Alamos acknowledge that his reputation pales beside those of his colleagues, J. Robert Oppenheimer, Hans Bethe, Enrico Fermi, Niels Bohr, Edward Teller, Rudolph Peierls, or Richard Feynman. Unlike Teller and Oppenheimer, Tuck never delved into the realm of politics. Unlike Bohr, Fermi, or Bethe, he has never been the subject of a full-scale biography. Feynman, Peierls, Victor Weisskopf, and Otto Frish all penned popular autobiographies, but Tuck's venture in that direction—a brief set of "Autobiographical Notes"—lies unconsulted in the archives of the Los Alamos National Laboratory.

Yet James L. Tuck was a crucial figure in the emergence of the Atomic West. Tuck was a transplanted Englishman whose 1943–45 discoveries proved vital to the development of the plutonium implosion weapons that were detonated at the Trinity test site in New Mexico and at Nagasaki, Japan, in July and August of 1945. The next year, he inaugurated America's first attempts to produce a controlled thermonuclear reaction. After a brief hiatus at Oxford University, he returned in 1950 to become an integral part of the postwar Los Alamos community. There he directed the Los Alamos portion of Project Sherwood (the umbrella term for the early fusion program) from 1952 to 1972. In 1958 he headed the team that produced the world's first laboratory thermonuclear fusion (confirmed finally in 1961). During the 1950s and 1960s, Tuck emerged as the most prominent, if not the most eminent, fusion scientist of his day. Everyone connected with the early atomic world recognized his name.

From the late 1960s until the late 1970s, Tuck took on yet a wider role. During those years he became a traveling Cassandra on the world's energy crisis, and a prominent spokesman for nuclear power. As a hobby, he turned himself into the nation's premier expert on ball lightning. Throughout his career, Tuck's eternal scientific optimism and endearing eccentricities made him a recognized figure in nuclear circles around the globe. The story of the Atomic West could not be told without him.

James Tuck was born January 9, 1910, to a middle-class family in Manchester, England. Educated at local schools, he took an Honours B.Sc. in general science at Victoria University of Manchester and then enrolled for a Ph.D. in physical chemistry at the same institution. During his postgraduate study, he fell under the influence of physical chemist Michael Polanyi and began a thesis on reaction kinetics. A chance meeting with maverick Hungarian refugee Leo Szilard led to his accepting an appointment in October 1937 as a Salter Research Fellow at the Clarendon Laboratory in Oxford, then directed by famed scientist Frederick A. Lindemann. He married Elsie Harper the same year.

Physicist R. V. Jones later recalled Tuck in those days as "a remarkable combination of social naivete and technical astuteness." Tall and handsome, he wore colored shirts and corduroy trousers that made him appear "more Oxford than Oxford." But his colleagues found him easily beguiled, and they often hoaxed him with a variety of practical jokes. Tuck himself described their Oxford stay as "bitter-sweet": "sweet because it is idyllic to be newly married and in Oxford, which is beautiful, [but] bitter because we were poverty-stricken and battered socially."[1]

Part of the social snobbery he met lay in academic insularity: in the late 1930s Oxford was a world unto itself. Its scientists scoffed at degrees from provincial institutions such as Manchester, and the lifetime appointment system of the Clarendon lab led to an ingrown and often out-of-date staff. Sir James Chadwick, Nobel laureate for his 1932 discovery of the neutron, once remarked that "in Cambridge those chaps couldn't have qualified as lab boys."[2]

From 1937 to 1939, Tuck worked on particle accelerators; and when Szilard fled Oxford for New York City, Tuck was left to design and build one almost by himself. The outbreak of the Second World War in 1939 diverted him into constructing emergency early warning radar systems for the defense of the British coast. In fact, he was working on the south channel coast when Lindemann, recently appointed to Winston Churchill's private staff, sent a telegram inviting him to become his scientific assistant.

Moving to Whitehall, Tuck was the only scientist among twelve specialists (economists, statisticians, etc.) on Churchill's personal staff. Lindemann remained his immediate superior, and working closely with that eccentric genius proved a constant challenge. Tuck was no "yes man," and they often disagreed violently. In one exchange, Tuck told Lindemann he had "had enough of his bloody double dealing" and stormed out of the office. In another, Lindemann fired him, so that he could "get a taste of the front line." Yet they always reconciled their differences.

Tuck's scientific duties proved equally challenging. At any moment he might be called upon to brief both Lindemann and Churchill on the current state of all British and Axis military research. Thus he kept abreast of developments in general weapons, aircraft, navigation, radar, poison gas, antitank weapons, and enemy technology in general.

Frustrated by office work, in 1943 Tuck began to explore the military and scientific gadgetry being developed by MD1 ("Winston Churchill's toyshop"). His knowledge of ordnance proved especially valuable in approaching a key scientific puzzle of the day—the powerful blast effect of shaped (hollowed out) explosive charges. Termed the Munroe effect, after the explosives expert who first discovered it in 1887, the focused blast of shaped charges was deemed crucial to the development of effective antitank weapons. Tuck devised a set of flash X rays, lasting a fraction of a microsecond, to record the changing configurations of the shaped charges both during and after detonation. Since this discovery led to major improvements in antitank weaponry, King George VI awarded Tuck the Order of the British Empire in 1943.[3] Simultaneously, the dean at Manchester University warned him that time was running out for the submission of his doctoral thesis, but that he could receive an extension (for a fee).

That same year, American scientists at the secret wartime laboratory in Los Alamos had run into major roadblocks in their plans to construct an implosion trigger for the plutonium weapon. Someone, perhaps Churchill, recommended Tuck's expertise. Accordingly, shortly after the 1943 Quebec Agreement that merged the American and British nuclear projects, Tuck was sent to Los Alamos as part of the British Mission. He remained there for the duration of the war.

Surprised to discover that the news of his experiments had preceded him, Tuck devoted most of his Los Alamos stay to the problems of implosion. Working with scientists Seth Neddermeyer and John von Neumann, he perfected a scheme whereby optical principles could be utilized to shape heavy explosive detonation waves, a process that is still classified. Years later, Tuck recalled Laboratory Director J. Robert Oppenheimer's speech to the Los Alamos Coordinating Council reporting that "for the first time, solid matter has been visibly compressed. Lens implosion was going to work."[4] Tuck's "lens system" of detonation eventually proved vital to the Trinity test, the Nagasaki weapon, and for virtually all nuclear weapons for several years afterward.

Although the precise details of Tuck's inventions remain secret, those in the know have always held them in the highest regard. Sir James Chadwick, overall head of the British Mission, listed Tuck's work on the implosion trigger as one of the British team's most significant contributions to the success of the Manhattan Project. R. V. Jones echoed that sentiment, arguing that without Tuck's contributions the weapons would not have been available in 1945.[5] The issue here revolved around timing. The mammoth plants at Oak Ridge, Tennessee, were not able to produce enough uranium 235 for a second uranium weapon. Devising an effective trigger mechanism for the plutonium spheres proved, perhaps, the most perplexing of all Los Alamos's problems. For better or worse, without James Tuck the plutonium bombs would not have been available for military use in July and August of 1945.

James and Elsie Tuck thoroughly enjoyed their Los Alamos stay. The rough Manchester edges that had so amused Oxford fit easily into a more democratic, western American environment. Thus, Tuck gladly accepted an offer to remain at Los Alamos after the war to assist the elaborate Crossroads atomic tests, scheduled for the spring of 1946 on the archipelago of Bikini. For these tests Tuck designed a number of recording devices to measure gamma-ray intensity. He also oversaw the building of about a dozen recording machines. In addition, he hoped to utilize the time during the long sea voyage to the Pacific island to write his Ph.D. thesis. Alas, however, a letter from his dean lay waiting for him when he arrived in Bikini; it informed him that the extended period for presenting his work had expired.

In August 1946, James and Elsie Tuck reluctantly left Los Alamos to return to Oxford. They did so in spite of receiving a letter from a colleague that warned Jim he should not expect his wartime successes to be reflected in his position at the Clarendon.

The Tucks found the austerity of postwar Britain very challenging. Their third-floor apartment had coal heat only, and everything had to be carried up the narrow stairs. During the winter of 1946–47 all their pipes froze. Jim used to shop for kidney and tripe ("edible offal") at the butcher shop on Saturday because the shopkeepers treated men better than women. He later recalled his admission to the Senior Common Room of Wadham College and strolling through the lovely gardens there as virtually the only happy recollections of his second Oxford stay.

Tuck's professional life met a similar series of frustrations. His major assignment was to oversee the operation of a commissioned betatron, but he watched helplessly as Britain's postwar economic problems steadily whittled down the size of the project. While the severe budget cutting saved several tons of steel, always in short supply after the war, it also meant his team ended up with "the largest accelerator in the world not able to produce mesons."

Postwar America suffered from no such economic misery, however, and when Edward Teller informed him of the new, exciting work about to begin in Los Alamos, he was sorely tempted. Soon Los Alamos Laboratory Director Norris Bradbury made a definite offer, and Tuck decided to emigrate. When Frederick Lindemann (now Lord Cherwell) heard about Tuck's negotiations with "foreign powers," he was furious, but he did write the necessary letters stating that Tuck's politics were completely safe. Those letters proved essential because one of Tuck's Oxford graduate students had become active in local communist demonstrations, and the McCarthy era atmosphere made any such associations dangerous.[6]

Because of his close connection with the British nuclear defense program—he had written the implosion handbook for them—Tuck began to develop personal qualms about his impending move. Thus he requested a year's grace to teach at an American university. Los Alamos agreed and consequently he spent the 1949–50 academic year at the Institute for Nuclear Studies at the University of Chicago. The Tucks enjoyed the intellectual life at Chicago (less so the climate), especially his collaboration with James (Keith) Allison and Herb Anderson in building a cyclotron. Working with Lee C. Teng, Tuck devised a scheme for deflecting the beam that became standard for all large cyclotrons.[7]

The University of Chicago was so pleased with his work that they invited him to remain as an associate professor, but the call of Los Alamos proved too strong. Teller had promised virtually unlimited research funds, and the Tucks—now with two adopted children—missed the energetic atmosphere of Los Alamos. Although they discovered that the postwar situation was considerably "less glamorous," they also found that the "old charm was still operative." The Tucks especially enjoyed the egalitarian spirit of the West, a world without "social ladders." Elsie Tuck often remarked that Los Alamos was the only American town she would ever live in. Locally their house became known as "little England."[8]

Upon his arrival in Los Alamos in 1950, Tuck resumed work he had initiated almost five years earlier. In the summer and fall of 1945, when the frenetic pace at Los Alamos was slowing down, many scientists had begun to broaden their interests. Tuck found himself repeatedly drawn into conversations with a group he termed "the thermonuclear wild ones"—Edward Teller, Stanislaw Ulam, Robert R. Wilson, and Enrico Fermi. These discussions started him thinking seriously about the possibility of controlled thermonuclear reactions.

When the war officially ended, the future role of Los Alamos was uncertain. Slowly the "first team" of scientists left for their peacetime university jobs. Members of the British Mission did the same. Intense political discussion in 1945–46 pointed to new legislation that would sharply redefine the rules of nuclear exchange—legislation that came to fruition with the passage of the Atomic Energy Act of 1946. After this, Tuck found himself a foreign national at America's only weapons laboratory, and therefore excluded from all weapons discussions. But Los Alamos needed his skills, and so Bradbury devised a title that would allow him to remain: "director of thermonuclear research." The designation so pleased Tuck that he kept a copy of the 1946 lab bulletin on display for several years.

The director of thermonuclear research immediately began to explore the subject in earnest. He theoretically examined the idea of colliding deuterium jets at high velocity, but could never produce a satisfactory experiment.[9] The few high-velocity jets he concocted were unable to create excess neutrons. Another scientist continued the experiments after Tuck departed Los Alamos, but he, too, left in about a year. In Tuck's words, "so ended the U.S. first foray into controlled fusion."[10]

When he returned to Los Alamos in 1950, however, Tuck resumed his earlier thermonuclear experiments and was assigned to T-Division, with Teller. His first task was to measure the relevant cross sections for deuterium-deuterium, deuterium-tritium, and deuterium-helium below 120 kiloelectronvolts. Gathering an outstanding team about him, Tuck spent a year on the project. Since their figures pointed more favorably to fusion than they had expected, they kept their results secret for about five years.

Shortly afterwards, Teller moved to California to continue his work on fusion weapons at the newly created Lawrence Livermore Laboratory. For reasons that are not entirely clear, Tuck elected to stay at Los Alamos, and henceforth devoted his attention largely to issues of fusion energy, not weapons development. Cautiously, he approached Bradbury for funds to conduct further experiments, and in February 1952, Project Sherwood was born.

The name derived from the search for funds to support the Los Alamos fusion proposal. Paul McDaniel of the Atomic Energy Commission met with Thomas H. Johnson, AEC director of research, about the possibility of closing down an old metallurgical project at the Hood Building of the Massachusetts Institute of Technology to divert funds for Los Alamos. Johnson quipped that they would be "robbing Hood" to pay "Friar Tuck" and that meant they were in "Sherwood Forest."[11] The name stuck, and Los Alamos, Princeton, and the University of California all began their "Sherwood" programs at about the same time.

Initially, however, Los Alamos took the lead. Tuck was the first person to erect an experimental model for fusion reactions. When a skeptic termed his device an "Impossibilitron," Tuck countered by naming it the "Perhapsatron." The bottom three floors of the northwest leg of the newly constructed Los Alamos Administration Building on the South Mesa were put at his disposal. Between 1945 and 1952, therefore, Tuck inaugurated both the first and the second fusion research programs at Los Alamos.

When Admiral Lewis Strauss assumed leadership of the Atomic Energy Commission in 1953, he became fascinated with this idea. Spurred on by Argentina's 1951 boast that émigré scientists had produced fusion in that country's laboratories, Strauss restructured the AEC bureaucracy and placed T. H. Johnson in charge of the overall program. Earlier Johnson had inaugurated a series of secret meetings that became known locally as the Sherwood conferences.[12]

About eighty scientists attended the first conference at the University of Denver in June 1952. Several sessions were held behind closed doors, a ruling that annoyed reporters covering the gathering. One newsman raised a number of eyebrows when he said, "If all you long hairs would quit this secret stuff and get on to finding out how I can use water instead of gasoline in my automobile, you might be of use."[13]

Project Sherwood remained classified for about six years. The security decision was based on the fact that if successful, controlled fusion would produce a new source of neutrons, and these, in turn, could be used to provide plutonium for weapons. Not until 1955–56 did information begin to leak out to the public through various speeches and articles. The mood changed under Dwight Eisenhower's Atoms for Peace program and, especially, with the Second United Nations Conference on the Peaceful Uses of Atomic Energy, in 1958. In fact the UN gathering in Geneva provided a showcase for controlled thermonuclear reactor experiments. By 1959 the United States had released most of the basic information regarding its programs.[14] Suddenly, fusion power was hailed as the savior of the human race.

The world's media quickly seized on the theme. Fusion power represented "the greatest discovery since fire." It promised "an almost limitless source of energy." But the more knowledgeable science writers cautioned that while the basic science behind the process was well known, there was little likelihood of any "sudden breakthroughs." One observed that the quest for fusion power was "undoubtedly the most difficult project ever presented to scientists and engineers."[15]

The skeptics knew whereof they spoke. Fusion occurs when elements at the low end of the periodic table combine (or fuse) to form heavier, more tightly bound nuclei, in the process releasing significant amounts of energy. The most likely candidates for this were deuterium, a commonly available isotope of hydrogen, and tritium, an expensive, man-made isotope of hydrogen. The theory had long been known; initially the scientists in wartime Los Alamos had hoped to complete a fusion as well as a fission program.

The problems, however, were legion. In order to overcome the Coulomb barrier (breaking through the atoms' like charges), the fuel atoms had to be heated to enormous temperatures so that they became a wholly ionized gas, or "plasma." This plasma then had to be confined sufficiently for random collisions to provide energy. Since no container could withstand such temperatures, strong magnetic fields emerged as the only way to confine the plasma. Containing a low-intensity gas by magnetic field, however, as Edward Teller once observed, was like trying to "confine a jelly with rubber bands."[16] Although the theory seemed clear, the experimental obstacles remained daunting.

From 1952 to 1972 James Tuck headed the Sherwood program at Los Alamos. In the process he created one of the world's leading fusion laboratories. At the start, he requested funding of $300,000; twenty years later, his budget ran to $4 million a year. (Two years later it reached $10 million.) Viewing his program as chiefly one of research, Tuck usually returned part of this money unspent, much to the frustration of the bureaucrats, but to the delight of the other fusion laboratories.[17]

Over the years Tuck devoted most of his energy to three containment systems, the pulsed high densities: Z pinch, theta pinch, and the picket fence. These systems demanded briefer confinement time than the lower density programs used by other laboratories: the Stellarator, Mirror Machine, and Tokamaks. Although Tuck became the first person to achieve successful fusion in the laboratory, his efforts to stabilize the containment system never produced the hoped for results.[18]

For most of the late 1950s and early 1960s, the American fusion community viewed Tuck as "first among equals." He served on a variety of important national committees, including the U.S. Fusion Steering Committee (which demanded fortnightly flights from Los Alamos to Washington) and the 1956 ad hoc committee on declassification. He alone presented papers at all eight of the secret Sherwood conferences.[19] His published works ran to about 100 articles (over a third classified). Only his essays in *Nature* (1971) and his entries for the McGraw-Hill *Yearbook of Science and Technology* (1960, 1962) reached a wider audience.[20]

In the early 1970s, however, fusion again moved onto the front pages of the nation's newspapers. In November 1971, Congress held a series of widely publicized hearings on the issue, at which directors of the nation's various fusion programs reported that if they had sufficient funds they could have a demonstration reactor on line by 1995.[21] The tactic worked, and fusion budgets leapt from $38 million in 1973 to $279 million three years later. The Arab oil embargo of the early 1970s added a political dimension to the search.[22] Some critics pointed out that the success of fusion would demand a total restructuring of the power industry, but they were quietly ignored.[23]

From the late 1960s forward, Tuck joined the chorus of public advocates for fusion (and fission) power. Freed from administrative duties at Los Alamos after his retirement in 1972, he became an international ambassador for fusion research. Although he wrote a few essays for public consumption, his chief forte proved to be the lecture platform. Over the years, he delivered invited lectures and seminars all over the world, from Novosibirsk to Winnipeg, from Canberra to Aberdeen. A marvelous public speaker—one high Los Alamos Lab official said he would give anything to be able to speak like him—Tuck reached thousands of people with his message.

He also spoke widely throughout the United States, giving lectures at fifteen American universities, his crusade culminating in the spring of 1974 when he served as Walker-Ames Distinguished Professor at the University of Washington in Seattle. His class, "The World's Energy Problem," was highly publicized by the university's physics department. One wishes that more student response had survived. There are, alas, only two student letters in the Tuck materials: one praising the class at great length; the other complaining about a grade.

Wonderfully enthusiastic and a great optimist, Tuck found the early promises of fusion almost irresistible. Since he had been at the center of the Los Alamos team that had conquered the seemingly unsolvable dilemmas of implosion, he doubtlessly felt that American (and world) science could repeat the success with fusion power. All one needed was time.

As Tuck viewed the world in the early 1970s, this element of time loomed very large indeed. Relying on the works of Thomas Malthus, whom he had read in Manchester, he usually began his talks with references to the population explosion. Then he would chart the world's known energy potential and point to the inevitable extinction of fossil fuels: coal, petroleum, gas, and oil shale. The world was nearing the end of the golden age of energy, he observed. Never would energy be so cheap again.[24] The fossil fuels were also adding so much carbon dioxide to the atmosphere that they constituted a genuine menace to the planet.

Thus, he told his audiences, "we had better hurry on to fission and fusion."[25] He once estimated that fission reactions could supply the world's energy needs for 50,000 years.

Although Tuck chose not to dwell on the problems connected with the spread of nuclear power, he never dismissed them completely. He acknowledged that a power plant might "pop" and that waste storage would always be difficult. Once he suggested establishing a series of "Reactor Parks" in isolated areas to handle such problems. He realized that enemy agents would probably try to steal fissionable materials from reactors, and he conceded that eventually someone might succeed in "cobbling together" a crude fission bomb. But all systems contained risks, he said. A 747 might crash into a football stadium. During his lifetime he had seen about 300 fission reactors go on line, and was convinced that fission was "a necessity for the future of man."[26]

For the last three decades of his life, however, Tuck's chief interest was fusion. In his speeches he always stressed the virtually limitless resources that fusion power would provide: deuterium was available in the ocean and tritium could be provided by other power plants. Only the natural limits of lithium might be a problem. While thieves might try to steal tritium (or even lithium), it would be virtually impossible to sell either one, except to other power plant operators. Since fusion reactors would contain only milligrams of fuel, they could never go out of control or explode. Thus, siting the reactors—always difficult for fission power plants—would never be a problem for their fusion counterparts. Even their waste heat could easily be utilized.[27] Although Tuck acknowledged that building a controlled thermonuclear reactor was "the most difficult but the most rewarding problem known in technical physics," he never gave up hope.[28]

When pressed for a probable fusion time schedule, Tuck always drew upon his Los Alamos past. The interval from Enrico Fermi's 1942 Chicago experiment of controlled fission to Britain's Calder Hall and the first American nuclear power plants had been about two decades. Thus in the mid-1970s he postulated that 1980 would be the probable birth date of controlled fusion. Competitive fusion plants could be expected sometime within the first decade of the twenty-first century.[29]

Tuck's prediction was only slightly optimistic. On November 10, 1991, in Oxford a team of scientists from Europe and Great Britain produced a two-second pulse of nearly two million watts of energy from their joint European Torus (JET) fusion reactor. Their multibillion-dollar project utilized a Tokamak design (pioneered by the Soviets) that produced temperatures twenty times hotter than the sun. Over 450 scientists composed the team, drawn from a large number of nations. Dubbing the experiment a success, the scientists celebrated the occasion with champagne.[30] Unlike the 1989 furor over the possible discovery of cold fusion, there was no question that this fusion energy was genuine.[31]

As might be expected, the newspapers gave the event considerable coverage. In their articles, the reporters struck several familiar chords: fusion energy was clean, abundant, and endless. Once it was achieved, both the greenhouse effect and world famine could be assigned "to the history books."[32] Unfortunately, James Tuck had died in 1980, but wherever his location, he surely must have smiled at these reports.

The 1991 discoveries also brought forth the critics, however, and this time they received a larger hearing. One writer observed that the scientists announced their "successful experiment" of fusion just days before their $5 billion budget was to be discussed by European Community finance ministers. Environmental writer John Vidal argued that the fusion promises of 1991 were simply repetitions of the utopian fission and fusion claims of earlier years. He noted that the project was dogged by a thousand unanswered questions, and that commercial reactors were unlikely to be available before 2040.[33] Moreover, the enormous cost—$20 billion so far and another $20 billion before anyone would know for certain if the method could be commercially viable—took funds from proven small-scale energy programs, such as solar, wind, biomass, and tidal power. These alternative sources of energy did not demand the massive centralization that fusion would entail; thus they would be much more suitable to the developing nations of Africa, South America, and Asia, where they were the most needed. One cynic paraphrased Lord Rutherford's criticism regarding fission and declared controlled fusion to be simply "moonshine."[34] In spite of massive funding and promises, the problems of fusion power seemed as baffling in 1991 as they had been when James Tuck inaugurated the first experiments. But in 1991, even the optimism had evaporated.

Tuck headed the Los Alamos dimension of Project Sherwood for twenty years, but the endless and increasing bureaucratic accounting methods required by Washington sorely tried his patience.[35] He sought relief by attacking a new range of scientific puzzles. He explored the phenomena of magnetic bird navigation, and learned a great deal about the issues of world energy. But he devoted most of his spare time from the late 1960s onward to a new interest: ball lightning.

By the 1960s, scientists fairly well understood the principles of sheet lightning and strike lightning. They also had a good grasp of the theory behind Saint Elmo's fire, the fuzzy lights that dance around the masts of ships or the wing tips of aircraft during storms. These were hardly new phenomena. Roman soldiers had reported how strange lights hovered around their spear tips when they stood watch during an electrical storm. The folklore regarding Saint Elmo's fire was similarly extensive.

Ball lightning—a medium-sized electrical sphere that popped through walls and windows, allegedly without damage—had been similarly observed for over two millennia. But it had always eluded rational explanation. The little sphere of light could hover, zigzag, or even bounce. It often disappeared with a "poof," sometimes leaving a burn mark behind. Occasionally, it vanished without a trace. Moreover, it was quite common; scientists estimated that ball lightning occurred about as frequently as tornados.

Over the years, tales had entered the folklore of many nations. One medieval scientist suggested that ball lightning occurred when a spark struck a devil who became so enraged he forgot himself and turned momentarily visible.[36] Other, more substantiated accounts, blamed it for killing both animals and people. The most famous of these stories involved a noted eighteenth-century Russian scientist at the St. Petersburg Academy who was trying to repeat Benjamin Franklin's experiments by flying a kite in an electrical storm. Midwestern American farmers allegedly removed telephones from their hooks during storms to try to discourage ball lightning visits.[37]

Much ball lightning folklore, however, reduced the sphere of energy to the category of nuisance. A nineteenth-century French peasant girl had one rise up her skirt and exit at her collar, terrifying her but doing no physical harm. A 1945 English Midlands housewife brushed one away involuntarily only to discover it had singed her dress and caused temporary numbness in her legs. Rocky Mountain forest lookouts allegedly included high stools so that rangers could perch on them while ball lightning danced around their feet. Airline passengers occasionally reported the sphere as bounding down the aisles. In *Present at the Creation*,

Secretary of State Dean Acheson described one that entered President Harry Truman's plane during a storm. *Nature* periodically carried articles on ball lightning, and a number of scientists put forth their opinions.[38]

In spite of scores of sightings, and even a few modest research programs, by 1969 nobody had been able to photograph ball lightning or duplicate it under laboratory conditions. Consequently, all ball lightning evidence retained a "nonscientific" dimension. At the most extreme it was regarded like UFO sightings, with every photograph under suspicion of possible fraud. Even Tuck admitted that ball lightning had provided the graveyard for many a scientific reputation.[39]

Nevertheless, from the late 1960s, Tuck threw himself into the subject with his usual intensity. During early 1969, he and a few colleagues began devoting their lunch hours twice a week to ball lightning experiments. Working with Robert Gordon of the photographic section of Los Alamos, he set up two 16mm cameras in front of several million dollars' worth of batteries and deliberately caused short circuits. These experiments produced a great deal of noise and some gigantic electrical discharges, but nothing that looked even remotely like ball lightning. In 1973, however, Tuck's experiments came to an abrupt halt. That year a new Los Alamos Lab director commandeered their space and equipment for his pet chemical laser project.[40]

With that, Tuck launched an even bolder effort. Submariner folklore contained a number of ball lightning stories. When enlisted men threw the wrong switches on their diesel electric generators, they occasionally caused fireballs to dance around their legs. While submarine officers scoffed at such tales, they were never present when the malfunction occurred. German, American, and British submariners had all witnessed the same thing. Using this as his guide, Tuck approached the U.S. Navy to let him board a diesel sub, in dry dock, deliberately short-circuit the system, and photograph the results.[41] The Navy, however, was in the midst of phasing out its diesel subs and could not be bothered. This, too, came to a dead end.

Although Tuck failed to duplicate ball lightning in a laboratory situation, he did have considerable success in bringing the phenomenon to the attention of the public. He gave his first ball lightning seminar in June 1969, and over the next decade delivered perhaps fifty seminars to 5,000 people on the theme.[42]

To aid his research, he devised a "Ball Lightning Report" which he freely distributed to such places as the Santa Fe National Forest and various newspapers across the land. It asked those who had seen the phenomenon to write up their experiences and send them to him. To help them categorize their tales, he included a questionnaire asking for specifics as to size, shape, color, brightness, heat or lack thereof, noise, odor, speed of movement, motion, disappearance, and so forth. He was especially interested in how ball lightning seemed able to enter walls and windows without breaking anything. He even wrote to airline pilots on this problem.[43]

The response proved overwhelming. People from nearby Sandia Peak in Albuquerque and from all across the country sent him their ball lightning stories. After a year, he had to discontinue the questionnaires because he and his secretary were swamped.[44] From those received, however, he compiled a list of "mean characteristics" of ball lightning. Ball lightning had a spherical or pear shape; it glowed with the brightness of a 100-watt lamp. Although sizes varied, it averaged about 6 inches (15 cm) in diameter, with colors from yellow to red. It floated for about five seconds, often hissed, frequently scorched things, and usually burst like a bubble, with a strong explosion, leaving an acrid odor.[45] But further than this he could not go.

As Tuck popularized the concept of ball lightning through his various talks, he always warned his audiences that he foresaw no practical application for his interest. "This is science for its own sake," he repeatedly said, "to solve a mystery."[46] In 1969, he received a small grant from the National Science Foundation to hire a summer student at Los Alamos to work on the subject. But the lack of immediate practical application doomed his request for a much larger grant from the Alfred P. Sloan Foundation.[47]

Such disclaimers of practical use were somewhat disingenuous. The link between ball lightning and the quest for controlled fusion seemed obvious, even to the amateur. In fact, Tuck's letters to both the Navy and the various granting agencies emphasized the importance of the research to basic science.[48]

In all, there were about ten theories as to the nature of ball lightning. These included a retinal afterimage caused by the psychological shock from a nearby lightning strike, burning marsh gas, lingering electrical fields after a lightning strike, or a type of electromagnetically confined hot ionized gas (plasma). Tuck hesitated to generalize, but he leaned toward the theory that ball lightning was an unusual plasma, consisting of cold positive and negative ions that somehow developed a surface tension like a soap bubble.[49] He was charmed by the British tale of a ball lightning sphere that had raced down a drain pipe into a barrel of rainwater, which then suddenly began to boil. From that, Tuck calculated the energy that the sphere contained. Tuck's fascination with ball lightning grew directly from his quest to unlock the secret of fusion. Perhaps Nature had solved the problem of stable magnetic confinement of plasma on her own.[50]

No account of James and Elsie Tuck would be complete without mention of their personalities. Described as "delightful together," they were universally well liked throughout Los Alamos. Besides being talented musically, Elsie Tuck was exceptionally well organized, and ran their affairs with a firm hand. Because she was so practical, Jim Tuck could let his imagination roam freely. As one friend noted, they complemented each other like characters in a Shakespearean play.

Every place that Tuck worked—Oxford, Whitehall, Chicago, or Los Alamos—produced a range of "Tuck stories." Those at Los Alamos rival the equally numerous "Oppenheimer stories," but while the Oppenheimer anecdotes often prove poignant, those involving Tuck invariably bring forth smiles and chuckles. Always "on stage," Tuck had a way of being at the center of things whenever they started to malfunction.

The Tuck stories have marvelous variety. How he kept a barber's chair in the basement of his home so that he could retreat there, smoke his pipe with his eyes closed, and simply think. How he planned to teach gorillas to do housework. How he drove his convertible to work in midwinter with the top down. How he would often arrive at a formal occasion dressed in a brown tweed jacket, Bermuda shorts, and mismatched socks, completely oblivious to his appearance. How his secretary stapled his cuffs together when he discovered he had forgotten his cufflinks. How he nailed a blackboard on the wall next to the dining room table so that his children could entertain guests during dinner by showing off their mathematical skills. How Elsie Tuck once called his secretary in dismay when she discovered her checks were bouncing, and his secretary opened Tuck's top drawer to find that he had forgotten to deposit the last several months' paychecks.[51] Tuck's obituary in *Physics Today*, written by a team of his Los Alamos colleagues, concluded with the same theme: "The fusion community has lost one of its strongest supporters and will miss his keen wit and idiosyncrasies—he was great fun to work and be with."[52]

James Tuck could assume the role of "comic relief" in Los Alamos—counterpoint, perhaps, to Oppenheimer's "tragic hero" image—for one reason: he completely avoided politics. His daughter Sarah once confessed that she never heard him utter a single political statement. The only exception might be his reply to historian Alice Kimball Smith's request in 1970 for his reactions to his wartime Los Alamos experience. There he confessed that he had a strange, recurring dream where he was fleeing from an encroaching mushroom cloud.[53] But one searches in vain for other political observations in the James Tuck manuscripts. Even his lectures on the world's energy problems skirted practical politics.

Where does James Tuck fit in the ongoing saga of the Atomic West? Was he, as Los Alamos Archivist Roger A. Meade once observed, the ultimate Don Quixote, the person who devoted his life to pursuing objectives that ever eluded his grasp?[54] Was he the quintessential scientist, the man who lived for scientific truth alone? Or was he a secret moralist, determined to discover an endless source of power to counterbalance the darker side of the atomic world?[55] All these interpretations are possible.

Yet I would suggest that James Tuck might be best understood as the Atomic West's "ultimate optimist." The open-minded zeal for scientific discovery that he brought to Oxford in 1937 never left him throughout his life. As his friend Arno Roensch recalled, he had an "innate curiosity about everything in the world."[56] The extensive funds available to him at Los Alamos, and the exciting intellectual atmosphere there, allowed him to explore many of these interests.

That his dreams have not yet been realized is surely not a moral fault. Too ill to respond to Three Mile Island in 1979, and gone before Chernobyl, he probably would not have altered his worldview even after these calamities. (He surely knew about the 1957 British nuclear accident at Windscale.) Besides, the breakthroughs continued to emerge. In December 1993, scientists at the Princeton Plasma Physics Laboratory produced 5.6 megawatts of energy, once again rekindling enthusiasm for "the holy grail of fusion ignition." U.S. Secretary of Energy Hazel O'Leary declared that this experience was "a great step in the development of fusion energy."[57] The emergence of yet another approach to fusion—using a chemical laser to ignite hydrogen fuel pellets—has increased contemporary optimism. Some scientists have suggested that commercial fusion power might be available by 2030.

If fusion power reactors ever do go on line, and the puzzle of ball lightning is "solved," James Tuck will be celebrated in song and story as one of humankind's "great beginners." The saga of the atomic era is firmly rooted in Los Alamos, and Los Alamos revolved around the genius and optimism of people like James L. Tuck. He formed an integral part of America's Atomic West.

NOTES

1. R. V. Jones, *Most Secret War* (London: Hamish Hamilton, 1978), 29–31; J. L. Tuck, "Autobiographical Notes," manuscript, Los Alamos National Laboratory, Los Alamos, New Mexico (hereafter LANL).

2. "Autobiographical Notes."

3. James L. Tuck, "Studies of Shaped Charges by Flash Radiography" (1943), and "A Note on the Theory of the Munroe Effect" (1943), both LANL; R. V. Jones, interview by author, Aberdeen, Scotland, December 1991.

4. "Autobiographical Notes."

5. Chadwick to Field Marshal Sir Henry Maitland Wilson, March 2, 1946, Chad. I 24/2, Chadwick Papers, Churchill College Archives, Cambridge, England. See also the transcript of the interview of Chadwick by Charles Weiner, 104–8, Chad. II 2/4; Jones, *Most Secret War*, 51, 80–83; and Jones, interview. See also Ferenc Morton Szasz, *The Day the Sun Rose Twice* (Albuquerque: University of New Mexico Press, 1984). I discuss the role of the British in detail in *The British Scientists and the Manhattan Project: The Los Alamos Years* (London: Macmillan, 1992).

6. "Autobiographical Notes"; James L. Tuck, "Lord Cherwell and His Part in World War II," LANL.

7. J. L. Tuck and Lee C. Teng, "The Regeneration Deflector," *Progress Report* III, chap. 8, Institute for Nuclear Studies, University of Chicago (July 1949–July 1950).

8. "Autobiographical Notes"; Sarah (Polly) Tuck, interview by author, Spring 1991, Los Alamos.

9. Amasa S. Bishop, *Project Sherwood: The U.S. Program in Controlled Fusion* (Reading, Mass.: Addison-Wesley, 1958), 15.

10. "Autobiographical Notes." The secondary literature on fusion history is growing steadily. Joan Lisa Bromberg has written a study for the U.S. Department of Energy, *Fusion: Science, Politics, and the Invention of a New Energy Source*

(Cambridge: MIT Press, 1983), while John Hendry and J. D. Lawson have produced a counterpart for the United Kingdom Atomic Energy Authority, *Fusion Research in the* UK (Harwell: AEA Technology, 1983). The most complete coverage is found in Robin Herman, *Fusion: The Search for Endless Energy* (Cambridge: Cambridge University Press, 1990), but she completely overlooks Tuck's contributions. See also chapter 2 of Eugene F. Mallove, *Fire from Ice: Searching for the Truth behind the Cold Fusion Furor* (New York: John Wiley, 1991).

11. Paul W. McDaniel to Harold Agnew, March 18, 1971, LANL.

12. *New York Times,* March 25, 1951; Bishop, *Project Sherwood,* 15, 76.

13. Speech by James L. Tuck at the Energy Resources Conference, October 15–17, 1958, Denver, Colorado, LANL.

14. Bishop, *Project Sherwood,* 159–60.

15. Richard F. Post, "Fusion Power," *Scientific American* 197 (December 1957): 73–83.

16. Teller, quoted in the *Guardian* (Manchester), November 11, 1991, p. 3.

17. J. L. Tuck, typescript of 1974 talk at the University of Colorado, LANL.

18. H. R. Hulme and A. McB. Collieu, *Nuclear Fusion* (London and Winchester: W. Y. Kennan Publications, 1969), 147.

19. Bishop, *Project Sherwood,* 193.

20. J. L. Tuck, "Outlook for Controlled Fusion Power," *Nature* 233 (October 29, 1971): 593–98.

21. *Hearings before the Subcommittee on Research, Development, and Radiation of the Joint Committee on Atomic Energy* (Washington, D.C.: Government Printing Office, 1972).

22. R. F. Post and F. L. Ribe, "Fusion Reactors as Future Energy Sources," *Science* 186 (November 1, 1974): 397–407.

23. See the three articles by William D. Metz on "Fusion Research," in *Science* 192 (June 25, 1976): 1370–23; 193 (July 2, 1976): 38–40; 193 (July 23, 1976): 307–9.

24. James Tuck, "World Energy Resources and Consumption," manuscript, 1974, LANL.

25. James Tuck, "On Nuclear Fusion Objectives," manuscript from talk given at the Culham Laboratory, UKAEA, September 17–19, 1969, 5, LANL.

26. Ibid.

27. James Tuck, paper at ALAA Third Fluid and Plasma Dynamics Conference, Los Angeles, June 29–July 1, 1970, LANL.

28. James Tuck speech for IEEE Region VI Conference on Energy Resources, Portland, Oregon, 1968, LANL.

29. James Tuck, "Outlook for Controlled Fusion Power, *Nation* 233 (October 29, 1971): 593–98.

30. *European,* November 15–17, 1991, p. 39; *Guardian,* November 11, 1991, p. 3.

31. Frank Close, *Too Hot to Handle: The Story of the Race for Cold Fusion* (London: W. H. Allen, 1990); John R. Huizenga, *Cold Fusion: The Scientific Fiasco of the Century* (New York: Oxford University Press, 1993).

32. *European,* November 15–17, 1991, p. 8.

33. *Guardian,* November 15, 1991, p. 31.

34. Ibid.

35. James Tuck, "Fireballs and Submarines," manuscript, LANL.

36. Cited in Paul M. Koloc, "A New Model for Ball Lightning," manuscript (1977) in Tuck materials, LANL.

37. James Tuck, "Ball Lightning," manuscript, LANL.

38. Harold W. Lewis, "Ball Lightning," *Nature* 107; copy, Tuck manuscripts. See also *Nature* 260 (April 15, 1976): 573.

39. Tuck, "Proposal to Alfred P. Sloan Foundation, November 13, 1970," LANL.

40. "Fireballs and Submarines," "Notes on Ball Lightning," Sherwood Seminar, June 2, 1969, LANL.

41. J. L. Tuck to Admiral Russell, August 29, 1970, LANL.

42. "Notes on Ball Lightning," Sherwood Seminar, June 2, 1961, and "Tuck Ball Lightning," both LANL.

43. Copy, Tuck manuscripts. See the coverage in the *Gazette* (Vineyard, Mass.), October 16, 1970; Los Alamos *Monitor,* January 13, 1980; Tuck to C. Kalota, May 20, 1970, LANL.

44. For a representative example, see Mrs. Albert R. Martin to Tuck, June 6, 1975, LANL.

45. Paul R. Krehbiel to Tuck, October 16, 1972; Ball Lightning Mean Characteristics, copy, LANL.

46. *Gazette* (Vineyard), October 16, 1970.

47. J. L. Tuck, "Ball Lightning: A Status Summary to November, 1971," LANL, LA–4847-MA.

48. See Tuck to Dr. Alvin Seift, December 30, 1970, LANL.

49. Proposal to the Alfred P. Sloan Foundation, November 13, 1970. He also phrased it as "a vortex ring composed of excited air having slowly decaying metastable states," Tuck, "Notes on Ball Lightning," II, LANL.

50. "Ball Lightning," 15. Harold W. Lewis, "Ball Lightning," undated article, Tuck manuscripts, 116. When Tuck died, his daughter had to fend off people who wanted all her father's ball lightning notes. Sarah (Polly) Tuck, interview.

51. Jerry and Arno Roensch, interview by author, Albuquerque, New Mexico, June 21, 1993. Carson Mark, interview by author, Los Alamos, New Mexico, Spring 1991. Cf. the Tuck stories in R. V. Jones, *Reflections on Intelligence* (London:

Heinemann, 1989), 238–42; Jones, interview; Sarah Tuck, interview; Molly Rodriguez, interview by author, Los Alamos, Spring 1991; Jerry and Arno Roensch, interview.

52. *Physics Today,* March 1981, pp. 87–88.

53. Alice Kimball Smith to Tuck, January 5, 1970, LANL. Tuck to Smith, January 1970, LANL.

54. Roger Meade, interview by author, Los Alamos, New Mexico, Spring 1991.

55. David J. Rose, "Controlled Nuclear Fusion: Status and Outlook," *Science* 192 (May 21, 1971): 797.

56. Jerry and Arno Roensch, interview.

57. Albuquerque *Tribune,* August 8, and February 9, 1994.

"Hotter Than a $2 Pistol"

Fallout, Sheep, and the Atomic Energy Commission, 1953–1986

Barton C. Hacker

THE SETTING

When it opened near Las Vegas in January 1951, only its novel purpose distinguished the Nevada Test Site from a host of other federally funded military projects dotting the western United States. Government officials, state and local alike, welcomed it for the promise of new money and new jobs. If local residents objected to the prospect of nuclear weapons testing in their backyard, they mostly kept their doubts to themselves. Atomic bomb testing looked like patriotism and national security, economic growth, and even tourist attraction. Disillusionment came slowly for many—a mushroom cloud's inlaid image still graced the sidewalk in front of Las Vegas city hall in 1981—but some learned more quickly. Operation Upshot-Knothole in spring 1953 taught the first major lessons.[1]

By 1953 the U.S. Atomic Energy Commission (AEC) and its contractors had completed three series of nuclear weapons tests, twenty "devices" in all having exploded on or above the arid southern Nevada landscape. Radioactive fallout from some of these tests had caused minor off-site damage—some slightly burned cattle and horses, a few broken windows—but the AEC, by settling the claims promptly, kept the public largely unperturbed.[2] Questions ran deeper within the test community. In mid-January 1953, one day short of two years since the first Nevada test, the AEC convened a study group to ponder radioactive fallout and the future of Nevada testing.[3] Upshot-Knothole, the fourth nuclear weapons test series, was scheduled to begin in March.

The fifteen panelists reviewed the reasons for testing and for the choice of a Nevada site, which in early 1952 the AEC had renamed the Nevada Proving Ground. Although they could not agree on whether or not the new name implied new functions, no one doubted the need for testing in Nevada. The major constraint remained on-site and nearby fallout; surface and tower shots posed greater problems than higher altitude tests, because they sucked up the most debris and spread the heaviest close-in fallout. Fortunately, the highest levels of fallout had so far coincided with the most sparsely populated wasteland; no one off-site had yet, to anyone's knowledge, been overexposed to radiation. That happy outcome owed something to careful planning but more to good luck, given the uncertainty inherent in any test program and the impossibility of making safety the top priority. The greatest care could only reduce, not erase, the risk, which the AEC perceived, perhaps rightly, as much in terms of public relations as health.[4] Such concerns gave the spring 1953 test series special significance. The future of testing in Nevada might hang in the balance when the panel met again to write a final report.

Although Upshot-Knothole posed no special threat, it did include more tests (ten planned, an eleventh added in progress) and lasted longer (two and a half months, from mid-March to early June 1953) than any of its three predecessors. It also produced the test program's first public safety crisis. Fallout on nearby roads and towns twice stirred the test organization to protective action. Highway roadblocks stopped cars to be vacuumed inside and washed outside, while public announcements urged residents of nearby towns to stay indoors. Modest, to be sure, but so was the risk of harm perceived: judging the danger small, the AEC felt it could act with restraint. Roadblocks and announcements nonetheless became the first public emergency measures ever taken off site to safeguard bystanders after a test. An intensive review by the panel on the proving ground's future convinced the AEC that nuclear weapons testing in Nevada remained viable. Although neighbors no longer seemed quite so willing to accept the government's judgment, the real crisis occurred within the AEC.[5]

Officials seemed shaken, not so much by the threat to public health as by the prospect of losing the Nevada site for testing. They firmly believed that fallout at the levels detected had injured no one, and their reassuring statements allayed most public fears. In opting to reassure rather than to inform, the AEC—its headquarters staff in particular—

followed a long-standing pattern. Convinced that test fallout posed only the most minor of hazards, they feared that trying to explain such small risks would simply confuse people or, even worse, cause panic. Overexposure could become a scare word, though technically it meant only exposure in excess of guidelines with their wide safety margins. Occasional moderate overexposure—the worst someone living near the test site seemed likely to face—ought to pose little or no health threat. But it might present another kind of threat if blown out of proportion by the news media. Excessive frankness could needlessly jeopardize the testing vital to American security. To avoid that risk, AEC spokesmen preferred to downplay or dismiss any hint of danger.[6]

By and large, the AEC strategy worked well enough in the aftermath of Upshot-Knothole. Despite a certain degree of skepticism, most people around the test site accepted AEC reassurances, a process abetted by the complete absence of any tangible symptom or effect on people. Not so easy to dismiss was evidence of animals apparently injured by fallout. Although first deemed minor, damage to livestock blamed on this latest series of tests became a large and growing issue. It started with horses grazing near the proving ground: evidence of beta burns was clear, the claims against the AEC quickly settled. Equally prompt was the response to a supposed link between cattle deaths and fallout in the same area; finding no sign of radiation damage, the AEC rejected the claims.[7] Such incidents had occurred before, and claims promptly settled or dismissed seemed almost routine. But this time the damage appeared not to be limited to horses and cattle.

Unfamiliar and often fatal symptoms displayed by thousands of sheep exposed to fallout from one or two shots proved hard to explain. The AEC learned about the damage months later, so could be certain about neither how many tests nor how much fallout. Finally, six months of study and experiment under AEC auspices yielded a public report in January 1954 that absolved radiation from any blame in sheep losses. Unfortunately, it offered nothing in place of fallout to account for the mysterious effects observed. Among those left unpersuaded by the AEC report were many of the aggrieved ranchers, who sued for damages. They lost in 1956, then again three decades later after apparently new evidence persuaded the trial judge to reopen the case.

Questions about fallout and sheep deaths have nonetheless persisted, at least partly because people have sometimes conflated the 1953 incident with other episodes. Allegations of government-caused sheep deaths in Utah seem to stick, not the specific times or agents.[8] This essay, however, focuses on the investigation conducted by the Atomic Energy Commission to determine whether or not radioactive fallout had caused, or contributed to, the sheep deaths of 1953. Making no effort to present an exhaustive account, I limit myself to sketching the pattern of events and to illustrating certain persistent aspects of AEC behavior displayed in the sheep investigation.[9]

THE PATTERN OF EVENTS

From a present-day viewpoint, the AEC's sheep investigation appears to have passed through three overlapping phases. A brief first phase, roughly spanning the first half of June 1953, centered on gathering field data on sheep in affected flocks. Meanwhile, a second phase of analysis, research, and negotiation began when AEC headquarters appointed Paul B. Pearson to coordinate the study and prepare the public report issued in January 1954. Finally, the AEC sought to persuade the owners, and the public in general, that radiation played no part at all in sheep deaths; this third phase led from Pearson's meeting with ranchers in August 1953 to their failed suit for damages in 1956 and its long-delayed postscript in the 1980s.

The AEC's sheep investigation opened June 2, 1953. Utah Commissioner of Health George A. Spendlove warned Gordon M. Dunning, an AEC staff member in Nevada for Upshot-Knothole, that unusually large numbers of ewes and lambs had died earlier that spring, and many others displayed odd symptoms.[10] All the injured animals belonged to flocks lately returned to Utah from winter pastures northeast of the proving ground. Dunning persuaded Spendlove to support an AEC investigation at the state level, the AEC promptly seeking help from other federal and state agencies. Teams of veterinarians and public health officers joined AEC officials to see surviving sheep from flocks that had suffered losses, talk with the owners and workers, and collect tissue samples for analysis. By June 18, this phase of the investigation was complete.[11]

From Utah pasture to Washington meeting room, no one doubted that radioactive fallout had struck sheep wintering northeast of the test site, and most assumed that fallout explained the damage. Dosimeter readings, whether from living animals or tissue samples, were high enough to implicate fallout in at least some of the puzzling symptoms observed.[12] Implicate—but not convict. Cause and effect had yet to be proved. Despite (or perhaps because of) inconclusive data, in fact, Washington opinion quickly shifted toward blaming ill and dying sheep on some as yet unidentified cause other than fallout. Malnutrition in an unusually dry year or toxic desert plants emerged as the chief suspects.[13]

Meanwhile, the second phase of the AEC effort began with Pearson assigned to coordinate the sheep study and issue a report. Himself a Utah native and graduate of Brigham Young University, Pearson had joined the AEC in 1949 after more than a decade teaching animal nutrition at Texas A&M. As chief of the biology branch in the AEC Division of Biology and Medicine, he seemed the logical choice to resolve the sheep questions.[14] To underpin the public report, Pearson organized a research program that included laboratory analyses of tissue samples, experimental studies of sheep exposed to radiation under controlled conditions, and field surveys of wildlife as well as livestock in areas hit by fallout.[15] Emphasis on analysis and interpretation of data should not obscure the fact that much, perhaps most, of the effort really involved negotiating an acceptable compromise between largely incompatible, if not immutable, positions: the conviction within the AEC that fallout had nothing to do with sheep deaths, and the view of many outside experts that radioactivity in some way contributed to killing sheep.

Genuine though the research Pearson sponsored might be, it was not likely to change minds in AEC headquarters. By early July, well before the findings were in, most AEC officials had concluded that fallout had no conceivable link to injured sheep. Pearson himself assumed from the outset that malnutrition or plant poisoning better accounted for sheep problems than radiation. This view henceforth dominated the investigation, at least for the AEC and its contractors.[16] Among the experts the AEC had called in to study the sheep problem, a University of Tennessee group lent the AEC its strongest support. Members of a long-term AEC-funded project keeping tabs on the Trinity cattle (animals exposed to fallout from the 1945 test at Alamogordo, New Mexico, and their descendants), they were familiar with radiation damage in livestock. Although radioactivity detected on and in their bodies clearly showed sheep to have been exposed to fallout, the Tennessee-AEC team concluded that nothing in the sheep samples they analyzed appeared remotely high

161

enough to have caused radiation sickness.[17] Two team members in particular, John H. Rust and Bernard F. Trum, both lieutenant colonels assigned to the project from the Army Veterinary Corps, devoted themselves assiduously over the next few years to marshaling support for that conclusion.[18]

Other non-AEC experts—from the federal Public Health Service and Department of Agriculture's Bureau of Animal Industry, and from state agencies and colleges in Nevada and Utah—though never unanimous in their views, remained less certain about crossing fallout off the list. The key question was, If not fallout, what? Range ecologist L. A. Stoddart of the Utah Agricultural Experiment Station ruled out malnutrition or plant poisoning as cause for most losses; so did W. T. Huffman, the Bureau of Animal Industry's local expert on stock poisoning by plants.[19] Radioassays of sheep tissue showed, according to veterinarian Arthur H. Wolff, acting chief of radiological health training at the Public Health Service's Cincinnati Environmental Health Center, "surprisingly high" thyroid radioactivity, although not high enough "to produce any *acute* syndrome or pathology."[20] The report from Robert C. Bay's Radiobiology Laboratory at the University of Utah Medical School reached much the same conclusion.[21] Although he wavered, William H. Hadlow, veterinary pathologist at the Public Health Service's Rocky Mountain Laboratory in Montana, finally decided against radioactivity as a possible cause, largely at Rust's urging.[22] Not so his colleagues Monroe A. Holmes, a Public Health Service veterinarian assigned to the Utah Department of Health, and James G. Terrill, Jr., chief of the Service's radiological health branch. Neither could see any solid basis for choosing among the alternatives.[23]

Those who had personally examined sheep in the field consistently tended to admit that radioactivity was at least contributory to their ailments, and some never retreated from believing it decisive—to the embarrassment of the Atomic Energy Commission that had sought their expertise.[24] The two major holdouts were Major Robert H. Veenstra, an army veterinarian attached to the Naval Radiological Defense Laboratory in San Francisco, and Robert E. Thompsett, a veterinarian in private practice who regularly consulted with the Los Alamos laboratory. Both were members of the first party of outside experts to see and sample the sheep in early June. Based on his analysis of the tissue samples he himself had collected, Veenstra judged radiation "at least a contributing factor."[25] Although subsequent AEC attempts to persuade him otherwise

162

failed, he refrained from making his views public.[26] Like Rust and Trum, Thompsett knew the Trinity cattle. Unlike them, however, he concluded that radiation was a major factor in the sheep losses, a view he never relinquished.[27]

Lack of consensus not only delayed the public report for months but also left lingering doubts about the report's integrity when it did appear. Meanwhile, in August 1953, the first formal meeting between AEC officials and sheep owners inaugurated the third phase of the AEC investigation. Stenographic records suggest that all nine sheep owners who attended, as well as the local veterinarian, were disturbed by events unlike any they had ever witnessed, by symptoms never seen before. Yet, on the whole, they seemed more puzzled than hostile, even when they received precious few answers. Policy constrained Pearson from discussing the conflict, polite but already growing troublesome, among his experts. Although he could do little more than promise to continue investigating, that seemed to satisfy the ranchers.[28] Pearson met with sheep owners again in January 1954, after the long-delayed public report at last appeared. This was the occasion when a perplexed rancher wondered what two men had meant the previous spring when they called one of his sheep "hotter than a $2 pistol."[29]

As more than one insider had noted from the outset, finding something other than fallout to blame for sheep injuries was crucial, but Pearson's efforts fell short.[30] Exculpating radiation left the case only half made; without the other half—a plausible alternative culprit—it fell flat. Yet once again the ranchers seemed more puzzled than angry, as Pearson promised still more research.[31] Further study has failed to sustain Pearson's conclusion. Radiation doses to sheep were almost certainly too low to have been the sole cause of death. Not so clear is whether doses were high enough to push stressed and weakened animals over the edge. Malnutrition, toxic plants, and other possible causes of death all have the same shortcoming: no proof strong enough to indict, not enough evidence to acquit. Despite the best efforts of many investigators, in the somewhat rueful words of a 1982 report, "the enigma of the 1953 sheep deaths has remained unsolved."[32]

Meanwhile, the issue went to court. Sheep owners filed five separate complaints against the United States, seeking damages for lost ewes and lambs. In 1956, Judge Sherman Christensen of the federal district court in Salt Lake City, after listening to testimony from both sides, rejected the sheep owners' claims on the merits. Finding overwhelming weight of evidence on the government's side of the argument, he judged that radiation could not be proved to have killed the sheep.[33] Surprisingly, the case returned to the same court a quarter century later. In contrast to most other fallout cases, this one had not been dismissed on grounds of sovereign immunity derived from the Federal Tort Claims Act of 1946.[34] Because it had been judged on the facts, new facts could make a difference. But how could new facts emerge so many years later?

They came from congressional hearings in the late 1970s. Both the AEC and its congressional sponsor, the Joint Committee on Atomic Energy, had passed from the scene. Unlike its predecessor, the new Department of Energy (DOE) did not answer to a single, usually friendly, congressional committee. How much things had changed became clear in 1978, when charges that troops in atomic maneuvers during the 1950s now suffered from high rates of radiation-caused leukemia led to House hearings. In contrast to the cordial welcome AEC witnesses had normally received from the Joint Committee, DOE spokesmen faced a decidedly hostile inquiry. Nor did it stop there, as other House and Senate hearings expanded the probe to the whole range of potential victims during that year and the next.[35] In 1979 one such hearing gave the still-unhappy sheep owners grounds to challenge the 1956 judgment against them.

The president's Secretary of Health, Education, and Welfare (HEW) had meanwhile formed the Interagency Task Force on Health Effects of Radiation to address the same issues that concerned the Congress. Testifying at the 1979 hearing as chairman of that task force, HEW General Counsel F. Peter Libassi implied that the government had withheld crucial evidence in the 1956 trial. In the same hearing, Harold A. Knapp, a mathematician once employed in the AEC's fallout studies branch, reported his reanalysis of the 1953 data that fixed fallout as the most likely cause of sheep deaths.[36] These views did not go unchallenged, but they carried weight enough to reopen the case.[37]

Bulloch v. United States resumed in 1981 before the same Judge Sherman Christensen who had presided in 1956. Relying on the 1979 hearing, lawyers for the sheep owners argued that the government had withheld relevant information during the first trial. In August 1982, Christensen found that it had. He cited the 1979 congressional hearing as the basis for his judgment of government misconduct: by withholding evidence that linked sheep deaths to fallout, the government and some of its witnesses had committed a fraud upon the court. Vacating his own 1956 judgment, he awarded court costs to the plantiffs and scheduled a new trial.[38]

The government appealed. A three-judge panel of the Tenth Circuit strongly disagreed with the trial judge on every score. They found both sides to have had access to all the relevant information in the first trial. What the 1979 congressional hearing revealed, they observed, was not new evidence but new attitudes, and one-sidedly at that. Accordingly, in November 1983 the panel set aside Christensen's finding of fraud and reversed his ruling on court costs and a new trial. Eighteenth months later the full court concurred, a decision confirmed the following year when the Supreme Court of the United States refused to hear the case.[39] So ended the long-running sheep trial, but not the persistent questions about what really happened.

WHAT DID IT MEAN?

Its handling of the sheep investigation betrayed certain unfortunate and persistent features of the Atomic Energy Commission's interaction with the world beyond its offices, and so offers a glimpse into the sources of growing public distrust. Of special significance in this instance, I believe, are the arrogance of officials who knew secrets and their underlying disdain for ill-informed outsiders. Manipulating public opinion, soothing public fears, deflecting public criticism, all loomed larger in AEC eyes—almost surely from nothing but the highest motives—than answering honest, if not always well-informed, questions. Nor were such practices directed only at the public. Two episodes that happened in the course of the sheep investigation will make this argument clearer.

In September 1953, AEC Chairman Lewis L. Strauss responded to an inquiry from Congressman Douglas R. Stringfellow of Utah with a brief status report on the sheep investigation. Strauss gave three reasons to dismiss fallout entirely as a factor in sheep deaths: (1) experimental lesions observed in sheep differed from beta burns induced in other animals; (2) cattle and wild animals ranging the same area as the sheep showed no signs of radiation burns; and (3) possible gamma exposure to sheep had not exceeded 5 roentgens, fifty times too low to produce any observable effects in domestic animals.[40] While each point was strictly true, each was also misleading. Sheep lesions did differ in some respects from beta burns produced experimentally, but resembled them in others. Strauss mentioned cattle and wild animals, but omitted the horses that had clearly suffered radiation burns, leading to claims the AEC had already settled. Finally, the crucial issue in sheep deaths was not external gamma levels, which truly fell well below anything likely to prove harmful, but ingested radionuclides, where no such proof existed.

The second incident involved Gordon Dunning's attempt to turn an ad hoc gathering of veterinarians into a panel that would conclusively absolve fallout as the cause of sheep deaths. Dunning held a Ph.D. in science education and had taught school for three years before joining the AEC in 1951. As a member of the biophysics branch in the AEC Division of Biology and Medicine, he often acted as liaison between AEC headquarters and the test organization.[41] Present in Nevada for Upshot-Knothole, Dunning was the AEC official who received the call from Utah about unusual sheep deaths and who persuaded the Utah health commissioner to support an AEC investigation.

On October 27, 1953, Dunning attended a meeting at Los Alamos intended to describe the early results from a study comparing skin damage suffered by Utah sheep with lesions produced by controlled beta irradiation of similar sheep in the laboratory. Clarence C. Lushbaugh, the biochemist who headed the Los Alamos research team, and his colleague, Health Division Chief Thomas L. Shipman, hosted the meeting. Two other AEC officials also attended, but the main guests were five of the veterinarians who had studied injured sheep in the field at AEC request—Monroe Holmes, F. H. Melvin, Robert Thompsett, Bernard Trum, and Arthur Wolff.[42] During the morning they saw the sheep and compared samples of their tissues under the microscope with slides made from Utah sheep and the beta-burned Nevada horses. Some thought they matched, some thought otherwise.[43] That afternoon, as the all-day meeting drew to a close, Dunning asked those present to sign a statement he had just drafted.

Dunning's statement began by sketching the facts of injured and dead sheep, then offered three reasons for exonerating fallout: (1) sheep elsewhere suffered the same lesions as those in regions of heavy fallout, and the heaviest fallout was not enough to produce the lesions anyway; (2) tissues from Utah sheep and experimentally burned animals compared under the microscope differed significantly; and (3) because it concentrated radioiodine in fallout, the critical internal organ was the thyroid, but calculations showed the Utah sheep could not have re-

166

ceived an exposure high enough to injure them. Lushbaugh and the five non-AEC veterinarians signed the statement. So did one AEC official. Dunning, who styled himself merely acting scientific secretary for the meeting, did not.[44]

Confusion surrounded both the meaning and purpose of Dunning's draft statement at the time, and it has remained controversial ever since.[45] At least one of the veterinarians thought his signature simply acknowledged his attendance at the meeting. Others worried whether or not signing committed one's agency as well as oneself. Dunning assured them it did not.[46] Apparently, he thought of those at the Los Alamos meeting as a committee or panel; from that viewpoint, his end-of-the-day attempt to secure a summary of their findings looked reasonable.[47] Participants, on the other hand, perceived themselves only as individuals invited to see some recent experimental results. To them, the broad scope of Dunning's hastily drafted statement might well appear puzzling.[48] It went far beyond anything that had been discussed that day. Indeed, only the second of Dunning's three reasons to absolve fallout of blame in sheep deaths—disparities between lesions observed on range sheep and lesions produced experimentally—bore on the main subject of the Los Alamos meeting, and the veterinarians could not agree on what mattered more: the differences or the similarities.

Dunning's other two reasons pertained only tangentially to the day's work. None of the veterinarians present could be expected to have expert knowledge of the first, that sheep outside the fallout area displayed the same lesions, even if fallout had been heavy enough to cause such lesions. They had not seen sheep on the Nevada ranges, only sheep returned to pastures in Utah. That might allow them to testify to having observed lesions, but all they could know about fallout patterns was what the AEC told them, and here was still another instance of literal truth in the service of falsehood: they heard only about low levels of fallout recorded, not that readings came only from roads and towns instead of the countryside where sheep grazed, or that only sheep in the fallout area showed symptoms.[49]

Ingested fission products as a source of damage posed another kind of question. In 1953 scientists perceived the degree of risk from fallout largely in terms of external gamma radiation; they thought the only short-term internal hazard of even minor significance to be radioiodine, since they knew that the thyroid concentrated iodine. No one at the Los

Alamos meeting would have been likely to challenge taking the thyroid as the critical internal organ.[50] At issue was how great the hazard, and whether or not radioiodine was the only fission product to worry about. Answers to such questions were not to be found by looking through a microscope at tissues exposed to beta rays. They may not even have been the right questions. Retrospectively, suspicion has centered on mixed fission products in the gastrointestinal tract, a source of damage largely overlooked in 1953.[51]

Meanwhile, Dunning clearly exulted over his Los Alamos coup. He promptly informed the Director of Information Services (the chief public relations officer in AEC headquarters) of his success. "After prolonged discussion I was able to get the group to agree to a series of statements which . . . members of the committee signed," he reported. "I doubt if we will ever obtain more positive conclusions from this committee than are contained in the attached statements."[52] Pearson quickly passed the good news to his chief, the Director of Biology and Medicine. What made it so pleasing to the AEC high command was the improved prospect of support from both the Public Health Service and the Bureau of Animal Industry when a public statement on sheep could at last be released.[53]

If AEC officials felt free to manipulate relative insiders like members of Congress or hired experts, they had even less compunction about misleading the public. In mid-August 1953, for instance, AEC headquarters refused to allow its Santa Fe Operations Office to release a statement that explained in some detail the apparent delay in closing the sheep investigation.[54] It permitted Santa Fe only to announce: "The investigation of sheep losses is continuing because the precise cause of death of the sheep has not yet been determined. When the investigation of the sheep losses is completed, the findings will be made known in a joint statement by the AEC and Public Health Service."[55]

The final report issued in January 1954 practiced the same deception. It ignored dissenting views:

> Considering all of the information and data available, it is now evident that the peculiar lesions observed in the sheep around Cedar City in the spring of 1953 and the abnormal losses suffered by the several sheepmen can not be accounted for by radiation or attributed to the atomic tests conducted at the Nevada Proving Grounds.[56]

Pearson apparently saw no need to mention the doubts still retained by Thompsett and Veenstra, who had examined sheep in the field at AEC request in June 1953, collected samples, and analyzed them in the laboratory. Both veterinarians remained unwilling in January 1954 to exonerate fallout from all blame. Nor were they the only doubters.

Pearson also sought to bolster his case by claiming the concurrence of federal and state agencies in the AEC finding. Initially the draft concluded: "This opinion is concurred in by the U.S. Public Health Service (HEW), the Bureau of Animal Industry, and the Departments of Agriculture and Health of the State of Utah." That had to be altered when Utah health commissioner Spendlove maintained his reservations against ruling out radiation as a factor in sheep deaths. The released version replaced the final phrase with: "This report has been reviewed by the Department of Health of the State of Utah."[57] Once again, disagreement remained unmentioned.

Such carefully crafted public statements, like Strauss's private letter to Congressman Stringfellow or Dunning's perplexing draft statement, adhered to the literal truth; they misled by what they omitted or downplayed or implied, not by what they stated. Probably no one thought of that as lying, but powerful officials facing little direct accountability in a secrecy-shrouded program found it easy to deny, dissemble, or mislead as a matter of course.[58] In fact, it can be all too easy for those high in government to forget how much their special knowledge derives from position rather than virtue. With access to privileged information, they may readily deem themselves wise enough to decide what costs their fellow citizens must risk paying by being uninformed.

NOTES

1. This chapter is based on research more fully presented in Barton C. Hacker, *Elements of Controversy: The Atomic Energy Commission and Radiation Safety in Nuclear Weapons Testing, 1947–1974* (Berkeley: University of California Press, 1994). Copies of all cited documents are available at the Coordination and Information Center, operated for the U.S. Department of Energy by Reynolds Electrical & Engineering Co., Inc., Las Vegas, Nevada. Many of the documents also have been published in congressional hearings; see especially House Committee on Interstate and Foreign Commerce, Subcommittee on Oversight and Investigations,

Low-Level Radiation Effects on Health, Hearings, 96th Cong., 1st sess., 1979. See also the joint hearing of the House Committee on Interstate and Foreign Commerce, Subcommittee on Oversight and Investigations; the Senate Committee on Labor and Human Resources, Subcommittee on Scientific Research; and the Senate Committee on the Judiciary: *Health Effects of Low-Level Radiation,* 2 vols., 96th Cong., 1st sess., 1979.

2. Hacker, *Elements of Controversy,* chaps. 1–3.

3. Committee to Study Operational Future—Nevada Proving Grounds [NPG], "Agenda for Meeting January 14, 1953 at SFOO [Santa Fe Operations Office], Albuquerque, New Mexico," n.d.; Committee on Operational Future of NPG, "Summary of Minutes," meeting of January 14, 1953. In early 1952 the Nevada Test Site became the Nevada Proving Ground; it reverted to its original name at the end of 1954.

4. Committee on Operational Future of NPG, "Report," May 11, 1953. See also Carroll L. Tyler [mgr., SFOO] to Kenneth E. Fields [dir., AEC Div. of Military Application (DMA)], May 11, 1953.

5. Hacker, *Elements of Controversy,* 89–105. How the perceived health risks from low-level radiation developed is one of the book's central themes, but see especially "Radiation Exposure versus Radiation Damage," 272–76, for a historical overview.

6. See Barton C. Hacker, "Radiation Safety, the AEC, and Nuclear Weapons Testing: Writing the History of a Controversial Program," *The Public Historian* 14 (1992): 31–53, esp. 46–53.

7. Gordon M. Dunning [AEC Div. of Biology and Medicine (DBM)] to Vincent G. Huston [chief, Test Section, DMA], "Information on Cattle and Horses Claimed to Have Been Damaged by Radiation from Fallout," June 11, 1953; AEC meetings no. 888, July 15, 1953, item 2, and no. 933, October 28, 1953, item 1.a; John C. Bugher [dir., DBM] to Marion W. Boyer [AEC gen. mgr.], "Death of Cattle Adjacent to Test Site," August 26, 1953, w/att. report by Paul B. Pearson [chief, Biology Br., DBM], same title, n.d.; AEC 604/2, "Death of Cattle Adjacent to Test Site," September 2, 1953; Joe B. Sanders [deputy mgr., Las Vegas Field Office (LVFO)] to Richard G. Elliott [dir., Off. of Information, SFOO], "Settlements on Horses and Blast Damage," October 9, 1953.

8. The 1968 escape of nerve gas from the Army's Dugway Proving Ground and the associated death of several thousand sheep apparently were a particular source of confusion, or so I surmise from several conversations. On the Dugway incident, see Elinor Langer, "Research Policy: United States," in CBW: *Chemical and Biological Warfare,* ed. Steven Rose (Boston: Beacon Press, 1969), 124; Seán Murphy, Alastair Hay, and Steven Rose, *No Fire, No Thunder: The Threat of Chemical and Biological Weapons* (New York: Monthly Review Press, 1984), 17.

9. For a much more detailed and fully documented narrative of the events

underlying the pattern, see Hacker, *Elements of Controversy*, chap. 5, "The Cost of Sheep."

10. Dunning to files, "Alleged Injury to Animals as Result of Tests at NPG," June 12, 1953; F. H. Melvin [veterinarian in charge, Salt Lake City, BAI] to Chief, Bureau of Animal Industry [BAI, U.S. Dept. of Agriculture], June 8, 1953; Warren B. Earl [dir., Div. of Animal Industry, Nev. Dept. of Agriculture] to John I. Curtis [Utah State Veterinarian], June 11, 1953; Monroe A. Holmes [veterinarian, Public Health Service (PHS), assigned to Utah Dept. of Health] to James H. Steele [chief, Veterinary PHS], "Compiled Report on Co-operative Field Survey of Sheep Deaths in S. W. Utah (Cedar City); by the U.S. Public Health Service, U.S. Department of Agriculture, B.A.I., the U.S. Atomic Energy Commission, the University of Utah Medical School, Utah Agricultural College, and Utah State Department of Health," n.d. (ca. August 15, 1953), 1–2; James G. Terrill, Jr. [chief, Radiological Health Br., PHS], "Interim Report on the Investigation of the Deaths of Sheep in Areas Affected by Atomic Fall-Out," August 21, 1953.

11. Sanders to files, "Alleged Damage to Stock on Range Lands Close to NPG," n.d. (ca. June 9, 1953); Dunning to files, "Alleged Injury"; Pearson to Bugher, "Livestock Losses around Test Site," June 21, 1953, 5; Holmes to Steele, "Compiled Report," 2–3; Sanders to files, "Trip to Cedar City, Utah, to Check with Stockmen, Perform Post Mortems on Afflicted Sheep and Obtain Location of Grazing Rights," n.d. (ca. June 15, 1953).

12. Dunning to Bugher, "Discussions on Alleged Radiation Injury to Animals and on Public Relations at the Nevada Proving Ground," June 12, 1953; AEC meeting no. 875, June 10, 1953, item 10; notes on radiation readings and samples collected at Cedar City, 6/13/53; "Data on Sheep Loss—Cedar City, Utah, Area: Second Preliminary Investigation," June 17, 1953.

13. Tyler to Fields, June 16, 1953; AEC meeting no. 877, June 17, 1953, item 8; Fields to Tyler, June 18, 1953; Tyler to Fields, June 19, 1953.

14. Fields to Tyler, June 16, 1953; Tyler to distrib., "Livestock and Mining Matters, Nevada Proving Grounds Area," June 26, 1953; Jaques Cattell Press, ed., *American Men and Women of Science: Physical and Biological Sciences,* 14th ed. (New York: Bowker, 1979), s.v. Pearson, Paul B.

15. Pearson to Bugher, "Sheep Losses in Utah and Nevada," June 12, 1953; Fields to Boyer, June 15, 1953; Pearson to Bugher, "Livestock Losses around Test Site," June 21, 1953.

16. Bugher to Lewis L. Strauss [Chairman, AEC], "Comments on Fallout Memoranda," July 8, 1953; AEC meeting no. 888, July 15, 1953, item 2; Pearson to Bugher, "Salt Lake City Conference on Livestock Losses," August 13, 1953; Allaire to files, "Report of Trip to Salt Lake City Meeting re Nevada-Utah Livestock," August 7, 1953; Terrill, "Interim Report"; Sanders to files, "Afflicted Animals— Vicinity of Nevada Proving Grounds," August 27, 1953.

17. Lt. Col. John H. Rust [Army Veterinary Corps, assigned to Univ. of Tennessee—AEC Project] et al., "Report of Farm Animal Survey at Nevada Test Site," June 16, 1953, p. 5; Rust, "Pathology Report on Special AEC Problem," n.d. (ca. June 24, 1953); Rust to Pearson, July 21, 1953. For a brief account of the Tennessee program and its findings, see J. Newell Stannard, *Radioactivity and Health: A History,* ed. Raymond W. Baalman, Jr., Report DOE/RL/01830-T59 (Richland, Wash.: PNL, October 1988), 1069–74.

18. Although Rust and Lt. Col. Bernard F. Trum [Army Veterinary Corps, assigned to University of Tennessee—AEC Project] appear frequently in these notes, the volume of their correspondence is scarcely suggested; for further citations, see Hacker, "The Cost of Sheep," cited above. Both went on to academic careers in 1959, Rust to the University of Chicago, Trum as director of an MIT-Harvard primate center (see Stannard, *Radioactivity and Health,* 1069). Philip L. Fradkin, *Fallout: An American Nuclear Tragedy* (Tucson: University of Arizona Press, 1989), 151–59, assigns them, especially Trum, a distinctly conspiratorial role in what he terms the AEC cover-up.

19. L. A. Stoddart, "Report on Livestock Conditions Adjacent to the Las Vegas Bombing Range," June 22, 1953; W. T. Huffman to H. W. Schoening [veterinarian in charge, Pathology Div., BAI], June 23, 1953; Holmes to Huffman, June 24, 1953.

20. Arthur H. Wolff to Holmes, June 24, 1953 (Wolff's emphasis). See also Wolff to Hadlow, June 10, 1953; Wolff, "Results of Radioassay of Tissues from Sheep in Southwest Utah," August 5, 1953.

21. Betsy J. Stover [radiochemist, Radiobiology Lab., Univ. of Utah Medical School] to Holmes, July 21, 1953, w/att. Stover to Holmes, "Report on Southern Utah Sheep," July 21, 1953.

22. "Test of Utah Sheep Sera Collected by Dr. Hadlow from Trip to 6/5/53," June 11, 1953; William H. Hadlow, Necropsy records of ovine females, nos. P53–353 and –354, June 30, 1953; Hadlow to Holmes, July 10, 1953; Hadlow to Rust, July 14, 1953; Rust to Pearson, July 21, 1953; Hadlow to Rust, July 27, 1953; Trum to John L. O'Harra [veterinarian, Nevada Dept. of Agriculture], August 28, 1953; O'Harra to Trum, September 5, 1953.

23. Holmes to Steele, "Compiled Report"; Terrill, "Interim Report."

24. Pearson to Allaire, July 22, 1953; Pearson to Bugher, "Salt Lake City Conference on Livestock Losses," August 13, 1953; Sanders to files, "Afflicted Animals" (see note 16 above); AEC 604/3, DMB report, "Sheep Losses Adjacent to the Nevada Proving Ground," November 4, 1953, p. 8.

25. Veenstra to William W. Allaire [chief, Operations Br., SFOO], June 17, 1953. For an overview of biomedical research at the Naval Radiological Defense Laboratory, which was established after Operation Crossroads in 1946 contaminated so many ships, see Stannard, *Radioactivity and Health,* 1064–69.

26. Veenstra to James E. Reeves [dir., Test Operations, SFOO], June 30, 1953;

Reeves to Holmes, July 3, 1953; Veenstra to Reuben E. Cole [dir., Engineering and Construction, SFOO], July 20, 1953; Pearson to Veenstra, October 19, 1953; Veenstra to Pearson, December 23, 1953. The most complete statement of Veenstra's skepticism about the AEC conclusion that radiation had nothing to do with sheep deaths appeared in his letter to Trum, April 7, 1955; it carries an unexplained notice that it "was not sent, has not been published and is confidential to the Department" (reproduced in *Low-Level Radiation Effects on Health*, 692–93).

27. Robert E. Thompsett to Cole, "Possible Radiation of Animals," n.d. (ca. August 3, 1953). Shortly before his death, Thompsett told a reporter that he still believed fallout had contributed significantly to the sheep deaths; *Deseret News* (Salt Lake City), March 8, 1979, as cited in Fradkin, *Fallout*, 294.

28. Shirley Foster [secretary to Stephen L. Brower, County Agricultural Agent, Iron County, Utah], "Notes from Meeting of Atomic Energy Commission, State Health Department, Livestockmen and Others, Held at the City and County Building, in Cedar City," August 9, 1953. A slightly different, anonymous version identifies speakers somewhat more fully: "Notes Taken at Meeting of Atomic Energy Commission, State Health Department, Public Health Department, Livestockmen and Others." See also Terrill, "Interim Report," 6; Sanders to files, "Afflicted Animals" (see note 16 above).

29. Transcript of remarks at "Meeting of Livestockmen and AEC Officials, January 13, 9:30 a.m., Fire House, Conference Room, Cedar City, Utah," n.d., w/ att. list of "Those in attendance at the meeting at Fire House in Cedar City, January 13, 1954, 9:30 a.m." See also Pearson to Bugher, "Report on Meetings in Utah on Sheep Losses," January 19, 1954.

30. AEC meeting no. 877, June 17, 1953; Allaire to files, "Report on Trip of June 10–16, 1953, re Livestock in the Nevada Proving Grounds Area," June 24, 1953.

31. "Meeting of Livestockmen and the AEC," January 13 (see note 29 above); AEC 604/5, "Study of Sheep Losses Adjacent to the Nevada Proving Grounds," February 17, 1954; AEC 604/6, "Study of Sheep Losses Adjacent to the Nevada Proving Grounds," May 6, 1954; Utah Agricultural Experiment Station, "The Effect of Level of Nutrition on the Pathology and Productivity of Range Sheep: First Progress Report, April 15, 1954 to January 15, 1955," n.d.

32. Lynn R. Anspaugh and John J. Koranda, eds., "Preliminary Assessment of Radiation Dose to Sheep Wintering in the Vicinity of the Nevada Test Site in 1953," draft rev. 3, UCRL-53242 (Livermore: Lawrence Livermore National Laboratory, April 2, 1982), "Introduction," 3. See also Koranda, Anspaugh, and Yook C. Ng, "Reconstruction of Radiation Doses to Sheep in Pennoyer Valley, NV, Exposed to Fallout from Shot Nancy in 1953," *Health Physics* 43 (1982): 105–6; Stannard, *Radioactivity and Health*, 969–70.

33. Charles F. Eason [AEC Office of Gen. Counsel] to Chalmers C. King [asst.

gen. counsel, SFOO], "(1) *Douglas Cory v. U.S.*—Civil C-22-55; (2) *A. C. Seegmiller & Myron Higbee, etc. v. U.S.*—Civil C-23-55; (3) *Lillian W. Clark, Admx., etc. v. U.S.*—Civil C-27-55; (4) *Nelson Webster v. United States U.S.D.C. for the D. of Utah,* Civil Action No. C-26-55; (5) *David C. Bulloch, et al. v. United States,* U.S.D.C. for the District of Utah—Civil Action No. C-19-55," 16 Mar. 1955, w/att. copies of complaints. The several suits were consolidated as *Bulloch et al. v. United States,* Civil C-19-55; the trial record is reproduced in *Health Effects of Low-Level Radiation,* 1:628–1404.

34. For a documented historical survey of how U.S. courts have treated fallout injury claims, see Hacker, *Elements of Controversy,* 266–72.

35. Ibid., 6–8, 259–60.

36. Testimony of F. Peter Libassi, in *Health Effects of Low-Level Radiation,* 1:69–226, at 98–99; Harold A. Knapp, "Sheep Deaths in Utah and Nevada Following the 1953 Nuclear Tests," June 18, 1979, ibid., 1:285–341. See also House Committee on Interstate and Foreign Commerce, Subcommittee on Oversight and Investigations, *"The Forgotten Guinea Pigs": A Report on Health Effects of Low-Level Radiation Sustained as a Result of the Nuclear Weapons Testing Program Conducted by the United States Government,* 96th Cong., 2d sess., 1980; C. Holden, "House Report Nails AEC for Sheep Deaths," *Science* 209 (1980): 1097.

37. Anspaugh and Koranda, eds., "Preliminary Assessment of Radiation Dose to Sheep"; L. B. Sasser et al., "Dose Assessment for Sheep Exposed to Fallout from Nuclear Test Nancy," PNL-4178 (Richland, Wash.: Pacific Northwest Laboratory, October 1982).

38. For a forceful, if one-sided, defense of Judge Christensen's judgment, see Howard Ball, *Justice Downwind: America's Atomic Testing Program in the 1950s* (New York: Oxford University Press, 1986), app. A. "The Long Journey of *Bulloch v. United States,* 1953—: Polaris Sighted?" See also R. Jeffrey Smith's two reports in *Science:* "Atom Bomb Tests Leave Infamous Legacy," 218 (October 15, 1982): 266–69; and "Scientists Implicated in Atom Test Deception," 218 (November 5, 1982): 545–47.

39. *Bulloch et al. v. United States,* 82–2245, 82–2352 (Civil No. C-81–0123C), U.S. Court of Appeals, 10th Circuit, November 23, 1983 (Slip Opinion). See also A. Costandina Titus, *Bombs in the Backyard: Atomic Testing and American Politics* (Reno: University of Nevada Press, 1986), 122–23.

40. Strauss to Stringfellow, September 25, 1953.

41. *American Men and Women of Science,* s.v. Dunning, Gordon M.

42. Melvin to Chief, MAI, October 29, 1953; Holmes to Steele, "Report of Conference Held at Los Alamos, New Mexico, on Utah Sheep Deaths and Experimentally Induced Beta-Radiation Burns on Sheep," November 9, 1953; [Wolff,] "Report of Trip to Los Alamos, October 26–29, 1953," n.d.

43. Holmes to Steele, "Report of Conference"; Wolff, "Report of Trip"; Trum to

Clarence C. Lushbaugh [Health Div., Los Alamos Scientific Lab.], November 4, 1953.

44. [Dunning,] "October 27, 1953, Los Alamos Conference on Livestock Losses," with signatures. On Dunning's self-perceived role, see Dunning to Committee on the Judiciary et al., September 10, 1984, w/att. comments, 9; cf. Dunning to Morse Salisbury [dir., AEC Div. of Information Services], "Alleged Radiation Damage to Sheep," November 3, 1953.

45. See, e.g., John G. Fuller, *The Day We Bombed Utah: America's Most Lethal Secret* (New York: New American Library, 1984), 80–83; Fadkin, *Fallout,* 154–55.

46. Lushbaugh to Dunning, February 12, 1981, as quoted in Dunning comments (see note 44 above), 10; Melvin to Chief, BAI, October 29; Holmes to Steele, "Report of Conference"; Wolff, "Report of Trip"; Trum to Henry A. Gill, Jr., March 13, 1982, as quoted in Dunning comments, September 10, 10. Cf. Trum to Lushbaugh, November 4, 1953.

47. Dunning comments, September 10, 9; Dunning to Salisbury, "Alleged Radiation Damage to Sheep," November 3, 1953.

48. Melvin to Chief, BAI; Holmes to Steele, "Report of Conference"; Wolff, "Report of Trip."

49. Sanders to Reeves, "Livestock Losses Vicinity of NPG," October 30, 1953. Cf. Terrill, "Interim Report."

50. Tommy F. McCraw to L. Joe Deal, "Possible Issues Related to Past Offsite Exposures around NTS [Nevada Test Site]," February 14, 1979; S. C. Black and G. D. Potter, "Historical Perspectives on Selected Health and Safety Aspects of Nuclear Weapons Testing," *Health Physics* 51 (1986): 17–33; Dunning to whom it may concern, n.d. [ca. 1986–89], w/att. "Comments on *Justice Downwind* by Howard Ball," 6.

51. Anspaugh and Koranda, eds., "Preliminary Assessment of Radiation Dose to Sheep"; Sasser et al., "Dose Assessment for Sheep."

52. Dunning to Salisbury, "Alleged Radiation Damage."

53. Pearson to Bugher, "Conference at Los Alamos on Beta Burns on Sheep," November 4, 1953.

54. Tyler to Fields, "Actions Proposed on NPG Livestock Losses," August 18, 1953.

55. Fields to Tyler, August 24, 1953.

56. AEC "Report on Sheep Losses Adjacent to the Nevada Proving Grounds," January 6, 1954, p. 1.

57. [Pearson] draft, "Final Report on Sheep Losses Adjacent to the Nevada Proving Grounds," n.d., 1; AEC, "Report on Sheep Losses," 1.

58. This argument is more fully developed in Hacker, "Radiation Safety, the AEC, and Nuclear Weapons Testing," 49–52.

III. LOCAL RESISTANCE

Alaska and the Firecracker Boys

The Story of Project Chariot

Dan O'Neill

If your mountain is not in the right place, just drop us a card.
Edward Teller in Alaska

Project Chariot was the U.S. Atomic Energy Commission's code name for a 1958 plan to create an instant harbor on the coast of Alaska by detonating several thermonuclear bombs. But amid noisy protests from Eskimos and a cadre of young Alaskan scientists, Project Chariot was canceled in 1962. This all-but-unknown episode might be seen as the first successful opposition to the American nuclear establishment. Chariot occasioned what was to that date the most comprehensive multidisciplinary environmental study conducted in advance of a federal project, prefiguring the modern environmental impact statement. It was perhaps the first specific project challenged principally on the grounds of ecological science, and protests over it served as a catalyst in redefining conservationists as environmentalists. The controversy also spurred Alaska Natives to hold the first-ever conference of all Alaska Eskimo people, to establish the first statewide Native newspaper, and ultimately to win a stunning victory in Congress for aboriginal land claims.

David Lilienthal, the first chairman of the AEC, has written that in the early 1950s there was a feeling within the agency that "somehow or other the discovery that had produced so terrible a weapon simply *had* to have an important peaceful use." Lilienthal hoped to atone for the bomb by promoting nuclear power plants. But a few years later, Edward Teller, the so-called father of the H-bomb, and his colleagues at the AEC's Lawrence Radiation Laboratory (LRL) in Livermore, California, conceived of the peaceful potentials of fission in even more ambitious terms. They proclaimed the redemption not just of nuclear technologies but of the nuclear explosion itself.[1]

The idea was born at a classified meeting held in February 1957 at

LRL—today called Lawrence Livermore National Laboratory (LLNL)—where Edward Teller was director. With worldwide pressure building to ban nuclear weapons testing, theoretical physicists at Livermore saw advantages in industrial and public works applications of nuclear explosives, which they hoped would be exempt from any test ban treaty negotiated. As Stephen Ambrose has written, "Teller and the AEC scientists and their friends were determined to continue testing. Their device was through 'peaceful explosions.' "[2]

The next summer, in June 1958, the AEC announced Project Plowshare, which, as the biblical reference suggests, would attempt to transform the nuclear sword into a peacetime tool. Harbors, canals, and mountain passes would be excavated, petroleum extracted from low-grade deposits, and ore bodies fractured to facilitate mining. Project Chariot would be the first Plowshare operation, and the AEC hoped it would be a prelude to an even more ambitious scheme. To the AEC, Project Chariot's main value was to yield cratering and radiation data necessary to plan a new sea-level Panama Canal to be excavated with nuclear explosives.[3]

For several reasons, Alaska struck Livermore planners as the ideal site for the experiment: the area was distant from population centers; it had plenty of coastline for testing in a marine environment; it seemed politic to test the technique on American soil before offering to export it; and like the West in general, Alaska was regarded as empty wasteland suitable for bombing ranges, dump sites for toxic wastes, and testing grounds for potentially hazardous technologies. As early as 1950, the AEC had considered—even secured presidential approval for—using the island of Amchitka in Alaska's Aleutian Islands as a continental nuclear test site.[4]

The Chariot plan was truly commensurate with Edward Teller's reputation for visionary ideas. Six thermonuclear bombs would be placed in a row and buried at a shallow depth. Four devices of 100 kilotons each would carve out an entrance channel. Two one-megaton bombs would excavate a turning basin.[5]

At 2.4 megatons, the explosion would be equivalent to 40 percent of all the firepower expended in World War II. Seventy million cubic yards of earth would be blasted as high as the stratosphere, while the sea rushed in to fill a keyhole-shaped crater. Practically all of the radiation produced would vent to the atmosphere.[6]

Most Alaskans first heard the words "Project Chariot" in July 1958 when Teller and his entourage from Livermore landed, unannounced, in Juneau, the state capital, to begin a traveling promotional campaign. At a hastily arranged press conference, Teller unveiled the plan to blast a harbor with nuclear explosives. Troubled by a postwar economic decline, his audience was eager for news of increased federal spending in Alaska. The site he proposed was near Cape Thompson on the northwest coast, about 30 miles from the Eskimo village of Point Hope. A study commissioned by LRL had shown the area to contain, according to Teller, "the highest quality proven coal deposits in Alaska." He claimed that by exporting coal, Alaska's "black diamonds can pay off better than its gold ever did or will." Moreover, he said, two-thirds of the project's estimated $5 million cost would be spent in Alaska.[7]

In selling the plan to Alaskans, Teller mixed flattery with frontier bravado. Scientists, he said, had "looked at the whole world" for the right place to host the technology, and found that Alaskans were "the most reasonable people." Furthermore, the AEC had refined the science of crater production to such a degree that they could "dig a harbor in the shape of a polar bear if desired."[8] Although other proposals were under consideration, he said, the harbor at Cape Thompson was favored. Planning for the shot had progressed so far that the atomic devices could be fired the following summer, provided that the harbor was economically justifiable and that Alaskan businessmen were ready to step in and develop it.

But Alaska businessmen, confirmed developers though they were, failed to see economic value in a harbor some 300 miles north of Nome: it would be ice locked by the frozen Chukchi Sea for nine months of the year. It wasn't that the frontier entrepreneurs were unenthusiastic about a free offer to move some dirt. They just wanted the hole to be useful, and suggested alternatives. Why didn't the AEC consider shortening the shipping lane to Bristol Bay, the world's richest fishing grounds, by blasting a canal across the Alaska Peninsula at Herendeen Bay, or a harbor on Norton Sound near Nome, or one on the Arctic coast to serve Umiat, where oil was known to exist?[9]

"I'm delighted," said Teller. "This is just the type of suggestion and objection we are looking for. . . . We came here to be partners with you, and because we want suggestions." By the time his group reached Fairbanks, Project Chariot seemed to be wide open: the Yukon, Susitna, or Copper River might be dammed with a nuclear explosion; harbors or canals might be blasted at a half dozen locations.[10] What Teller did not say, however, was that some two months earlier his laboratory had already proposed, in a classified application to the Department of Interior, the withdrawal from the public domain of a chunk of the Cape Thompson hinterlands nearly the size of Delaware. In fact, even as Teller spoke in Fairbanks encouraging his audience to consider various "geographic engineering" possibilities, his associates on the ground at Cape Thompson were selecting the Ogotoruk Creek drainage as the new harbor site and planning where the nuclear devices might be placed.[11]

Still trying to find economic justification for the Cape Thompson harbor, Teller tried to recruit George Rogers, a long-time Alaska resident and Harvard-educated economist. Rogers recalled that the physicist

> invited me to breakfast . . . [and] he gave the pitch again. . . . Then I said well, the Native people, they depend on the sea mammals and the caribou. He said well, they're going to have to change their way of life. I said what are they going to do. Well, he said, when we have the harbor we can create coal mines in the Arctic and they can become coal miners.

Not eager to advise the Eskimos to abandon an established economy and culture rooted in gathering food from the land and sea, in exchange for low-wage underground work and the expectation of black lung disease, Rogers shifted the focus of the discussion to economics, mentioning the short shipping season. But Teller simply "said we'll just have to create warehouses and tank farms to retain these things until the season opens." Reminded that the coal deposits the physicists seemed to be referring to were on the back side of the Brooks Range, hundreds of miles from the proposed harbor site, Teller said it was not a problem, a railroad would be built. Agape, Rogers asked if Teller had any idea what these things would cost to construct in the Arctic. "By this point he realized I was not the economist he wanted, so he changed the subject totally and said time is running out, where would you advise me to buy my souvenirs?"[12]

Teller reported the results of his Alaska visit in a classified letter to General Starbird, director of military applications at AEC: "In discussing the usefulness of such a harbor with groups in Alaska we found no one who could justify at this time the harbor on an economic or military basis." Though the AEC was publicly adamant that Plowshare projects had no military connection, the letter reveals that Teller had consulted with Alaska's General Frank Armstrong regarding the strategic advantages of nuclear excavations at various sites.[13]

Without the justification of economic development or the unacknowledged but hoped-for military value, Teller began to rethink Project Chariot, envisioning now "a partial experiment, that is, firing only one or two shots to get scaling information." Then, shortly after the Livermore group returned from Alaska, the Neptune test (October 1958) conducted at Nevada produced an unexpected and striking result that supported Teller's modified plan. Though sometimes referred to within nuclear testing circles as the first nuclear cratering experiment, Neptune was designed to be a contained explosion—the crater and escape of radioactivity were entirely accidental. When test officials returned to the site (having beat a hasty retreat at the appearance of flying boulders, arcing streamers of dust, and a rising steam cloud), they were surprised to see a relatively large crater considering that the device had been buried fairly deep and that the magnitude of the explosion (yield) had been low. They were surprised also to note that a relatively small percentage of Neptune's total radioactivity had escaped to the atmosphere.[14]

Neptune revealed that, up to a point, crater size increased with depth of burial, while the venting of radiation decreased steadily with depth. The physicists already knew that to make the largest possible crater, the bomb should be buried at a specified depth according to the bomb's yield. Now they realized that by burying the bomb somewhat deeper than this optimal depth, they could excavate a hole nearly as large but reduce the vented radiation to fairly low levels. And this was important news to Plowshare's promoters.

Before the principle could be applied to large-scale explosions near populated areas, however, it would need to be tested in a remote location. "An experiment," wrote Teller in a January 1959 classified letter, "using two to three 20 KT explosions plus two at about 200 KT would serve this purpose. . . . As a consequence, the Chariot concept has been revised to provide for this experiment."[15]

Scaled down to 460 kilotons, just 19 percent of the original 2.4 megaton blast, the Chariot detonation was now strictly an engineering test. The smaller crater could not serve as a harbor to oceangoing ships, and thus lost any value as a demonstration of useful applications of nuclear explosions. (In 1960 the Chariot shot was again reduced, this time to 280 kilotons.)

As the Livermore scientists regrouped, and as a result of Chariot's cool reception from some quarters in Alaska, the AEC in Washington, D.C., seemed to abandon the project. When the idea was presented at the Second International Conference on Peaceful Uses of Atomic Energy in Geneva in 1958, the Soviets charged that it was a thinly veiled attempt to continue testing nuclear explosives and circumvent the provisions of an emerging test ban treaty. Even U.S. allies saw Chariot, 180 miles from Siberia, as an unnecessary obstacle to negotiations. At the conference, AEC commissioner Willard Libby, and later, AEC chairman John McCone speaking in Washington, indicated the project had been shelved because Alaska business leaders were disinclined to invest in harbor facilities at Cape Thompson.

Livermore responded by launching a vigorous drive to enlist support in Alaska. That LRL enjoyed relative autonomy from AEC in Washington is evident in the recently expressed views of Gerald Johnson, who ran the Plowshare program at Livermore:

> The thing people need to realize is that in those days in the Laboratory we could go directly to the top. We didn't go to the President, but we'd go to the Joint Committee [on Atomic Energy] or we'd go directly to the commissioners. We didn't feel we had to work with anybody in between. . . . It wasn't a normal bureaucratic structure. Now the structure resented that. The people down the line—well, people like John Kelly [director, Division of Peaceful Nuclear Explosives, AEC] felt like they were running the Plowshare program. We never felt he had very much to do with the Plowshare program in terms of running it, and we'd ignore him if he tried to tell us to do something we didn't want to do. . . . We were the operators . . . and he was just another contract administrator.[16]

Teller toured Alaska promoting his dream "to engage in the great art of geographic engineering, to reshape the earth to your pleasure." Delivering the University of Alaska commencement address at Fairbanks in June 1959, he said such a project "needs big people . . . and big people are found in big states." In Anchorage, when Teller was questioned about the possibility of other nuclear projects in Alaska, his rhetoric became even more swaggering: "If your mountain is not in the right place, just drop us a card," he said.[17]

Because of Teller's energetic salesmanship, the repackaged Chariot plan was well received in Alaska in 1959. Presented with the choice of affirming the plan or losing the atomic construction project for their new state, Alaskan opinion leaders rallied behind Project Chariot. Newspaper editors, chambers of commerce, labor unions, the legislature, even church leaders and university administrators, now jumped at the chance to "center world scientific and economic attention on Alaska just at a time when we are moving into statehood and inviting development," in the words of a *Fairbanks Daily News-Miner* editorial published the previous summer, three weeks after Congress passed the Alaska statehood bill. The editorial seemed to view the nuclear explosion as just the sort of pyrotechnic fanfare that ought to mark the Great Land's entry into the Union: "We think the holding of a huge nuclear blast in Alaska would be a fitting overture to the new era which is opening up for our state."[18]

The unqualified endorsement of the proposal is striking considering that most Alaskans were hypersensitive about federal domination. As one long-time resident said, "Alaska had been a step child of the United States over the years. We were governed by Washington, D.C., you know. For years and years and years just totally neglected, just totally disregarded. Statehood came along and we still had big battles with Outside financial interests which pulled the strings of most of the big enterprises in Alaska." And though this antipathy toward the federal government was a hallmark of Alaskan journalism, when big federal dollars were at stake the editors seemed to urge Alaskans simply to trust Uncle Sam to do right by them. As requested by the AEC, and led by the Alaska press, chambers of commerce statewide campaigned to get out the "vote" for Project Chariot.[19]

Bishop William Gordon, the famous "Flying Bishop" and powerful leader of the Episcopal Church in Alaska, squelched even the *mention* of concern over Project Chariot by members of the Alaska Council of Churches in the minutes of its annual meeting. When a young minister named Richard Heacock introduced a motion opposing Chariot to the committee on social concerns, Gordon saw to it that the motion was not contained in the committee's report. Screwing up his courage, Heacock presented the resolution directly on the floor of the annual meeting and moved that it be referred to the committee for study:

And that motion carried. But then Bishop Gordon subsequently made a motion that the statement not be included in the minutes of the assembly of the Alaska Council of Churches. . . . It's in good hands, he said. And when I said, whose hands? the response was, the Atomic Energy Commission's.[20]

Eventually Bishop Gordon's confidence in the AEC diminished as he came to believe that the government scientists were "not much concerned about the people in the area." He credited Heacock and other clerics with helping him to see Chariot "in a larger light."[21]

Chariot promoters drew on the popular image of Alaska as a barren wasteland, always referring to the harbor site as a "bleak spot" that was "located in the wilderness, far away from any human habitation." This sentiment was expressed perhaps at its naked best by Robert Atwood, longtime editor and publisher of the *Anchorage Times* and erstwhile Chariot booster. In a 1989 interview, Atwood showed that the intervening thirty years had not heightened his sensibilities with respect to the value of either biological or cultural diversity: "It is a wilderness with no trees, no nothing! Nobody would want to live there." Almost three years passed before any AEC official bothered to explain the project to the people who would be most affected by it, the Eskimos of Point Hope, just thirty miles from ground zero.[22]

Like the Bikini Islanders, whom the AEC had abruptly uprooted from their homeland to accommodate nuclear weapons testing, the Eskimos of Point Hope apparently lacked any sort of political clout. They were few in number, nonwhite, and not uniformly proficient in the English language.

But the village had a long tradition. Point Hope, or Tikiraq, as it is called in the native Inupiaq language, is said to be the oldest continuously occupied settlement in North America. It is situated at the tip of a low spit of land which juts like a finger into the Chukchi Sea (the word Tikiraq means "index finger"). This geography is undoubtedly related to the community's longevity; it is the ideal place to intercept whales on their migration north. The community had a unique sense of cohesiveness and solidarity, and a "strong tradition of self administration of local affairs."[23]

The people of Point Hope were also fortunate to have in residence a young graduate student from McGill University named Don Charles

Foote. Foote had landed the AEC contract to research the "human geogra-phy" of the Cape Thompson region, and his laborious researches docu-mented the people's dependency on caribou taken near there. He also raised a host of questions about the safety aspects of the proposed nu-clear explosion and maintained a close liaison with the village council, explaining in lay language the potential hazards posed by radiation. When AEC representatives finally did visit Point Hope, they found a hundred villagers waiting in the community hall and two tape recorders set up on the head table.

Speaking at Point Hope on March 14, 1960, representatives of the AEC told the Eskimo audience that none of the nuclear tests in the Pacific had significantly contaminated fish with radiation such that the fish were unfit to eat; that radioactive fallout from the Chariot blast would be too small to measure with radiation detection equipment; that the half-life of the harmful constituents of fallout would be so short that "some [radioac-tive isotopes] would be gone in a matter of hours, others will take longer"; that people at Point Hope would not feel the seismic shock of the explo-sion; that a two-year study of forty-seven cattle in the Nevada desert offered evidence as to the harmlessness of fallout on the Arctic tundra; and that once Japanese survivors who received "very great exposures" at Hiroshima and Nagasaki recovered from radiation sickness, they suffered no further effects. And the Eskimos got it all down on tape.[24]

The Point Hopers had read for themselves in magazines of the disas-trous 1954 Bravo shot at Bikini which spewed lethal levels of radioactiv-ity over 7,000 square miles of the Pacific. Some of the villagers had served in the war in the Pacific, even participating in the cleanup of Nagasaki. "We really don't want to see Cape Thompson blasted," a tiny but fearless Kitty Kinneeveauk told the men from the AEC, "because it [is] our homeland. I'm pretty sure you don't like to see your home blasted by some other people who don't live in your place like we live in Point Hope."

David Frankson, a whaling captain and president of the Village Coun-cil, made the point even more emphatically to the AEC representatives: "We Council at the Point Hope that sent the protest letter to Atomic Energy Commission stating that we don't want to see the blast down there. And when we say it we mean it! For any reason." He told the agency representatives that the next time they came to Point Hope they ought to bring along one of the five AEC commissioners. The AEC did just that the following summer. But in a meeting lasting more than four hours, Commissioner Leland Haworth had little effect on the steadfast opposition of 300 assembled Point Hopers.

In 1960 and 1961 the AEC made presentations in more than a dozen villages in northwestern Alaska. For whatever reason—greater distance from the proposed blast, greater interest in the prospects for employment, a less thorough understanding of the potential health effects, or differences in various groups' disposition toward militant activism—the proposed Chariot explosion seems not to have particularly troubled the residents of other villages. Only at Point Hope were any significant questions or objections raised.[25]

By 1961 the Point Hope Village Council had written letters to the AEC, the secretary of the interior, and the Association on American Indian Affairs (AAIA). They expressed informed concern over the health hazards of radiation, and they questioned the right of the Bureau of Land Management to transfer to the AEC land that the Point Hopers claimed. To President Kennedy, the women of the Point Hope Village Health Council wrote expressing fear that radiation would contaminate the animals upon which the people's health depended:

> All the four seasons, each month, we get what we need for living. In December, January, February and even March, we get the polar bear, seals, tomcod, oogrook, walrus, fox and caribou. In March we also get crabs. In April, May and June we also hunt whales, ducks, seals, white beluga, and oogrook. In July we collect crow-bell eggs from Cape Thompson and Cape Lisbourne and store them for the summer. . . . In the middle of September many of our village go up Kookpuk River for the fishing and caribou hunting until the middle of November.[26]

From AAIA, Point Hope secured legal and investigatory services and underwriting for the first-ever meeting of all the Alaskan Eskimos. The Eskimos convened in Barrow in 1961 to discuss Native rights and issued a report calling for the revocation of the AEC's permit to occupy lands at Cape Thompson, which the village of Point Hope claimed. The language of the opening lines of their report is hauntingly reminiscent of the cries for aboriginal rights by American Indians a century earlier:

We the Inupiat have come together for the first time ever in all the years of our history. We had to come together in meeting from our far villages from Lower Kuskokwim to Point Barrow. We had to come from so far together for this reason. We always thought our Inupiat Paitot was safe to be passed down to our future generations as our fathers passed down to us. Our Inupiat Paitot is our land around the whole Arctic world where we Inupiat live.[27]

The following summer, at Tanana, the Athabaskan Indians of Alaska's Interior met for the first time since 1913. They followed the Barrow model to organize in defense of aboriginal rights and land issues. Also in 1962, in response to a recommendation made at the Barrow meeting, the first statewide Native newspaper, *Tundra Times,* was established. Under the editorship of Howard Rock, an Inupiat from Point Hope, the paper served to politically sensitize and unify all Alaska Natives. This flurry of activism marked the beginning of a new era of political accomplishment for Alaska Natives which reached its apex in 1971 with the passage of the historic Alaska Native Claims Settlement Act. The 40 million acres of land conveyed by the act exceeded all the land held in trust for all other American Indians. And the nearly $962 million in compensation for lands already given up nearly quadrupled what all other Indian tribes had won from the Indian Claims Commission over its twenty-five-year history.[28]

On another front, scientists at the University of Alaska initially greeted Teller's announcement of Project Chariot with some skepticism and some opportunism. As one said later, "A good field biologist will do damn near anything to get back in the field again." If the operation was truly a peaceful use of the atom, they argued in 1958, then national security imperatives did not preclude incorporating bioenvironmental studies into the plan.[29]

At a tense meeting on the Fairbanks campus in January 1959, a group of young biologists objected to the claims made by the Livermore scientists, whom they privately called "the firecracker boys." The biologists pointed out "conflicting and crudely misleading statements about the possible biological effects of this explosion and the entire weapons testing program of the AEC." They said they were "embarrassed" to have to point out that Chariot could not possibly yield useful biological results, as the AEC claimed, unless "a carefully considered experimental design" was planned. Shortly, such studies were approved and the University of Alaska critics became contract employees of the AEC.[30]

John N. Wolfe of the AEC's Division of Biology and Medicine (DBM) developed the program of studies. It included forty-two investigations in geology, hydrology, meteorology, vegetation, studies of birds, mammals, zooplankton, and tundra ponds, oceanography, fisheries, archaeology, human geography (which brought Don Foote to Point Hope), and existing radiation levels.

While it seems that the idea for a comprehensive, integrated study originated with biologists at the University of Alaska, Wolfe was the man who pulled it off. Working within a Cold War era AEC—an agency of considerable institutional inertia, unaccustomed to abdicating power— Wolfe persuaded the AEC to publicly declare that the Chariot shot was contingent on the results of an environmental study. It was a milestone in public policy. And the studies began three years before Rachel Carson's 1962 book *Silent Spring,* the environmental wake-up call which has generally served historians as the convenient starting point for the age of ecology.

Though he called himself "the only defender of the program here at DBM," Wolfe persisted in arguing that "it is scarcely too early in the Atomic Age to give considerable attention to the environment which supports man on this planet." He successfully resisted the pressure of superiors who said "we want something blankety fast and dirty." And according to one AEC official, when Edward Teller charged that the environmental program was "nothing but a gigantic ecological boondoggle," Wolfe rebutted, "Without it, Chariot would only be a thud in the mud."[31]

The report, finally published as *Environment of the Cape Thompson Region, Alaska* in 1966, years after the Chariot controversy had been resolved, was said to be the most comprehensive bioenvironmental program ever done. "Nowhere in the free world at least," wrote Wolfe in 1961, "and probably nowhere else, has such an assemblage of bioenvironmental researches been carried on simultaneously in the same location encompassing both land and sea environments." Because the Chariot study was, at least ostensibly, intended as a planning tool, it can be considered the first de facto environmental impact statement. It certainly provided a model for the early official ones required after the passage of the National Environmental Policy Act of 1969.[32]

The Cape Thompson studies also presaged the need to give attention to cultural realities in impact assessment. Don Foote's research on human geography revealed that the Eskimos were dependent on hunting caribou in the area destined to be contaminated by Chariot's fallout. At the same time other researchers noted that the most harmful radionuclides in fallout from worldwide atmospheric testing seemed, somehow, to be moving with unusual efficiency through the Arctic food chain. Eskimos were inexplicably showing body burdens (radioactive material absorbed) higher than those of residents of the lower states, even though the amount of fallout on the ground in the Arctic was a tenth that of more temperate latitudes. For some reason, the caribou, and the Eskimos who ate them, appeared "to be higher in Sr90 [strontium 90] content than any other group in the world."[33]

The key to the puzzle was the lichen, a rootless tundra plant that derives its mineral nutrition from airborne dust. It was an ideal organism to capture fallout. As the caribou grazed on the lichen, they gleaned fallout from many acres and retained it in their tissues and bones. When an Eskimo ate several caribou each year, he further concentrated in his body the strontium and cesium once scattered over many square miles of tundra.

As the environmental picture became clearer, several of the scientists developed strong opposition to the Chariot detonation. The University of Alaska's new president, William R. Wood, discounted their objections. "If the United States government decides that the project is a safe one," he told the press in August 1960, "there is no reason for concern." Wood had recently arrived from the University of Nevada, which received millions of dollars in AEC grants during the 1950s and 1960s.[34]

University of Alaska biologists were further angered when the AEC— particularly John Wolfe—mischaracterized the researchers' preliminary reports in statements to the press. The agency's supposedly independent Environmental Committee also seemed to be ignoring the preliminary findings in deference to AEC's stated objectives. After complaining formally to AEC, the biologists sought President Wood's help. Instead of intervening on behalf of his faculty, Wood let it be known he opposed any attempts by the scientists to set the record straight, which he later characterized as "negative opposition" and "continued sniping." One university administrator remembers him saying that perhaps it was not in the best interest of the university to rehire members of the staff if they felt strongly against the activities of the agency that was providing money for their research. There was no tenure at the University of Alaska then, and before long the two most vocal Chariot critics, William Pruitt and Leslie Viereck, learned that their contracts were not being renewed.[35]

Besides losing their jobs, the professors reported being blacklisted. Learning that Pruitt had been asked to join the zoology department at Montana State University, Dr. Wood put the MSU president in touch with the AEC. As a result, the MSU administration rejected the unanimous recommendation of its zoology department and blocked Pruitt's appointment.[36]

Pruitt's next two National Science Foundation grant proposals were turned down. And while on a visiting professorship at the University of Oklahoma, he heard that an AEC representative had visited the campus to caution college administrators about him. After his aged mother was interrogated by the FBI, Pruitt emigrated to Canada.[37]

But the critics of Chariot gained momentum by enlisting support from national advocacy groups. The Wilderness Society adopted a resolution in September 1960 disapproving of Project Chariot and urging its abandonment. In May 1961 the *Sierra Club Bulletin* reprinted a lengthy and critical account of Project Chariot originally published by the tiny, Fairbanks-based Alaska Conservation Society. The next month, Barry Commoner's Committee for Nuclear Information in St. Louis devoted a whole issue of its bulletin to the controversy. In these narratives, arguments were grounded in incipient environmentalism, rather than conservationism. Now the rationale for caution was not the old logic of conserving a magnificent landscape or an endangered species. It was based instead on a more holistic concept of environmental protection: insidious degradation of the natural world was possible because of the invisible interconnectedness of things. In the late spring of 1962 the *New York Times* reported that "Project Chariot may well be dead, killed by adverse publicity about its effects on Alaskan Eskimos and their hunting grounds."[38]

Barry Commoner sees Chariot as a turning point, both personally and historically. As he commented in a 1988 oral history interview: "Looking back on my career in environmentalism, it is absolutely certain that it began when I went to the library to look up lichens in connection with the Chariot program. That's a very vivid picture in my mind. I realized that we're dealing with an ecosystem here." Commoner, who by 1970 was on the cover of *Time* magazine as the apparent leader of the new movement, reflected: "I think, in so far as I had an effect on the development of the whole movement (which I did, I have to admit), Project Chariot can be regarded as the ancestral birthplace of at least a large segment of the environmental movement."[39]

At the same time that public concern began to coalesce, two other matters served to rein in Chariot. Data from the environmental studies revealed several flaws in the plan. Besides the lichen-caribou-man pathway for radiation uptake, there were geophysical problems with the Cape Thompson site. Even though AEC press releases continued to claim that the site was technically "well suited," internal correspondence at the time acknowledged that the studies showed the harbor's water would thaw surrounding permafrost, resulting in "a serious deterioration of the crater slopes." Furthermore, whatever scientists might learn about the effects of saturation on crater slope stability in permafrost soils, it could not be applied to soils in warmer locations (such as Panama) where the AEC hoped to excavate. And the meteorological studies showed that dominant northerly winds made a landward disposition of fallout impossible. The AEC knew that directing fallout toward the sea was preferable from a biological standpoint (due to the sea's greater capacity for dilution), and it publicly stressed that dosages to Eskimos would be kept as low as possible. Nevertheless, Chariot planners privately favored sending the fallout over the tundra in order to monitor its movement through the environment. Thus, they considered the steady offshore wind a hindrance to a "meaningful radioactivity experiment."[40]

Besides the environmental study having done its job all too well, the other factor leading to Chariot's demise was the development of technical information from recent nuclear tests. The Danny Boy shot in March 1962 apparently confirmed LRL radiation release models. And the Sedan shot, set for that summer in Nevada, was designed out of "frustration," as "an alternate to Chariot," to answer many of the same questions.[41]

By April 1962, Livermore officials concluded that "the Chariot project should be canceled"; but they were concerned that the decision might create "serious political problems." LRL planners had always been sensitive to any change in the design which "looks like another retreat to mollify local demands." So when Livermore director John S. Foster finally wrote the AEC in Washington on April 30, 1962, to recommend cancellation, he pointed out: "Such an action could have repercussions which would adversely affect the whole Plowshare program."[42]

In Washington, the AEC considered the problem. John Kelly, director of the AEC's Division of Peaceful Nuclear Explosives, listed several factors that argued for the project's continuation. First, the agency had spent nearly $4 million on surveys of the blast area and wanted a return on its money. Second, although the experiment was "four years old and obsolescent," it would still provide some useful data. And third, officials worried that "since Chariot has been vigorously criticized from this standpoint of safety . . . its cancellation will contribute to the skepticism on the safety of nuclear excavation."[43]

But Kelly also listed arguments against continuing with Project Chariot, and these held greater sway. Other tests more cheaply conducted in Nevada could address some of the experimental questions. Stewart Udall's Department of the Interior, which was charged with protecting Indian land rights until Congress should address the issue, was disinclined to grant AEC the necessary land withdrawal. And, though he did his bureaucratic best not to say so plainly, Kelly admitted that the environmental studies did raise safety concerns. After first predicting that the chance of harm to local inhabitants would be exceedingly remote, he conceded "there are some uncertainties within the parameters involved in some of these predictions however that can only be resolved by proceeding with an experiment." In other words, the uncertainty of the program's safety was one reason not to go ahead.

Finally, Kelly addressed the public opinion consequences of canceling Project Chariot. His "Information Plan" was intended "to minimize, insofar as possible, adverse criticism of the Commission's decision to cancel Project Chariot by providing a publicly convincing explanation of the reasons for canceling the project." He called for a public announcement, "carefully timed to coincide with a convincing event which documents the technical rationale for the decision. Project Sedan will be such an event. Therefore, it is proposed to include, in the second post-shot announcement of the results of Project Sedan, the announcement of the cancellation of Project Chariot."

In May 1962, Kelly began the process of "terminating all Chariot activities" while cautioning Livermore that it was "important that all concerned with this program be careful that their actions or words are not such that they can be interpreted as indicating that the Commission has canceled Chariot."[44]

Shortly after the Sedan shot in Nevada, an AEC press release noted that the AEC "has decided to defer, for the present, any recommendations to The President on whether to conduct the experiment." The accompanying fact sheet noted that "some of the data originally planned to be obtained from Chariot are now available or may be developed from other experiments." In mid-1963, after LRL abandoned Chariot, public announcements still insisted that "no final decision has been made by the AEC as to conducting the proposed nuclear experiment." Even as late as 1989, the Department of Energy's chief historian was unable to say whether his agency had ever formally admitted canceling Project Chariot.[45]

The opponents of Project Chariot—the Eskimos, the biologists, and the conservationists—were denied a clear-cut acknowledgment of their success. But their victory is as stunning as it is historic. They took on Edward Teller and his dream to use nuclear explosions in the "great art of geographic engineering,"[46] and they turned it into one of the first stirrings of the environmental movement. And something larger than Chariot was knocked off course as well. Bogged down also was Teller's headlong rush to establish Plowshare as a highly visible affirmation of fission. Indeed, the civilian application of nuclear energy, other than for electric power generation, never regained its momentum.

On the surface, Project Chariot is a tale of conflict, even scandal, involving passionate, radical, pioneering people. But it is more than that. Chariot illustrates why the most cherished institutions of a free society—a democratic government, a free press, the university, even the church—cannot necessarily be accepted as seats of objectivity and candor. The lesson Chariot offers is that a free society must be a skeptical one, that rigorous questioning and dissent protect, rather than subvert, our freedoms.

* * *

In 1992, thirty years after Project Chariot's cancellation, dozens of William Pruitt and Leslie Viereck's friends and colleagues campaigned for a symbolic reinstatement of the two men at the University of Alaska. In the spring of 1993, Pruitt entered U.S. territory for the first time since immigrating to Canada in 1965. On May 6, 1993, he touched down in Fairbanks, and three

*days later the university awarded Pruitt and Viereck honorary doctorate de-
grees. In part, the University of Alaska conferred its highest honor in recognition of the very actions for which the men had lost their jobs three decades
earlier.*[47]

NOTES

Funding for this research came from the Alaska Humanities Forum with support from the National Endowment for the Humanities. I would also like to
acknowledge and thank Jim Carothers and Steve Wofford of Lawrence Livermore
National Laboratory (LLNL) for their professionalism regarding my access to internal documents, Ernest Campbell of the Nevada Operations Office (NVOO) for his
near total recall of events thirty years old, and Bernie Maza and Yvonne
Townsend of the Coordination and Information Center (CIC) for really excellent
archival service. I am especially indebted to the late Don Charles Foote for his
writings and his collection of historical materials dealing with Project Chariot.

1. David Lilienthal, *Change, Hope and the Bomb* (Princeton: Princeton University Press, 1963), 109.

2. Stephen E. Ambrose, *Eisenhower: The President,* 2 vols. (New York: Simon
and Schuster, 1983–84), 2:568.

3. Gerald W. Johnson, oral history interview, July 7, 1989, in Dan O'Neill,
"Project Chariot: A Collection of Oral Histories," 1989 (hereafter, O'Neill, "Proj-
ect Chariot"), 202–3, Alaska Humanities Forum, University of Alaska Fairbanks
Archives (hereafter UAF Archives).

4. Richard G. Hewlett and Jack M. Holl, *Atoms for Peace and War* (Berkeley:
University of California Press, 1989), 535; Richard L. Miller, *Under the Cloud: The
Decades of Nuclear Testing* (New York: Free Press, 1986), 130.

5. Teller to E. C. Shute, January 26, 1959, declassified with deletions, in document no. 0070391, Coordination and Information Center (CIC), U.S. Department of Energy, Las Vegas, Nevada. *Note:* LLNL also has the Teller letter, but
refused a number of requests to declassify several pages of it, including the
writer's name. The CIC copy has only minor deletions.

6. Forty percent is based on the 6 megaton figure in Linus Pauling, *No More
War!* (New York: Dodd, Mead, 1983), 5; all would vent: Gary H. Higgins, letter to
author, August 29, 1989.

7. *Anchorage Daily Times,* July 16, 1958; two-thirds of $5 million: *Fairbanks
Daily News-Miner,* July 16, 1958.

8. *Fairbanks Daily News-Miner,* July 15, 17, 1958.

9. *Fairbanks Daily News-Miner,* July 15, 1958.

10. Ibid. (AP story out of Juneau).

11. Classified application: C. M. Bacigalupi to D. Kilgore, May 20, 1958, classification canceled February 17, 1989 (LLNL); associates on the ground: U.S. Atomic Energy Commission, *Project Chariot Phases I-V: Project Manager's Summary Report,* August 1964, 1–3.

12. George Rogers, oral history interview, April 1986, in O'Neill, "Project Chariot," 655, UAF Archives.

13. Teller to A. Starbird, August 15, 1958, classification canceled February 17, 1989, LLNL.

14. Ibid. (quotation); first cratering experiment (and hasty retreat): James Carothers, in oral history interview of Ralph Chase, transcript dated 1986, LLNL.

15. See note 4 above.

16. Gerald W. Johnson, oral history interview (this portion of interview not transcribed), July 7, 1989, UAF Archives.

17. Edward Teller, commencement speech to University of Alaska, transcript of recording by D. C. Foote, Foote Collection, UAF Archives (first two quotations); *Anchorage Daily Times,* June 26, 1959 (third quotation).

18. *Fairbanks Daily News-Miner,* July 24, 1958.

19. Celia Hunter, oral history interview, September 20, 1988, in O'Neill, "Project Chariot," 619, UAF Archives.

20. Rev. Richard Heacock, oral history interview, February 22, 1988, ibid., 730.

21. Rev. William Gordon, telephone interview, December 12, 1993, author's notes.

22. *Jesson's Weekly,* August 18, 1960 (first quotation); *Fairbanks Daily News-Miner,* January 10, 1959 (second quotation); Robert Atwood, oral history interview, February 27, 1989, UAF Archives.

23. Don Charles Foote, "A Human Geographical Study," in Norman J. Wilimovsky and John N. Wolfe, eds., *Environment of the Cape Thompson Region, Alaska* (Oak Ridge, Tenn.: U.S. AEC, 1966).

24. Tape recording made by Keith Lawton of March 14, 1960, meeting at Point Hope, Alaska, UAF Oral History Collection, UAF Archives; see also Don Charles Foote, partial transcript of tape recording of March 14, 1960, meeting at Point Hope, Foote Collection, UAF Archives.

25. AEC, *Project Chariot Phases I-V,* August 1964, B-16 to B-22.

26. Point Hope Village Health Council to John F. Kennedy, March 3, 1969, no. 16872, CIC.

27. "A Statement of Policy and Recommendations Adopted by the Point Barrow Conference on Native Rights, Barrow, Alaska, November 17, 1961," reprinted in *Indian Affairs: Newsletter of the Association of American Indian Affairs,* no. 44, December 1961.

28. Tanana conference: *Fairbanks Daily News-Miner,* June 23, 25, 26, 27, 1962;

Robert D. Arnold, *Alaska Native Land Claims* (Anchorage: Alaska Native Foundation, 1978), 147–48.

29. William O. Pruitt, oral history interview, March 2, 1988, in O'Neill, "Project Chariot," 348, UAF Archives.

30. T. Saunders English, statement read to H. B. Keller and A. V. Shelton, January 9, 1959, President's Papers, UAF Archives.

31. Wolfe to E. Patty, May 5, 1960, President's Papers, UAF Archives (first quotation); John N. Wolfe, "The Ecological Aspects of Project Chariot," *Proceedings of the Second Plowshare Symposium,* May 13–15, 1959, UCRL-5676 (second quotation); Wolfe to J. Philips, March 5, 1962, LLNL (third quotation); quoted in E. Campbell to Wolfe, December 1, 1972, no. 131349, CIC (fourth and fifth quotations).

32. Most comprehensive: Ralph Sanders, *Project Plowshare* (Washington, D.C.: Public Affairs Press, 1962), 79. See also AEC press release, "Plowshare Program Fact Sheet—Project Chariot," revised August 1962, p. 4; John N. Wolfe, "Comments on Biological Aspects of Report by St. Louis Committee for Nuclear Information," attachment to General A. W. Betts to A. R. Luedecke, August 2, 1961, in no. 75525, CIC (quotation); model for EIS: M. L. Merritt and R. G. Fuller, eds., *The Environment of Amchitka Island, Alaska* (Oak Ridge, Tenn.: Energy Research and Development Administration, 1977), iv. See also E. Campbell to J. Kirkwood, March 5, 1970, no. 130821, CIC, in which the "Chariot Environmental Program Plan, July 1959" is transmitted as aid to planning the Amchitka environmental studies required under NEPA.

33. Barry Commoner, *The Closing Circle: Nature, Man, and Technology* (New York: Knopf, 1971), 54; Barry Commoner et al., "Biological Risks from Project Chariot," *Nuclear Information,* June 1961, 12 (quotation).

34. *Jesson's Weekly,* August 18, 1960 (quotation); AEC grants: James W. Hulse, *The University of Nevada: A Centennial History* (Reno: University of Nevada Press, 1974), 142.

35. Albert W. Johnson, "Science, Society and Academic Freedom," undated paper presented to the Association of University Professors, A. W. Johnson Papers; W. R. Wood to C. T. Elvey, August 20, 1962, President's Papers, UAF Archives (first quotation); Wood to Wolfe, February 4, 1963, President's Papers, UAF Archives (second quotation); not in the best interest: Johnson, 6.

36. William B. Stern, "ACLU Probes Pruitt Case," *Polar Star,* October 18, 1963, p. 1.

37. Pruitt, interview (note 29 above), 377.

38. Wilderness Society resolution: reprinted in no. 13811, CIC; *Sierra Club Bulletin,* May 1961; *Nuclear Information,* June 1961; *New York Times,* May 13, 1962, p. 71.

39. Barry Commoner, oral history interview, April 27, 1988, in O'Neill, "Project Chariot," 284, UAF Archives.

40. AEC press release, "Plowshare Program Fact Sheet—Project Chariot," revised August 1962 (first quotation); J. S. Foster to J. S. Kelly, April 27, 1962, LLNL (second and third quotations).

41. Johnson, interview (note 3 above), 222–23.

42. Foster to Kelly, April 27, 1962, LLNL; W. N. Hess et al. to G. W. Johnson, January 5, 1961, LLNL; Foster to Kelly, April 30, 1962, LLNL.

43. John S. Kelly, *Report to the General Manager by the Director, Division of Peaceful Nuclear Explosives,* in AEC 811/104, no. 75574, CIC.

44. Kelly to Foster, received May 18, 1962, LLNL.

45. AEC press release, "Project Chariot Decision Held in Abeyance," August 24, 1962; AEC, "Plowshare Program Fact Sheet—Project Chariot," revised August 1962; AEC press release, "AEC Transfers Chariot Camp to Navy Research Office," April 18, 1963; DOE historian: Benjamin Franklin Cooling, letter to author, November 27, 1989.

46. Teller, commencement speech (see note 17 above).

47. Dan O'Neill to Committee to Nominate Honorary Degree Recipients, May 23, 1992.

Radical Initiatives
and Moderate Alternatives

California's 1976 Nuclear Safeguards Initiative

Thomas Wellock

E dward Teller was furious. With trembling hands and flushed face, the father of the hydrogen bomb confronted two engineers outside a California hearing room. His voice rising, he finally screamed at them, "You are traitors." For Sierra Club lobbyist John Zierold, who witnessed the exchange, it was unnerving to watch a man of Teller's stature come unhinged in public.[1]

No one present needed to be told what the exchange was about. The two engineers had quit their nuclear engineering jobs with General Electric to join a campaign for a 1976 voter initiative to halt nuclear plant operation and construction. As threatening as it sounded, Teller's outburst seemed odd considering the initiative's slim chances of success, for the nuclear industry had already turned public opinion against it.[2] After the 1973 oil embargo, the idea of voters shutting down nuclear plants was considered absurd.

That the engineers' actions might bring down the industry petrified Teller. "Goddamn, I've got to defeat the nuclear initiative," the scientist confessed to a reporter.[3] He was not alone in his fears. Adversaries spat on each other, debate flared into shouting matches, and each side routinely branded its opponents liars. Short tempers abounded in a campaign in which fundamental values were at stake.

Teller, a Hungarian refugee from Nazi Germany, believed that technology in a democratic society could elevate civilization to higher levels of dignity and achievement. Nuclear power would create energy abundance, spread American democracy and civilization, and end the "pollution of poverty." Whatever its flaws, scientists and engineers were best off seeking reform within the system and not through open dissent that could wreck enthusiasm for the "peaceful atom."[4]

The engineers had lost Teller's technological optimism. As children of the Cold War, they feared poverty less than a decline in the quality of their middle-class existence. Technology had not been the magic solution to their generation's concerns. Government and scientific control of nuclear power appeared to threaten democracy, the environment, and world peace. Unlike Teller, they saw their profession as part of the problem, and only open disagreement could solve it.[5]

Coming from within the nuclear community, the engineers' revolt made it easy for a nuclear booster's fears to run wild. The contest had national and international implications for the atom's future. "Proposition 15" made nuclear power an issue in the 1976 presidential elections and inspired six similar ballot measures in other states and Switzerland. Proposition 15's success, industrialists feared, might create an antinuclear domino effect.[6] They breathed easier when Californians rejected Proposition 15 by a two-to-one margin in June. Antinuclear initiatives in the other states lost by similar margins five months later. The American people were not ready to turn their backs on the country's most highly touted energy option. Antinuclear activist David Pesonen surmised, "All their lives, people are told to connect the good life with industrial technology. With progress. We threatened all that, we scared them, and they backed away."[7]

It was a dubious victory for the nuclear industry. More remarkable was the fact that the election had been held at all. A third of the voters wanted to shut down nuclear power, and many more citizens were uneasy about its use. Capitalizing on the public dread of nuclear hazards whipped up by the campaign, antinuclear politicians in the California legislature pushed through three bills expanding the state's power to restrict nuclear plant construction. This achievement, just days before the Proposition 15 vote, provided a modest alternative to the ill-fated initiative.

The central drama of Proposition 15 was the confrontation between the worldview of antinuclear activists and the growth-oriented priorities that had informed socioeconomic policy in the country throughout its history. The dramatic success of the alliance between the federal government and scientific expertise during World War II produced a consensus supporting federal control over a host of policy areas, particularly civilian nuclear power.[8] Nuclear boosters believed that the state needed to promote peaceful uses of atomic power through a policy both controlled by federal administrators, scientists, and sympathetic politicians and insulated from the average citizen. Such insulation was justified because nuclear power was essential for economic growth and social stability.[9] To muster sufficient support to defeat the initiative, pronuclear advocates relied on the time-honored rhetoric of public trust in scientific authority and economic need for nuclear power.

At its root, Proposition 15 was an attempt to infuse society with new values. The postwar period marked America's transition toward markedly different priorities and values. As historian Samuel Hays demonstrated in his study of the modern environmental movement, suburban expansion, greater disposable wealth, education, and the rise of service industries encouraged society to value physical and spiritual amenities whose monetary value was unclear. These "nonmaterial values," as I call them, included greater personal freedom and health, a protected ecosystem, and a pleasing, pollution-free environment. Nonmaterialist values gained a measure of popularity especially among young, well-educated white Americans. When searching for solutions to the harmful effects of modern society, such as pollution, nonmaterialists argued for a return to simpler lifestyles, local amenities, and community power. In the words of Jerry Brown (governor of California, 1975–83), Americans had to accept "a world with limits to its resources and a country with limits to its power and economy."[10]

These values first emerged in changing patterns of consumption and a desire for aesthetic amenities. Outdoor recreation, for example, mushroomed in popularity and increased the demand for parks. As Americans began to fear threats to their health from industrial pollution, pesticides, and radioactive fallout, aesthetics fused with these newer concerns to form the basis for a new environmental movement. Environmentalism provided the seminal ideas and activists for a host of other movements, including antinuclear activism.

As a younger, better educated generation reached maturity by the early 1970s, nuclear opposition expanded beyond environmentalism to encompass a coalition opposed to the centers of authority supporting nuclear power. The Proposition 15 coalition included the left, or progressive, wing of the Democratic Party. They cared more about participatory democracy and personal empowerment than the employment and economic growth issues that historically concerned liberals.[11] Progressives expanded objections to nuclear power from the aesthetics and safety

202

issues favored by moderate environmentalists to a fundamental critique of government, industry, and scientific authority. Unwilling to accept risks imposed on them by scientific elites, peace groups and former New Leftists joined the nuclear opposition to challenge the corporate and federal power structure.[12] For these groups, nuclear power was a symbol of what was wrong with America.

Proposition 15 provided an outlet for Californians troubled by the country's direction following economic, social, and political upheavals of the 1960s and early 1970s. As financially secure as many of them were, California activists perceived a fragile world strewn with perils. In the early 1970s, potentially catastrophic problems of economic and environmental decline, a crisis of authority, and weapons proliferation supplanted much of the middle-class and baby-boomer concern over the Vietnam War and urban conflict. The country, they believed, was headed toward restricted personal freedom, environmental catastrophe, and possibly global conflict. Only new values could alter the nation's direction. Antinuclear activists were not in accord on the degree of social change necessary. Moderate groups like the Sierra Club wanted only greater public sensitivity to the environment. At the other end of the spectrum, millennial religious groups believed that their antinuclear message could transform society and usher in a new age of peace and brotherhood. In between, populists, former New Leftists, and antiwar activists gravitated to nuclear issues to alter public attitudes about corporate power, weapons proliferation, and democratic control of technology.

California offered the opportunity for these activists to advance citizen democracy through a Progressive, and largely Western, political device—the initiative. Little used until the early 1970s, the initiative process allowed them to challenge scientific authority and nuclear regulation by establishing the average citizen as arbiter of the once exclusive debate over the atom. Proposition 15 advocates did not win the campaign or achieve the utopian goals of its most zealous allies, but they raised public doubts about nuclear safety and won nuclear legislation that transferred future regulatory control from the federal government to states and localities.

The legislative victory also followed from the success of antinuclear activists in building upon the California government's historically large role as a regulatory agency in such areas as agriculture, energy, and water resources. Environmental activists allied with a network of Sacramento bureaucrats, politicians, and sympathetic scientists to bring alternative energy ideas into public forums. The antinuclear network used Proposition 15 and state government regulatory capacity to pry concessions from the electric industry and seize a victory from the initiative's defeat. By overcoming the efforts of the utility industry and passing bills that ultimately forbade future reliance on the atom, antinuclear forces achieved a triumph unmatched in any other state.

The Proposition 15 controversy offers a practical lesson in the interest group politics of the 1970s and how new public values are written into law. Antinuclear activists achieved success through the political and bureaucratic resources of a dynamic western state. This fusion of grassroots work, political lobbying, and scientific talent created an atmosphere conducive to new legislation. Although they were seen as such, the nuclear bills were not a cynical maneuver by legislators to prevent a more radical solution from becoming law. Quite the reverse. The initiative acted as an opening wedge to force legislation with new values on the political order. The older pro-growth philosophy had to accommodate nonmaterial values.

TURNING TO STATE SOLUTIONS

The antinuclear movement turned to the states after local interventions and federal lobbying proved generally unsuccessful. Activists took heart in the Atomic Energy Commission's dissolution, the nuclear industry's poor sales, and scattered victories over power plants, but the atom's supporters still won most of the battles. The nuclear proponents were strong enough to prevent further erosion of federal support for nuclear programs. They halted antinuclear attempts to pass legislation such as a construction moratorium, cuts in funding for the experimental breeder reactor, and a repeal of the Price-Anderson Indemnity Act. The latter bill provided special insurance protection to the industry in the event of a serious accident.

Locally, perennial activists such as David Pesonen, a San Francisco attorney, had grown cynical about the possibility of stopping nuclear power. He had led the first successful power plant battle at Bodega Bay, California. But the AEC and its successor, the Nuclear Regulatory Commission (NRC), were making it harder for activists by prohibiting questions, at construction hearings, about government subsidized insurance, generic reactor safety problems, and waste disposal. Pesonen hoped to find some other "political device" to stop the nuclear industry.[13]

In 1973, the leaders of the antinuclear movement convened a summit meeting at the home of MIT physicist Henry Kendall, leader of the Union of Concerned Scientists (UCS). Represented were the key antinuclear groups such as consumer representatives from Ralph Nader's organization, public interest lawyers, environmentalists from Friends of the Earth, and scientists with UCS. Their numbers were small and they knew it. David Comey, an activist from Chicago, joked that they represented the "ruling presidium of the antinuclear cabal." They were a capable bunch, but their past victories would not compensate for the grim prospect of an exploding market for reactors. Jim Harding, leader of the Friends of the Earth's antinuclear activities, thought nuclear power was an "unstoppable industry." Most opponents, he recalled, would have "gladly come to terms with [only] 200 reactors" in the United States.[14]

The gathering decided that the power of the states might be the means of striking at the soft underbelly of federal control. The strategy seemed doomed since earlier attempts to use state power had resulted in judicial defeat. The 1971 *Northern States* decision had declared that federal laws preempted the states' police power when setting safety standards for radioactive hazards. Despite this setback, activists in California hoped to apply state power to other aspects of nuclear construction and operation ignored by the ruling. Pesonen and Richard Spohn, a California Ralph Nader associate, decided to seek antinuclear legislation in Sacramento.[15]

David Pesonen. Merely to utter his name in the presence of a California utility executive would evoke curses and dread. The state's most persistent nuclear foe was back again. In 1964, Pesonen had reduced the Pacific Gas and Electric Company's Bodega Bay excavation for a nuclear complex to a $4 million duck pond. In this antinuclear battle, the young activist displayed the motives and values of the later movement. The Berkeley graduate's objection to nuclear power stemmed from his attraction to New Left thought, especially democratic control of technology. He railed against the power vested in a "small elite corps of nuclear experts" as citizens participated in an "abject worship of technology."[16]

In an emotional moment of conversion while heading to an anti-nuclear meeting in Sonoma County, Pesonen saw that nuclear power was a moral as well as a political issue. "It was a beautiful evening, a touch of fog," Pesonen recalled. The Sonoma landscape evinced a soft mysteriousness, a quality menaced by industrial and nuclear develop-ment. "I had a feeling of the enormousness of what we were fighting; that it was antilife. I had an insight into the mentality of it, I began to see it as the ultimate brutality, short of nuclear weapons."[17] The revela-tion compelled him to fight nuclear power for the next decade.

The utilities might have been relieved when in the mid-1960s Pesonen took a break from hounding them to pursue a Berkeley law degree. But upon graduation as valedictorian, he returned, a more formi-dable opponent, to lead the Sierra Club's opposition to PG&E's ill-fated nuclear project at Point Arena and brought antinuclear litigation against the utility. Environmentalist David Brower noted that Pesonen was the "only man I know of who has two nuclear reactor skulls hanging from his belt."[18] Pesonen would prove he had no intention of resting on his laurels.

Pesonen and Spohn approached state assemblyman and environmen-tal ally Charles Warren in early 1973, hoping to persuade him to include restrictions on nuclear power in his energy conservation legislation. Warren was sympathetic but because antinuclear legislation had no pub-lic or political constituency, he advised the two men to create support by qualifying an antinuclear initiative. An initiative might give Warren a reason to hold hearings, raise awareness, and perhaps even introduce legislative solutions. Pesonen had considered this difficult and expen-sive option as a last resort. But the two activists agreed to navigate the hazardous waters of California's initiative process.[19]

Pesonen's reluctance to pursue an initiative was justified. California is now famous for its ballots replete with citizen-generated initiatives, but this was not always the case. By the 1960s, this Progressive tool had become a device only wealthy interest groups could afford. Gathering qualified signatures was a bureaucratic nightmare. Few groups could raise the large sums of money for a campaign. When initiatives did qualify, voters, often confused and irked by their complexity, struck them down at a rate of four to one.[20] The advantage of pursuing an initiative, however, was that it would draw in peace groups and left-wing populists to antinuclear activism. In the process, these groups would revive the initiative and transform the antinuclear cabal into a movement.

POPULISTS AND PEACE ACTIVISTS JOIN THE MOVEMENT

When it came to popular democracy, Ed Koupal was a latter-day Tom Paine. A disgruntled used-car salesmen, he revolutionized the initiative system by tapping into a growing egalitarian, anti-authoritarian sentiment in the nation. This Ford dealer from Sacramento, feeling that he had been betrayed in a local political matter, began viewing politics as a conspiratorial "web of corruption."[21] Forsaking his career as a salesman, he deserted his home and furniture and moved his family to Los Angeles to be near a population center for signature gathering.[22] Learning from his failures, including an attempt to recall Governor Ronald Reagan, Koupal formed the People's Lobby, which he staffed with young activists, and launched a successful initiative to simplify laws governing the petition process. He used his sales ability to pioneer cheap mass signature gathering methods that became a campaign standard.[23] Without the work of Koupal, an initiative would have been impossible for the antinuclear movement.

In the early 1970s, Koupal's democratic instincts led him to join the nuclear power opposition. His objections were not over science and safety but political power. Proponents used the aura and mystery of nuclear power, he believed, to mask their usurpation of authority. The safety issue, then, was less significant than the right of the people to decide what risks were worth taking.[24] Koupal wanted to use this skepticism of authority to promote the initiative process. "One of the great things about the initiative," he insisted, "is that ordinary citizens can go directly to the people with the great issues of the day, like nuclear power—bypassing the politicians, powerful lobbies, special interest groups, and state legislatures."[25] The People's Lobby placed the Clean Environment Act, Proposition 9, on the June 1972 ballot. The omnibus initiative attacked nearly every conceivable polluter and included a five-year moratorium on nuclear plant construction. A broad coalition of industry opponents waged a successful campaign against a measure they claimed would strangle economic development.[26] Undaunted, Koupal joined the new antinuclear initiative coalition to try again.

Remnants of the sixties antiwar activism spilled over into the initiative through the Another Mother for Peace organization. Formed in 1967 by fifteen Beverly Hills women, including actress Donna Reed, the Mothers for Peace became a national organization with over 230,000 members in 1971.[27] During the period of anti–Vietnam War activism the Mothers showed only passing interest in civilian nuclear issues,[28] but the war movement's decline encouraged them to shift their focus. New members, mostly young mothers, expressed concern for the environmental effects of weapons production and nuclear power on their children.

The Mothers for Peace rejected nuclear power as an immoral energy source. Differing from environmental organizations, the Mothers' history of peace activity steered them to link civilian power and nuclear weapons proliferation and the genetic hazards that radiation posed to children.[29] They promoted a maternal image in the sixties, and they continued to do so in antinuclear campaigns. The organization had begun with the popular slogan, "War is unhealthy for children and other living things." In the seventies they modified "War" to "Radiation" for antinuclear campaigns, and they joined the antinuclear initiative coalition as protectors of children and generations unborn. The addition of Another Mother for Peace broadened the critique of nuclear power to problems of war and humanity.[30]

Activists worked together to form a state coalition called People for Proof, and went to work on an initiative proposal.[31] The authors first had to overcome the notion that moratorium legislation would shut down the entire nuclear industry.[32] Most activists wanted to shut down nuclear power, but they had to balance their own desires with an alternative acceptable to a still pronuclear public. What they needed was a measure ending nuclear power without admitting it. It was somewhat duplicitous, but a frontal assault seemed doomed to failure.[33] A number of sources advised the activists to challenge federal preemption through the state's power to control land use within its borders. To win on these grounds required a narrow view of federal authority.

The final form of the initiative, later called Proposition 15, took shape in early 1974. The measure was designed to halt construction and reduce the operation of existing nuclear plants unless three objectives were met: federally subsidized accident insurance, reactor safety, and waste disposal. The Price-Anderson Act's ceiling on liability in the event of a nuclear accident had to be lifted by Congress or waived by the utility. This stipulation was especially pernicious since it exposed the industry to unlimited damage claims. A second condition required a two-thirds vote by the state legislature declaring that reactor safety systems worked. Finally, there had to be a solution to the waste disposal problem. Otherwise, operating reactors would be phased out by 1987.[34] The act seemed fair by only specifying conditions of operation and not arbitrarily shutting down all reactors. Activists admitted in private that the Price-Anderson waiver in particular could never be met.

With the objective of qualifying the initiative for the November ballot, People for Proof kicked off a campaign in March 1974.[35] Organizers had garnered some impressive allies, including Friends of the Earth (FOE), the Sierra Club, California Public Interest Group, and Another Mother for Peace. With the support of such major organizations, People for Proof appeared to be a serious threat to the nuclear industry.

The conversion to antinuclear activism by the Sierra Club and the more aggressive Friends of the Earth indicated that environmentalists were now united in opposition to nuclear power. Early opposition had come from environmental ranks, but the general movement often favored nuclear energy during the 1960s when their concerns were scenic preservation and pollution; dams and the use of fossil fuels appeared worse threats. But militant environmentalists prodded the movement to focus on the human health hazards that industrialism posed through toxins such as radioactive wastes.[36] In 1974, after years of acrimonious debate on nuclear power, the national board of the Sierra Club took no moral position and offered a pragmatic statement of disapproval only until problems with waste and safety were solved. The leaders of the club's California chapters were more ideologically opposed to nuclear power than the national organization.[37]

Having split with the Sierra Club on nuclear power a few years before, the Friends of the Earth refused to "mistake growth for progress," and stressed a democratic and moral position. FOE attacked the ethics of nuclear waste, control of the industry by big business, the links between nuclear power and weapons, and the prospect of irreversible genetic damage.[38] FOE believed in local control and democratic answers like the initiative. By contrast, the Sierra Club was leery because initiatives had a poor record in being able to withstand court challenges; the organization was more comfortable with legislative dealings and was the most effective environmental lobbyist in Sacramento.[39]

But hopes for this coalition proved unfounded. FOE and Sierra Club leaders in California tried to gather signatures and support, but soon discovered there was no constituency even in their membership. Commitment was high at leadership levels, but below them there was little awareness of nuclear dangers. Without the financial resources for a professional petition drive, there were too few volunteers, mostly drawn from California's counterculture, chasing too many signatures. People for Proof suffered from poor accounting practices, and hippies resisted enforced discipline. There was conflict between northern and southern California wings of the movement. San Francisco area activists, the bulk of the organization, resented what they perceived as poor management by southern leaders.[40]

Internal strife opened the door for Pesonen to take control of the movement. With the signature drive in disarray, some Bay Area volunteers approached him for advice. He had helped launch the initiative, but the demands of his law practice limited his involvement in signature gathering. He convinced activists to scrap the campaign and begin anew with him as leader. Ed Koupal did not go quietly.[41] He wanted to use the California initiative as a platform for his dream of creating a national initiative process. Through a new group called Western Bloc, he aimed to push antinuclear initiatives in other states and thereby create popular support for this democratic tool.[42] Pesonen was more interested in the immediate goal of passing the initiative in California. He was determined to squeeze Koupal out of a leadership role in the new effort. In a carefully arranged meeting in August 1975, Pesonen won election as chairman of a newly named organization, Californians for Nuclear Safeguards (CNS), which absorbed People for Proof. To bring better management to the new effort, CNS hired campaign professionals Robert Jeans and Larry Levine. Operating out of Pesonen's law office basement, Dwight Cocke took over the signature drive.[43]

Even with the quelling of factional disputes and better organization, Californians for Nuclear Safeguards still faced the basic problems of money and personnel. Pesonen secured $5,000 from the Union of Concerned Scientists,[44] but with little else the antinuclear movement was almost certain to fail, again. What Pesonen needed was the impossible: a thousand affluent, idealistic, motivated individuals. Lucky for him, this was California.

CREATIVE INITIATIVE: A MIDDLE-CLASS MILLENNIAL MOVEMENT

Little in Pesonen's years of activism prepared him for the nonprofit Creative Initiative Foundation (CIF). The Palo Alto based group was composed largely of wealthy and middle-class professional couples drawn from the San Francisco Bay area's burgeoning white-collar communities. In December 1974, the leadership of Creative Initiative contacted Californians for Nuclear Safeguards to learn more about their campaign. Having no previous knowledge of Creative Initiative, Pesonen and other CNS leaders found themselves on a stage before a thousand of the best-dressed, most attentive activists they had ever seen. Pesonen was an excellent speaker, but this group required little convincing. The morning presentation ended when Creative Initiative leader James Burch told the members to break for discussion. Those who returned to the auditorium would do so as members of a new political organization to oppose nuclear power. Nearly all returned and made large donations. Burch counted the mound of money and checks and uttered, "twenty thousand dollars."[45] Pesonen and his associates gaped at Burch as the audience burst into applause.

Yet Creative Initiative offered more than money. Pesonen now had at his disposal a staff of lawyers and advertising executives. The women of Creative Initiative provided critical labor to the effort. Although many of them held jobs, the majority did not and were willing to devote a great deal of time to the cause. They were eager to learn Koupal's methods and hit the streets in search of signatures.[46] Thus Pesonen drove home from the meeting with a six-inch stack of checks on the seat beside him, trying to figure out what made Creative Initiative members tick. Their energy was exhilarating, but their complete unity was unnerving. They seemed too naive, he thought, and defeat might crush them. For the moment, however, their optimism wiped away all his fears. He was happier than he had been in months.[47]

Pesonen was not the only individual baffled by Creative Initiative. Their enemies often described them as a "quasi-religious cult." They were not a formal religion, although their philosophy was an eclectic amalgam of world religions. They were not a cult, but they committed themselves to building a strong community culture. Intense encounter sessions built a strong bond and a startling degree of unanimity.

211

Members were like many middle-class Americans who in the late 1960s and 1970s had grown uncomfortable with their lives and experimented with new lifestyles and philosophies.[48] The difference was Creative Initiative's turn to religious millennialism. Elements of the group dated from the 1940s, but CIF's modern form emerged two decades later. In the early 1960s a group of Palo Alto women began discussing their concerns about post–World War II family life and society. They had achieved the ideal of the American way of life, but found it empty and threatening. The Cuban missile crisis left them uneasy about their children's future. They exemplified Betty Friedan's discontented women in *The Feminine Mystique* who found that family life "wasn't enough and wanted greater power to influence society." The group tried to reconcile traditional family expectations with social responsibility, and to balance male and female roles. Their title (Creative representing a traditional feminine quality, Initiative a masculine one) signified their striving for balance.[49] Balance was also the key to their social goals. They believed that America's male-dominated society was too enamored of economic growth and neglected quality-of-life values. A holistic worldview was needed if civilization was to survive.

The women of the organization resolved to lead a millennial movement to a more moral and peaceful world. Specifically, 1975 and 1976, as the International Women's Year and America's bicentennial, they thought, would usher in a "New Order of the Ages" of racial brotherhood and peace.[50] To achieve this transformation, they sought an issue that affected all levels of society. In the wake of the 1973 oil crisis, the most obvious issue was energy. They were drawn to the "small is beautiful" ideas of economist E. F. Schumacher, whose opposition to the "ethical, spiritual, and metaphysical monstrosity" of nuclear power derived from religious roots.[51] Schumacher's advocacy of decentralized and small-scale energy sources pointed the way to a safer and more ethical alternative. By contrast, nuclear power represented to them an apocalyptic threat to the world and was symbolic of humankind's disregard for future generations and limits. To leave a legacy of toxins represented the ultimate crime against humanity. For Creative Initiative, Proposition 15 was the perfect vehicle to a more peaceful age.[52] CIF formed a political action organization, Project Survival, to campaign for the initiative.

The women of Project Survival joined the final signature drive in early 1975 and fanned out over the Bay Area and the state's Central Valley cities. They arrived by the carload to work a city's shopping centers and homes. With Koupal's petition methods, they collected nearly 250,000 signatures. The women capped off their drive with a "Call for Information" for hearings on nuclear power. On May 5, 1975, the initiative qualified for the June 1976 ballot with 400,000 valid signatures.[53] Assemblyman Charles Warren kept his word to Pesonen and announced fall hearings on Proposition 15.

Creative Initiative also moved beyond nuclear power to bring their millennial message to the populace. The educational presentations balanced rational "masculine" arguments with appeals to motherhood, future generations, and predictions of catastrophe. One announcement declared, "We are irreversibly committed to one million deaths from nuclear radiation. . . . We must take immediate action. All other problems of human welfare take second place."[54] The "feminine principle must lead," the women announced, as they launched a colorful parade of four hundred "rainbow women" in Sacramento wearing pantsuits in the colors of the rainbow. In a solemn evening "way of the light" ritual, the "warriors of the rainbow," including a multiracial group of women, accepted a covenant to wage a nonviolent war to inaugurate the new age.[55] Creative Initiative had brought to the antinuclear movement a moral outrage at what male domination had done to society and a desire by women for greater power.

Project Survival saved the Proposition 15 campaign at a price. The group brought vitality to the initiative effort, but other activists did not always greet them with open arms. These well-to-do members envisioned remaking lifestyles in a manner counterculture activists did not. Their odd mix of conservative lifestyle and group discipline alienated other activists, making cooperation difficult. The Palo Alto group also had difficulty conveying their message to the public. Their displays offended many who thought their regimentation anathema, even fascist, to an individualistic society. CNS leadership quickly moved to tone down Project Survival and persuaded the group to pursue more narrow educational efforts in support of Proposition 15.[56] But it remained a persistent problem for the antinuclear campaign to balance practical needs and public image with the more utopian goals of some of its coalition members.

ASSEMBLY HEARINGS AND LEGISLATION:
GROWTH ADVOCATES LOSE THE DEBATE

When the initiative qualified, industry-sponsored opposition made its debut. The nuclear industry could count on groups who believed energy and economic growth were necessary to maintain social stability and trusted scientists and scientific rationality as the means to the common good. It was a traditional coalition of conservatives, business and industry associations, labor organizations, and pro-growth politicians. An impressive list of America's scientists signed on to oppose the measure. Proposition 15, they argued, would shut down safe nuclear power, stifle economic growth, cost the state jobs, impoverish the poor, raise utility rates, pollute the air, and increase dependence on Mideast oil. The jobs-and-growth theme attracted Republicans and New Deal Democrats alike.[57] Former Governor Edmund "Pat" Brown (Jerry Brown's father), long a champion of large government projects, announced he would assume leadership of the opposition: "Let us not forget one key reality: Either we continue to develop our domestic energy sources, or this nation is programmed for economic and eventually social disaster." Despite such posturing, Pat Brown was a politician who knew how to straddle issues. He hinted at some future legislative compromise.[58] In the meantime, the opposition's first task was to prepare for the hearings held by an all too familiar foe, Charles Warren.

The nuclear industry fared poorly during the hearings, and a review of the decade-long conflict over energy policy in California helps explain why.[59] Pesonen's victory at Bodega Bay initiated a series of canceled nuclear projects and resistance by local government bodies. In the 1960s, state resource officials stepped in to overcome obstacles to power-plant construction. State agencies enjoyed a long history of promoting and regulating resources use.[60] But initially they had limited authority, and power-plant siting turned into a war between local groups, environmentalists, and the electric power industry. It was nearly impossible to find an acceptable site for a nuclear plant. The stalemate, however, set a precedent for California regulators to assume a greater role in energy matters. It remained an open question whether pronuclear or antinuclear forces would shape the philosophy behind new state regulation.

In the early 1970s, the utilities made the first move and asked the state to create an agency with broad power to bypass local officials and expedite construction plans. In the utility version, the agency would have no authority to encourage conservation or develop its own estimates of state power needs. Instead, the utilities' calculations of electrical demand would form the basis for long-term planning. The industry lobbied Sacramento lawmakers with graphs and charts depicting exploding electrical demand and predictions of imminent blackouts.

There was a time when utilities could expect the understaffed and part-time state legislature to do what they asked simply out of ignorance, but by the 1970s the California legislature had changed dramatically. Full-time, professional lawmakers had the resources to create their own options. Reform legislation expanded committee staffs to allow for independent evaluation of legislative proposals. As a result, one citizen committee ranked the California legislature the best in the country. With this new level of independence, legislators refused to take the utility estimates at face value. Democratic assembly speaker Robert Moretti tasked land-use-committee aide Emilio "Gene" Varanini with looking deeper into the energy issue. Varanini's experience as a naval academy graduate, training as a general staff officer, and service with the CIA left him ideally suited to integrate technical expertise, policy, and politics. He recognized that information was power and that he needed expertise to challenge the utilities. With a Ford Foundation grant, he enlisted the Rand Corporation to study California's energy future.[61]

The results were an environmentalist's dream. Rand published its work in 1972 in the devastating *California's Electricity Quandary* report. Researchers considered utility needs through the end of the century and estimated that California would need a 1,200 megawatt power plant along its beautiful coast *every eight miles.* "This rate of growth cannot continue," the study warned, "for it would theoretically outstrip the ability of society to finance, build, and even find room for the generating facilities—to say nothing of supplying them with fuel nor of their impact on the environment." As for nuclear power, Rand dismissed the "headlong rush" to construction as unwarranted in the face of emerging safety and environmental problems. Limiting demand was the most rational solution.[62]

The Sierra Club played a central role in the tone of the Rand study. An environmental consciousness among the Rand authors appears to have influenced the results. Two of the principal authors, Richard Ball and Ron Doctor, were active Sierra Club members. Doctor was, as one observer remembers, "violently opposed" to nuclear power and active in the antinuclear movement.[63] In these and later instances, environmental groups influenced energy policy through experts who shared their values.[64] The Rand study was the first serious challenge by environmentalists and their experts to the utility industry's vision of a future with no energy limits. The report was the opening wedge for the state to gain control over energy planning and for environmentalist values to filter into policy debate.[65]

The study's most important convert was Charles Warren. A relative novice on environmental issues, Warren chaired the land-use subcommittee hearings on the Rand report.[66] By the end of the six days of testimony, Warren later admitted, "My life was changed."[67] He was stirred by the testimony of the Union of Concerned Scientists' representatives Henry Kendall and Daniel Ford. The Los Angeles assemblyman quickly established a friendship and alliance with Kendall. Warren's conversion excited Kendall, for the legislator was in a position to expedite substantial energy legislation. Convinced that the utilities' pro-growth "demand accommodation" philosophy was a prescription for disaster, Warren immersed himself in creating legislation to limit energy growth and nuclear power.[68]

But Warren had to hide his antinuclear intentions. Ronald Reagan was the governor in 1973, and an avid fan of the peaceful atom (he left office after 1974). Warren presented a bill to the governor that, he explained, was not antinuclear but aimed at rational management to reduce power plant construction. Warren knew, however, that he could attack nuclear power with his bill, since most utility construction projects were nuclear plants anyway. But Reagan bowed to utility pressure and vetoed the measure in early October 1973.[69]

Events, however, soon revived the fortunes of the energy bill. The Arab oil embargo of October 1973 alerted the nation and Californians to the need for an energy policy. Governor Reagan similarly realized the need, and his aides turned to Warren to revise the vetoed bill.[70] Warren's legislation gave the utilities an energy commission, and in return the state wrested responsibility from the industry to manage energy demand.[71]

The Warren legislation worked nonmaterial values favoring limited growth into the state's legislative framework. To slow the nuclear juggernaut, the assemblyman included sections on resource conservation and research for alternative power sources. With the right leadership, the

California Energy Commission could force electric companies to pursue slow-growth policies and stop building power plants. Moreover, Warren's legislation provided a framework to regulate nuclear power (later nuclear legislation was incorporated into the act). He bided his time for a chance like Proposition 15 to expand state control of nuclear power again.[72] At the initiative hearings, Warren's antinuclear vision and Varanini's technical staff enabled the energy committee to do more than passively listen to the pros and cons of nuclear power; it could formulate its own solutions.

The hearings on Proposition 15 opened in October 1975 with anticipation by activists and dread by the nuclear industry. This was the first public forum devoted to raising awareness of nuclear power issues. The "specter of a nuclear moratorium" had haunted the industry for some time. The fifteen days of hearings took on a life-or-death importance as both sides rushed in "platoons of goons," as Varanini remembered. Publicly, Warren claimed he would not introduce legislation from the hearings and would only create a voter's guide.[73] Industry organizations considered the legislators to be "obviously biased against nuclear power, and . . . sure to make this known, officially or unofficially." Industry officials grumbled that the legislators had "ganged up" on pronuclear witnesses in an "inquisition in which industry is presumed to be guilty."[74]

Analysts, however, faulted the industry for failing to win the hearings debate.[75] Industry spokespersons could not clearly refute the antinuclear witnesses' accusations about poor nuclear safety. What were the assemblymen to think when Edward Teller championed nuclear power despite his misgivings about nuclear power safety? And Nobel Prize–winning physicist Hans Bethe, when asked if the Emergency Core Cooling System was adequate, remarked: "I do not know, and the people who know much more about it . . . do not know either. [But these experts have] the feeling that it will work. The best you can do is to rely on the feelings of people who have studied it."[76] Some listening to this were stunned. "My God!—they really don't have the answers, do they?" one woman in the room blurted out.[77]

Industry witnesses did convince the committee that Proposition 15 was poorly written; its two-thirds majority vote requirement in the legislature was too harsh; it would have severe economic consequences; and it would shut down nuclear power.[78] They could not show that reactor safety and waste disposal problems were well in hand. For every industry expert to testify, antinuclear activists presented one of their own. "After listening to 120 learned witnesses who could not agree on the merits of the Initiative or the safety of nuclear power," the committee concluded, "it is clear that no objective conclusion *can* be drawn."[79] Initially, committee members were uncommitted. By the end of the hearings, nearly all considered the initiative defective, but they opposed unregulated nuclear power.[80] The hearings neutralized pronuclear expertise and provided a justification for state regulation.

In January 1976, the Warren committee members filled this power vacuum with legislation free of the "harsh" provisions and "procedural problems" of the radical nuclear initiative.[81] The four bills restricted the construction of new nuclear plants but exempted those under construction. Two of the bills forbade new construction until the Nuclear Regulatory Commission found facilities for fuel reprocessing and waste disposal. A third bill prohibited construction for one year while a study looked into Teller's recommendation for burying nuclear power plants. A final bill, which did not survive, required power plant operators to waive the Price-Anderson exemption and assume full liability for any accident. The energy commission established under Warren's 1974 legislation would determine whether the NRC and the industry had met the conditions of the bills. The legislature would approve the commission's findings by a simple majority.

The new moderate legislation posed a dilemma for the nuclear industry and a lesser one for initiative supporters. The Proposition 15 forces feared that the Warren legislation could end all chances for the initiative. Nonetheless, CNS recognized the bills as substantive legislation and that passage would represent a victory. CNS decided it could pursue both a radical and a moderate solution. "I think it's courageous of this committee to venture into this area," Pesonen declared in what became their standard response, "but it certainly isn't going to dampen our efforts to campaign for the initiative." A few activists claimed they always intended the initiative be a radical, provocative way to force the state legislature to act. Most eventually came to a fatalistic understanding of this strategy and accepted it.[82]

Pronuclear forces opposed Proposition 15 because the initiative was extreme in eliminating the nuclear option at a time when the nation needed every energy source it could find. But if they were to use their influence to halt the bills, then Warren's committee and Governor Jerry Brown, who at the time was heating up for a presidential bid, would actively support Proposition 15. The pronuclear forces therefore decided to keep the bills alive and negotiate changes.[83] Throughout the spring, Warren and environmental lobbyists played on industry fears about Proposition 15 to win concessions. Meanwhile, antinuclear activists had a surprise that scared the wits out of the nuclear industry.

LOSING FAITH

Project Survival provided the most sensational story of the campaign, and one that best exemplified the clash of old and new values. General Electric nuclear engineers within Creative Initiative had been discussing how the morality of nuclear energy fit into their worldview. They had once dreamed of bringing a cheap, limitless source of energy to the nation. Now three of them saw great trouble in the long-term dangers of the nuclear fuel cycle and reactor safety. Could they work for an industry that posed strong intergenerational risks? What could they do about the threat of sabotage and nuclear proliferation? If they stayed with GE, could they help eliminate the risk to reactor safety posed by human error? Dale Bridenbaugh, Gregory Minor, and Richard Hubbard concluded that they could not. They would leave the industry. On February 2, 1976, these engineering managers, each the father of three, exited the gates of GE's San Jose plant for the last time. They distributed copies of their resignations to the *San Francisco Chronicle,* the *New York Times,* and the *Los Angles Times.* Nuclear power was a "technological monster," they told the press. "The issue we face is not the survival of an industry, rather it is the survival of mankind."[84]

These resignations altered the context of the debate over nuclear power. Activists had other scientific support, but now they could boast of endorsements directly from the nuclear industry. Moreover, by forsaking their careers for principle, these men had unimpeachable motives. The engineers' decision roiled the nuclear industry well out of proportion to the accusations leveled as rumors spread of other defections. Despite fears that they would tell "where the bodies are buried," the trio offered no damaging information to the Joint Committee on Atomic Energy (JCAE). Their objections centered on what degree of risk was acceptable, possible human error, and a philosophical rejection of a technology that left its problems to be solved by a generation unborn. What made their stand so unnerving was that they had been members of the faith, the nuclear family.[85] How were the true believers to explain this apostasy?

As Edward Teller had done, the atom's defenders branded the men traitors and irrational. Within weeks, the shaken nuclear industry counterattacked by focusing attention on the three engineers' affiliation with Creative Initiative. Not everyone thought the group enchanting. Many found its close-knit structure and intimacy invasive and intimidating. Former members claimed Creative Initiative insisted on a "party line."[86] Others called CIF a cultlike "force for robbing men and women of their individuality and turning them into willing slaves of the leaders of the group." Pronuclear advocates such as Congressmen Mike McCormack claimed the three engineers were "pressured" by CIF in an "orchestrated ploy." He pronounced a decree of excommunication on the three men: "In two years they'll be totally forgotten by the public, frozen out of the industry, and of no further use to the people who exploited them. They'll be dead." McCormack's hyperbole contained an element of truth. Creative Initiative was hamstrung in refuting cult labels because there *was* strong peer pressure. "We were hard on each other. And I think we overstepped boundaries," one member later admitted.[87]

The engineers' public resignation proved to be a tactical mistake, as the focus shifted from educating the public about nuclear power to arguing ideology and motivations. As the campaign dragged on into the spring, debate degenerated into shouting matches, name-calling, and wild exaggerations of the opposition's position. In the battle of ideologies, CNS's message was at a disadvantage. Nonmaterialism had a distinct following, but the growth ethic spoke to a wide audience. As the country struggled with economic malaise, it was hard for the antinuclear movement to avoid charges of elitism.[88] Pronuclear forces devised their own version of the "people versus elites" theme by portraying the "neo-religious, radical environmentalists" as a "privileged few" willing to let the average citizen freeze in the dark and caring little for blue-collar workers who would lose their jobs if nuclear plants closed.[89] There was some truth to this charge, since antinuclear activists and general supporters of Proposition 15 tended to be younger and more educated than the typical "no" voter.[90]

Instead of defending specific attacks on nuclear safety, a debate the

Warren hearings proved was unwinnable, the "No on 15" campaign focused on economics. Proposition 15 became a draconian "shutdown initiative" that would cost the state jobs, and the average homeowner thousands of dollars in higher electric bills. Still smarting from the shocks of the recent economic downturn and rising fuel prices, most Americans were concerned about their immediate problems. For the average citizen, protecting future generations and a "small is beautiful" message paled before protection of America's energy supply.[91] By the time of the balloting, pronuclear forces gloated that they had thousands of people, journalists, and organizations chorusing: "It's too drastic. It's a shutdown." The American people refused to follow the three engineers in a revolt against nuclear technology. It was a "masterful campaign," CNS media coordinator Larry Levine admitted.[92]

The disparate groups forming CNS failed to speak with the same unity as their opposition. Scientific authority still carried ample influence among voters, and CNS worked hard for scientific endorsements. They had achieved some notable success in gaining the backing of the American Federation of Scientists, the three GE engineers, and Nobel Prize winners Linus Pauling and Harold Urey. But through this authoritative facade surfaced populist, counterculture, and emotional pleas that appealed mostly to the converted. An undecided voter was sure to find the pronuclear message that "California Scientists Urge No on 15" more convincing than "Why the Doobie Brothers Want You to Vote Yes on Proposition 15." For similar reasons, CNS's switch in advertising strategy had little influence on opinion. CNS ran photos of children in emotional ads emphasizing nuclear power's long-term hazards. They also contrasted corporate support of the "No on 15" campaign with their more populist effort.[93] Voters considered these arguments distractions to a more specific debate over the wisdom of the initiative. In a slow and steady progression, support for the initiative slipped.[94]

SEIZING A VICTORY AND EXPANDING STATE POWER

But the industry strategy of portraying the initiative as extreme left a gap for Charles Warren and the Sierra Club lobbyists to push the nuclear bills through the legislature. While PG&E and other electric companies dragged their feet, Southern California Edison openly supported the bills and offered to work with Warren's committee to insert compromise language.[95] Assembly speaker Leo McCarthey, Charles Warren, and the Sierra Club's gifted lobbyist John Zierold worked in a bruising battle to keep the bills alive. The utilities agreed reluctantly to remain neutral on the legislation while Warren, McCarthey, and Governor Brown took a similar position on Proposition 15.[96] With sufficient compromises to pacify the utilities, opposition leadership shifted to Democratic Senator Ralph Dills for the floor fight. At the top of his lungs, Dills attacked the "no-growth" philosophy of the bills as so much "gobbledegoo." "Let's do something manly for once," he exhorted his colleagues, "and turn this baby down." The lawmakers ignored this hairy-chested oratory, and the three bills passed the legislature. Governor Brown signed them into law on June 3, 1976, just days before the balloting on Proposition 15. "This kills the initiative," crowed Proposition 15 opponent Lieutenant Governor Mervyn Dymally.[97]

Why did the utilities accept the compromise? Unlike Warren's 1974 energy legislation, these bills offered the utilities nothing to compensate for their concessions. The utilities, observers believed, had the influence to stop the bills. By April, moreover, opinion polls showed majorities against Proposition 15. By June a large no vote was certain. Support by Brown and others was unlikely to rescue the initiative. The nuclear industry could have had it all—a defeat of both Proposition 15 and the nuclear bills.

The industry believed the future of the atom was at stake. The energy crisis, nonexistent orders for nuclear plants, and the burgeoning antinuclear movement had eroded industry optimism. A half dozen antinuclear initiatives in other states awaited utilities in November, and they needed to win them all. Antinuclear elements were planning to move to nonviolent, direct-action tactics against nuclear plants. A close victory was insufficient to stem this tide. The industry wanted a win, a big one.[98]

The voters gave the nuclear industry its wish in the June 8 primary, striking down Proposition 15 by a two-to-one margin. Industry lobbyist and former congressman Craig Hosmer exulted: "We have broken the back of the opponents—that vast collection of food faddists, perennial bitchers, deep-breathers, nature lovers and anti-establishment counterculturists who came together in California"; and *Time* called the vote a "go-ahead" for nuclear power.[99] In one sense, these views were correct. Polling indicated that citizens thought nuclear power was necessary in scarce times and opposed shutting it down.[100] Activists' grand dream of a national moratorium was dead. The public still believed in the atom as a savior of the nation's energy future.

But the large margin of defeat masked just how much progress the antinuclear movement had made with public opinion. A third of the voters were now committed to shutting down nuclear power regardless of electric supply. The significance of this fact was not lost on David Pesonen, who told reporters, "A million and a half people were willing to vote to shut down nuclear power. Those people are firm and will not go away." Even those who voted against Proposition 15 were wary of a pronuclear energy policy. Majorities believed the nation was better off investing in alternative energy sources and conservation, even at a risk to living standards.[101] The "shutdown" theme of the pronuclear campaign made the ballot an inaccurate gauge of public concern for nuclear safety and waste disposal. The large no vote represented a desire to protect basic energy supplies and a rejection of a radical proposal.[102] A more moderate initiative might have changed the results. By demanding safety in a benign way, the nuclear bills were a closer approximation of public sentiment.

Charles Warren's legislation was a state's rights rebel yell against the federal government's control of the peacetime atom. Richard Maullin, chairman of the California Energy Commission, described the new authority vested in his commission as a "new facet of energy federalism. We will be holding the federal government to the test."[103] In 1978, the Energy Commission used the nuclear bills to halt the Sundesert Nuclear Project in southern California and institute a moratorium on further nuclear construction plans.

The courts were the only possible industry refuge. Legal opinion assumed the initiatives and even Warren's legislation would fall before federal preemption. Nuclear industry lawyers asked the courts to take a broad interpretation of federal powers under the Atomic Energy Act of 1954. They asked the justices to declare that the real motive behind state laws was to regulate reactor safety, not land use.[104] The lawyers were right, of course, but Gene Varanini wrote the final Warren committee report on Proposition 15 knowing the document would be the focal point of any legal challenge. He took a wide berth around the safety issue and justified California's regulation of nuclear power as an economic necessity. State regulation of nuclear construction was essential,

Varanini wrote, because waste disposal problems were "largely economic or the result of poor planning, not safety-related." In 1983, the Burger Court, in their unanimous landmark decision, accepted Varanini's arguments at face value, concluding that "inquiry into legislative motive is often an unsatisfactory venture." This decision paved the way for other states to follow California's lead and adopt similar legislation.[105]

Antinuclear moderates could take heart that they had helped pass legislation and raised attention and wrecked nuclear power's future in California. Public awareness of nuclear safety issues had skyrocketed to nearly 95 percent.[106] In the future, voter initiatives would be far easier for antinuclear activists to wage. It was finally respectable to question America's commitment to nuclear power.[107]

These and earlier successes by California activists are at odds with the conclusions of recent scholars. They contend that the antinuclear movement had minimal influence, and that economic considerations were the prime reasons for the industry's demise.[108] There is little doubt that economics played a crucial role. But generalizations of national trends do little to explain the importance of what was largely a local movement. Time and again, California activists proved they were the best in the nation at defeating nuclear power. Their success did not depend on economic arguments, but on the state's political and cultural resources.[109]

The direction, however, was shifting away from moderate elements who had provided the movement with its victories. The coalition that came together for Proposition 15 drifted apart as the nuclear industry declined. Peace groups and Creative Initiative moved on to weapons issues in the early 1980s. Populist elements within the movement had strengthened the initiative process, but the national initiative envisioned by Ed Koupal faded with his death in March 1976 and with the defeats of the other state nuclear initiatives. Nuclear power would not be the means to popular democracy or social transformation. The movement shifted to those promoting a radical approach. "We're feeling very disillusioned about the legal and legislative channels for stopping nuclear power," one California activist pointed out. "Our new method is disciplined, nonviolent direct action."[110]

But what of the pronuclear idealists? Those apostles had lost much in this fight. They could only watch with alarm as the nation's commitment to their worldview and the respect accorded them, once almost mystical, weakened. What solace could they take in this muddled com-

224

promise? There was little for an individual to do but lash out at enemies. When Edward Teller branded the former GE engineers traitors, it was to a vision of the nation that fewer individuals were sharing. The best label for that vision is the American Dream. To Teller and many Americans, the dream still meant economic growth, confidence, and a way of life without limits.[111] Because the energy crisis demonstrated the risks associated with fossil fuels, nuclear power appeared to them the only way to save the dream. But the California initiative indicated that Americans were less sure of the old values. Room for new ones had to be found.

NOTES

1. John Zierold, interview by author, June 23, 1992, telephone tape recording; and anonymous source, telephone interview by author, June 8, 1993, handwritten notes.

2. William L. Rankin, Stanley M. Nealey, and Barbara D. Melber, "Overview of National Attitudes Toward Nuclear Energy: A Longitudinal Analysis," in *Public Reaction to Nuclear Power: Are There Critical Masses?*, ed. William R. Freudenburg and Eugene A. Rosa (Boulder: Westview Press, 1984), 41–68.

3. *Telegram-Tribune* (San Luis Obispo), October 20, 1975.

4. *Telegram-Tribune*, October 18, 1975, 1 (quotation). Edward Teller, *Energy from Heaven and Earth* (San Francisco: W. H. Freeman, 1979), 155, 158–67, 310–12.

5. The link between ideology and scientists has been described in Stanley Rothman and S. Robert Lichter, "Elite Ideology and Risk Perception in Nuclear Energy Policy," *American Political Science Review* 81 (1987): 396–97.

6. *Nucleonics Week,* 17 (May 6, 1976): 7, and 17 (May 27, 1976): 2.

7. *Los Angeles Times* (hereafter *LAT*), June 10, 1976, 1.

8. Brian Balogh, *Chain Reaction: Expert Debate and Public Participation in American Commercial Nuclear Power, 1945–75* (Cambridge: Cambridge University Press, 1991).

9. Steven Del Sesto has described the nuclear power controversy as a contest between two worldviews. See Steven L. Del Sesto, *Science, Politics, and Controversy: Civilian Nuclear Power in the United States, 1946–1974* (Boulder: Westview Press, 1979), 181–208.

10. On the postwar shift generally, see William H. Chafe, *The Unfinished Journey: America Since World War II* (New York: Oxford University Press, 1986). See Samuel P. Hays, *Beauty, Health, and Permanence: Environmental Politics in the United States, 1955–1985* (Cambridge: Cambridge University Press, 1987), 1–39, 490, 527–

43. Other scholars have more generally demonstrated Hays's thesis for the United States and most Western nations: Ronald Inglehart, *The Silent Revolution: Changing Values and Political Styles Among Western Publics* (Princeton: Princeton University Press, 1977); Inglehart, *Culture Shift in Advanced Industrial Society* (Princeton: Princeton University Press, 1990); and Daniel Yankelovich, *New Rules, Searching for Self-fulfillment in a World Turned Upside Down* (New York: Random House, 1981; Bantam Books, 1982). Jerry Brown quoted in Peter N. Carroll, *It Seemed Like Nothing Happened* (New York: Holt, Rinehart, and Winston, 1982), 323.

11. Progressivism has become a popular term, especially among San Francisco politicians, to describe what is usually thought of as the "liberal" wing of today's Democratic Party. I prefer "progressive" to "liberal" since the meaning of the latter term was undergoing significant changes in the 1960s and 1970s. Liberal is particularly confusing for this story because avid supporters of nuclear power, such as Edmund "Pat" Brown (governor of California, 1959–67), considered themselves liberal in the older sense of the term. Previously, the liberal coalition included pro-growth politicians, labor unions, and business elites that supported development projects, but these groups rarely opposed nuclear power.

12. The link between nonmaterialist values and intolerance for involuntary risk is detailed by Mary Douglas and Aaron Wildavsky. These new values encouraged a suspicion of authority and involuntary risks, such as nuclear power, imposed by institutions. Only voluntarily assumed hazards are acceptable. The public must therefore have a voice in assuming all risks. See Mary Douglas and Aaron Wildavsky, *Risk and Culture: An Essay on the Selection of Technological and Environmental Dangers* (Berkeley: University of California Press, 1982), 158–60. See also Michael Thompson, Richard Ellis, and Aaron Wildavsky, *Cultural Theory* (Boulder: Westview Press, 1990).

13. Quoted in William J. Lanouette, "The Nuclear Power Issue," *Commonweal* 103 (July 30, 1976): 489, and Gene [Coan] to Mike [McCloskey], May 15, 1974, Sierra Club Records, Bancroft Library, University of California, Berkeley, carton 191.

14. Jim Harding, interview by author, El Cerrito, California, January 1, 1994, tape recording.

15. *Northern States Power Co. v. Minnesota*, 447 F. 2d (8th Cir. 1971). David Pesonen, interview by Ann Lage, rough draft of transcript, used by permission. This idea eventually evolved into the goal of using California and possibly other state initiatives to force the passage of national moratorium legislation by the time of America's bicentennial. See "Summary of Organizational Meeting of October 26–7, 1974," Sierra Club Records, carton 119.

16. Pesonen to Edgar Wayburn, September 26, 1963, Sierra Club, San Francisco Bay Chapter Records, Bancroft Library, carton 30. The fight over the Bodega reactor is chronicled in: J. Samuel Walker, "Reactor at the Fault: The Bodega Bay

Nuclear Plant Controversy, 1958–1964: A Case Study in the Politics of Technology," *Pacific Historical Review* 59 (1990): 323–48; Thomas Wellock, "The Battle for Bodega Bay: The Sierra Club and Nuclear Power, 1958–64," *California History* 71 (Summer 1992): 192–211, 289–91; and Balogh, *Chain Reaction,* 240–58.

17. Quoted in Sheldon Novick, *The Electric Wars: The Fight over Nuclear Power* (San Francisco: Sierra Club Books, 1976), 241.

18. Friends of the Earth, *Not Man Apart,* July 1973, p. 9.

19. Charles Warren, interview by the author, Sacramento, July 2, 1992, tape recording; and Pesonen, interview.

20. "Initiative Makes a Big Comeback as Groups Seek to Bypass Legislature," *California Journal* 3 (August 1972): 229–30.

21. For a discussion of the importance of Ed Koupal to the modern initiative process, see David D. Schmidt, *Citizen Lawmakers: The Ballot Initiative Revolution* (Philadelphia: Temple University Press, 1989), chap. 3; quotation, 42.

22. Diane Koupal-Hyde, interview by author, Santa Rosa, California, June 7, 1992, tape recording.

23. One of Koupal's star pupils was Howard Jarvis, who would lead California's Proposition 13 tax revolt. Koupal's methods are best described in People's Lobby, *National Initiative and Vote of Confidence (Recall): Tools for Self-Government* (Los Angeles: People's Lobby Press, 1977); and Schmidt, *Citizen Lawmakers,* chap. 9.

24. Koupal believed a "nuclear web" of conspiracy existed to thwart citizen efforts to control the atom. People's Lobby even drew a picture of this web, illustrating the ties of influence that politicians had with the nuclear industry. Koupal thought this web was a chance creation "by the circumstances of finances and employment, and in some cases, marital and nepotistic ties." Because of these links, elected officials become "contemptuous of voters and disdainful of the public at large." *People's Lobby Newsletter,* November-December 1975; and quoted in Jerome Price, *The Antinuclear Movement* (Boston: Twayne Publishers, 1982), 101.

An example of the inability of some pronuclear spokesmen to understand the motivations of the opposition occurred when scientist Hans Bethe, in a public lecture, favorably compared nuclear power hazards to automobile deaths. A woman in the audience responded, "But we choose, we the people choose, to drive automobiles, and we choose not to have nuclear power!" See "Hans Bethe Recounts Some Frustrations as a Nuclear Spokesman," *Nuclear Industry* 22 (November 1975): 20. See also Spencer Weart, *Nuclear Fear: A History of Images* (Cambridge: Harvard University Press, 1988), 339–43; and Douglas and Widalsky, *Risk and Culture,* 126–51.

25. Quoted in McKinley C. Olsen, *Unacceptable Risk: The Nuclear Power Controversy* (New York: Bantam Books, 1976), 12; and *San Francisco Chronicle* (hereafter *SFC*), April 7, 1975, p. 9.

26. Schmidt, *Citizen Lawmakers,* 51; Richard Spohn to Ralph Nader, July 4,

1974, Union of Concerned Scientists Archives, Massachusetts Institute of Technology, Institute Archives and Special Collections, carton 33 (hereafter UCS Archives).

27. See untitled description of the group dated October 11, 1972; Another Mother for Peace, "Look What We Did Together in 1970–71," July 1971; and "Look What We Did Together in 1971–72," July 1972, Another Mother for Peace Records, Swarthmore College Peace Collection, Swarthmore, Pennsylvania, box 1 (hereafter AMP Records).

28. Dorothy B. Jones to Elizabeth [Hogan], March 23, 1970, AMP Records, box 3.

29. See correspondence between Dorothy Jones, John Gofman, and Elizabeth Hogan from 1970 to 1973 in AMP Records, box 3; and AMP, "The Nuclear Presence in Los Angeles County," in March 1976, AMP Records, box 1.

30. AMP, "Another Mother for Peace Newsletter," December 1972, and Winter 1974, AMP Records, box 1.

31. Pesonen, interview; Ilene Lengyel to Friends, April 3, 1973, UCS Archives, carton 33; and Alvin Duskin, interview by Yuko Hirabayashi, San Francisco, June 16, 1992, tape recording.

32. The idea of a moratorium was popular for some years in antinuclear circles. The citizens of Eugene, Oregon, enacted a four-year ban on construction in 1970. This victory inspired some national activists like John Gofman, and some efforts were made in 1972 to pass moratorium measures. The general assessment was that "moratorium" was too closely associated with Vietnam peace campaigns. See Olsen, *Unacceptable Risk,* 13; Daniel Pope, " 'We Can Wait. We Should Wait.' Eugene's Nuclear Power Controversy, 1968–1970," *Pacific Historical Review* 59 (August 1990): 349–73; John W. Gofman and Arthur R. Tamplin, *Poisoned Power: The Case Against Nuclear Power Plants* (Emmaus, Penn.: Rodale Press, 1971), 227–42; Rich Sextro to Lowell Smith and Sid Moglewer, December 22, 1973, Richard Sextro personal files.

33. Handwritten notes, "Moratorium Group Meeting," December 2, 1973, UCS Archives, carton 33; Pesonen, interview; and Larry Levine, interview by author, June 24, 1992, telephone tape recording.

34. The best explanation of the mechanics of Proposition 15 is John H. Barton and Charles J. Meyers, "The Legal and Political Effects of the California Nuclear Initiative," in *The California Nuclear Initiative: Analysis and Discussion of the Issues,* ed. W. C. Reynolds (Stanford: Institute for Energy Studies, Stanford University, April 1976), 1–36.

35. *LAT,* March 12, 1974, sec. 2, p. 1.

36. Hays, *Beauty, Health, and Permanence,* 173, 205.

37. "Club Board Adopts New Policies: Nuclear Power, Oil Shale, Energy," *Sierra Club Bulletin* 59 (February 1974): 15. For a discussion of the Sierra Club's evolution on nuclear policy, see Brock Evans, "Sierra Club Involvement in

Nuclear Power: An Evolution of Awareness," *Oregon Law Review* 54 (1975): 607–21.

38. Hugh Nash, ed., *Progress As If Survival Mattered* (San Francisco: Friends of the Earth, 1977), 7–10, 25–62. See also, "15 Reasons to Vote Yes on 15," *Not Man Apart,* June and Mid-June 1976; Novick, *Electric Wars,* 184–95; Egan O'Connor, "Moratorium Politics," *Not Man Apart,* May 1973, 10–11; Eugene Coan et al., "Nuclear Power and the Sierra Club," November 1977, pamphlet.

39. The Sierra Club's national position on nuclear power was more conservative than that of the local California chapter leadership. California activists, especially in the San Francisco and Los Angeles areas, moved to endorse the initiative very early in 1974, while the national board of directors would not do so until 1976. Richard Sextro, interview by author, June 17, 1992, Berkeley, tape recording; Ted Trzyna to SCRCC Members, January 18, 1974, Sierra Club Records, carton 191; Rich Sextro, personal files; and Joseph Fontaine and Phillip Berry, "Nuclear Safety Initiative," *Sierra Club Bulletin* 61 (March 1976): 21–22.

40. Gene [Coan] to Mike [McCloskey], May 15, 1974, Sierra Club Records, carton 191; Richard Sextro, interview; and Spohn to Nader, UCS Archives, carton 33; Dwight Cocke, interview by author, San Francisco, July 21, 1992, tape recording; Schmidt, *Citizen Lawmakers,* 51; and Pesonen, interview.

41. Duskin, Cocke, and Pesonen, interviews.

42. Schmidt, *Citizen Lawmakers,* 59; "Citizens Organize Western Bloc," *Critical Mass* 1 (August 1975): 1, 4; and Laura Tallian, *Direct Democracy: An Historical Analysis of the Initiative, Referendum and Recall Process* (Los Angeles: People's Lobby Press, 1977), 111–19.

43. "Minutes of Steering Committee Meeting," August 23, 1975, September 21, 1975, and October 25, 1975, Rich Sextro personal files; Pesonen and Cocke, interviews.

44. Rob Duboff to all participants of Organizational Meeting of October 26–27, November 1, 1974, Sierra Club Records, carton 119; and Pesonen, interview.

45. Pesonen, interview; James Burch, interview by author, Palo Alto, June 17, 1992, tape recording; Wileta Burch, Beverley Sorensen, Jane Kroll, and Fredricka McGlashan, interview by author, Palo Alto, July 1, 1992, tape recording (hereafter Creative Initiative, interview); and Cocke, interview.

46. Sheldon Novick, *Electric Wars,* 242–49; Pesonen, Burch, Creative Initiative, and Cocke, interviews.

47. Pesonen, interview.

48. For a discussion of the shifting cultural patterns in the 1970s, see Yankelovich, *New Rules;* and Inglehart, *Silent Revolution.*

49. Creative Initiative, interview. For a detailed history of Creative Initiative, see Steven M. Gelber and Martin L. Cook, *Saving the Earth: The History of a Middle-Class Millenarian Movement* (Berkeley: University of California Press, 1990).

50. Creative Initiative program, "The Time Is Now"; attached to Paul C. Valentine to J. Anthony Kline, May 13, 1975, Governor Edmund G. Brown, Jr. Papers, Doheny Memorial Library Department of Special Collections, University of Southern California Archives, Los Angeles, carton E-26-10 (hereafter Brown Papers).

51. E. F. Schumacher, *Small Is Beautiful: Economics As If People Mattered* (New York: Harper and Row, 1973), 145.

52. Creative Initiative and Burch, interviews; and Novick, *Electric War,* 242–49; "The Time Is Now."

53. *LAT,* May 6, 24, and 9, 1975; Creative Initiative, interview.

54. Quoted in Gelber, *Saving the Earth,* 256.

55. "The Time Is Now"; Creative Initiative, interview.

56. Cocke, interview.

57. No on 15 Committee, *California Energy Bulletin* (Spring 1976): 1.

58. *LAT,* May 7, 1975, sec. 2, p. 1 (quotation). Pat Brown's ability to shift his position on issues was legendary; see Roger Rapoport, *California Dreaming: The Political Odyssey of Pat & Jerry Brown* (Berkeley: Nolo Press, 1982). On legislative compromise see Bruce Keppel, "Nuclear Power: California's Next Big Initiative Battle," *California Journal* 6 (June 1975): 202–3; and "A Labor Committee Against Proposition 15," *Nucleonics Week* 17 (April 22, 1976): 7.

59. This discussion is drawn from Thomas Wellock, "Critical Masses: Opposition to Nuclear Power in California, 1958–78" (Ph.D. diss., University of California, Berkeley, 1995), chap. 3; and Maureen Fitzgerald, "Has the State Government Done Its Part?" *California Journal* 4 (June 1973): 188–94.

60. Gerald D. Nash, *Government and Economic Development: A History of Administrative Policies in California, 1849–1933* (Berkeley: Institute for Governmental Studies, 1964).

61. The effectiveness of the professionalized legislature has been questioned in recent years, but the institution has generally been considered a modest success. See Charles G. Bell and Charles M. Price, "20 Years of a Full-Time Legislature," *California Journal* 18 (January 1987): 36–40; Citizens Conference on State Legislatures, *The Sometimes Governments: A Critical Study of the 50 American Legislatures* (New York: Bantam Books, 1971); *San Diego Union,* April 15, 1971, sec. B, p. 3; and Emilio Varanini, interview by author, July 2, 1992, Sacramento, tape recording.

62. Rand Corporation, *California's Electricity Quandary,* 3 vols. (Santa Monica: Rand Corporation, 1972); vol. 3, *Slowing the Growth Rate,* by R. D. Doctor et al., vi (every eight miles); vol. 1, v.

63. Varanini, interview; Ronald Doctor, interview by author, December 13, 1993, telephone tape recording; and John Zierold, "Environmental Lobbyist in California's Capital, 1965–1984," an oral history conducted in 1984 by Ann Lage, Sierra Club History Series, Regional Oral History Office, Bancroft Library, 1988, 96–97.

64. *California's Electricity Quandary,* vol. 3, vi. Sierra Club scientists also gained access to the energy debate during the Proposition 15 campaign through other studies. In one instance, Richard Sextro, a Lawrence Radiation Laboratory physicist, worked on an Energy Development and Research Administration study of California's energy needs. Sextro, a Sierra Club leader in the Proposition 15 campaign, considered nuclear power a "monster" and rejected the claims of nuclear scientists to objectivity. Other scientists involved in the Proposition 15 campaign served on an oversight board for a Federal Energy Administration–sponsored study of Proposition 15's possible effects. Historian Brian Balogh's *Chain Reaction* discusses the decline of nuclear power through the formation of alliances, or "issue networks," of politicians, scientists, and political activists. As Balogh might describe it, Varanini, the Sierra Club, and its scientific allies constructed a broad-based issue network to drag energy industry experts into the public arena. They were able to blunt any effort by the federal government to influence the California initiative debate through government-sponsored studies. Rich Sextro to Lowell Smith, Sid Moglewer, December 22, 1973, Rich Sextro files; Varanini, interview; John Zierold, "Environmental Lobbyist," 96–97; William E. Siri et al., *Impacts of Alternative Electrical Supply Systems for California, and Analysis of Supply-Demand of Electricity for the Twelve Western States, 1973 to 1990* (Lakewood, Colo.: Western Interstate Nuclear Board, 1976); Center for Energy Studies, *Direct and Indirect Economic, Social, and Environmental Impacts of the Passage of the California Nuclear Safeguards Initiative* (Austin: University of Texas, April 1976), 29; and Brian Balogh, *Chain Reaction,* 19–20 and 149–50.

65. *California's Electricity Quandary,* vol. 3, 105.

66. California, Legislature, Assembly Committee on Planning and Land Use, Subcommittee on State Energy Policy, *State Energy Policy Hearings* (February–March 1973), 6 vols.

67. Charles H. Warren, "From the California Assembly to the Council on Environmental Quality, 1962–1979: The Evolution of an Environmentalist," interview by Sarah Sharp, in *Democratic Party Politics and Environmental Issues in California, 1962–1976,* Regional Oral History Office, Bancroft Library, 1986, pp. 19–21.

68. Varanini and Warren, interviews. Warren's conversion to an environmentalist ethic was complete. He was troubled by the disparities between Western nations and the Third World. Even as a state assemblyman, he viewed his legislation in international terms and tried to bring holistic management practices to issues such as food supply, natural resources, and energy consumption. He became a committed "Malthusian," believing growth itself was the enemy. Warren thus opposed nuclear power construction in part because of the expanded consumption it would encourage. Charles Warren, "Parson Malthus Tolls the Bell," *Sierra Club Bulletin* 60 (March 1975): 7–10, 24, 31.

69. For the development of Warren's relationship with the antinuclear move-

ment and his intentions in writing state energy legislation, see his correspondence with Kendall in the UCS Archives, carton 33, folder "California Assembly Hearings"; Warren to Reagan, July 13, 1973, UCS Archives, carton 33; Varanini, interview; Gary D. Simon to Henry W. Kendall, October 5, 1973, UCS Archives, carton 33.

70. Varanini, interview.

71. "Concession or Compromise? How the New Energy Act Should Work," *California Journal* 5 (July 1974), 239; and Varanini, interview.

72. "Concession or Compromise?" 239; Warren, "Evolution of an Environmentalist," 25; and Warren to Kendall, May 17, 1973, UCS Archives, carton 33.

73. "Nuclear Power in the U.S.: Chaos Reigns Supreme as 1975 Opens," *Nucleonics Week* 16 (January 16, 1975): 1; Varanini, interview; "The California Initiative Organizers Filed Some 500,000 Signatures," *Nucleonics Week* 16 (April 10, 1975): 8.

74. Atomic Industrial Forum, "Report on Warren Committee Hearings," October 14, 15, 21, and 22, and November 4 and 5, 1975, from the personal files of James Burch, copy in possession of the author.

75. Even industry publications admitted industry witnesses fared poorly. See *Nucleonics Week* 17 (January 15, 1976): 2; and James K. Staley, "California Initiative Hearings: Industry's Showing Faulted," *Nuclear Industry* 23 (January 1976): 9–11.

76. Edward Teller and Hans Bethe, testimony before California Assembly, Committee on Resources, Land Use and Energy, *Hearings on the Nuclear Initiative* (hereafter *Assembly Hearings*), October 22, 1975, vol. 4, 16.

77. Staley, "Industry's Showing Faulted," 10.

78. Michael Peevey, *Assembly Hearings,* December 2, 1975, vol. 12, 46–56; and Katherine Dunlap, *Assembly Hearings,* December 10, 1975, vol. 15, 58–60.

79. See especially *Assembly Hearings,* October 28 and 29, 1975, vols. 5 and 6; and California Assembly, Committee on Resources, Land Use and Energy, *Reassessment of Nuclear Energy in California: A Policy Analysis of Proposition 15 and Its Alternatives* (May 10, 1976): 4.

80. Staley, "Industry's Showing Faulted," 10.

81. *SFC,* January 23, 1976, 6. At least one scholar has seen the bills as a conspiratorial effort to co-opt the antinuclear movement's agenda and forestall the victory of the initiative. This interpretation fails to consider the motives of Charles Warren or other committee members. See Jerome Price, *The Antinuclear Movement* (Boston: Twayne Publishers, 1982), 99–104.

82. Pesonen, interview; and *SFC,* January 23, 1976, p. 6. Duskin and Levine, interviews.

83. Warren hinted publicly and told the Winner/Wagner campaign managers in private that he would support the initiative if the bills failed. PG&E concluded

that Brown, Warren, assembly speaker Leo McCarthey, and a number of newspapers would have changed their position on Proposition 15 if the utilities "killed" the three surviving bills. Warren, interview; Pacific Gas & Electric Co., "Proposition 15: The What and Why of Its Defeat," James Burch files.

84. Dale Bridenbaugh to N. L. Felmus, February 2, 1976; Richard B. Hubbard to Abdon Rubio, February 2, 1976, copies in the possession of the author. The story of Bridenbaugh's decision is detailed in Gail Sheehy, *Pathfinders* (New York: Morrow, 1981), chap. 16.

85. "Four Resignations Radically Change Complexion of the Nuclear Fight," *Nucleonics Week* 17 (February 12, 1976): 1–2; and "Debate on Safety Stirs Senate," *Nuclear Industry* 23 (February 1976): 2–5.

86. *SFC,* February 12, 1976, p. 1.

87. McCormack's prediction proved wrong. The three engineers formed the consulting firm MHB Associates, which is a smashing success. *Oregonian* (Portland), March 17, 1976; *Spokane Chronicle,* February 27, 1976; "Creative Initiative Foundation: An Enigma Against Nuclear Power," *Nucleonics Week* 17 (March 11, 1976): 9, and Sheehy, *Pathfinders,* 373. Creative Initiative, interview.

88. No on 15 Committee, "Why We Oppose Proposition 15" (n.d.), pamphlet, Rich Sextro files; *SFC,* June 7, 1976, p. 32; *California Energy Bulletin,* 3.

89. *Press-Democrat* (Santa Rosa, California), March 18, 1976, p. 4; No on 15 Committee, *California Energy Bulletin* (Spring 1976): 1–8; John Simpson testimony, *Assembly Hearings,* 14 (December 9, 1975), 10; and "Annual Banquet Speech is a Stem-Winder by Mike McCormack," *Nuclear Industry* 22 (December 1975): 3–5.

90. Alexander J. Groth and Howard G. Schultz, "Voter Attitudes on the 1976 Nuclear Initiative in California," *Environmental Quality Series* 25 (Davis, Calif.: Institute of Government Affairs, December 1976): 20–21.

91. "$40 Billion Cost, $7,500 per Family, Seen for California," *California Energy Bulletin,* 1; and *SFC,* March 31, 1976, p. 13. A good example of the nuclear experts' prophecy of doom is an article by Hans Bethe that the pronuclear forces referred to often in the Proposition 15 campaign. Bethe warned that nuclear power was the "only source" available to meet most of America's energy needs. Without rapid expansion the country faced "unemployment and recession, if not worse." H. A. Bethe, "The Necessity of Fission Power," *Scientific American* 234 (January 1976): 21–31.

92. Pacific Gas and Electric, "Proposition 15: The What and Why of Its Defeat," James Burch files. Pesonen later admitted that "much of the public saw us as dishonest . . . and it hurt." Levine and Pesonen, interviews.

93. *SFC,* June 4, 6, and 7, 1976; *LAT,* June 7, 1976; Project Survival, "The People Are For Yes on 15, Big Money Is Against Yes on 15," pamphlet, Richard

Sextro files; "15 Reasons to Vote Yes on 15," *Not Man Apart,* June and Mid-June 1976; and see Proposition 15 literature in Sierra Club, San Francisco Bay Chapter Records, carton 9.

94. Rich Sextro meeting notes, Richard Sextro personal files. In March, Proposition 15 actually led in the polls by a 48 to 45 percent margin, but by June it lagged 27 to 54 percent. *SFC,* March 4, April 16, and June 4, 1976.

95. *SFC,* March 9, 1976, p. 6.

96. Governor Jerry Brown was supportive of Warren's efforts, but did not become involved in the legislative negotiations. He and his aides, in Warren's words, did "absolutely nothing" to ensure passage of the legislation. "Brown and Nuclear Safety," *Yodeler* (June 1976); Varanini, Zierold, and Warren, interviews. "California Utilities Appear to be Able to Live with the Three Nuclear Bills," *Nucleonics Week* 17 (June 10, 1976): 3.

97. *SFC,* May 12 and 13, June 1 and 2, 1976; Warren picked up key support by exempting the proposed Sundesert project from the underground reactor feasibility study. See Warren-Alquist State Energy Resources Conservation and Development Act, §25534.1–5.

98. "California: One Down, Many to Go," *Nuclear Industry* (June 23, 1976): 32; *Nucleonics Week* 17 (January 1, 1976): 1–2, and 17 (April 8, 1976): 3. On utilities outside California, see Robert T. Person to Shareholders of Public Service Corp. of Colorado, May 17, 1976, Sierra Club Records, carton 20; and *New York Times,* May 23, 1976.

99. Tim Nicholson, "No Truce in the New A-War," *Newsweek,* June 21, 1976, p. 61; "A Go-Ahead for Nuclear Power," *Time,* June 21, 1976, p. 62.

100. Deborah R. Hensler and Carl P. Hensler, *Evaluating Nuclear Power: Voter Choice on the California Nuclear Energy Initiative* (Santa Monica: Rand Corporation, 1979), 10.

101. Pesonen quoted in Atomic Industrial Forum, *Info,* June 1976, p. 1. Groth, and Schultz, "Voter Attitudes," 11, 15, and 37.

102. *LAT,* June 10, 1976; Hensler, *Nuclear Power,* 10; and Groth and Schultz, "Voter Attitudes," 10.

103. Quoted in Mary Ellen Leary, "California's Nuclear Initiative: The Best Possible Defeat," *The Nation* 223 (August 14, 1976): 104–7.

104. ". . . But Lawyers Predict Anti-Nuclear Bills Face Court Upsets," *Nuclear Industry* 23 (January 1976): 11–13.

105. Varanini, interview; and California Assembly, *Reassessment of Nuclear Energy,* 18. *Pacific Gas & Electric Co. v. State Energy Resources Conservation and Development Commission,* 103 S. Ct. 1713 (1983). On the legal implications of California's nuclear legislation, see Eric Charles Woychik, "California's Nuclear Disposal Law Confronts the Nuclear Waste Management Dilemma: State Power to Regulate Reactors," *Environmental Law* 14 (1984): 359–463. On the significance of the

Supreme Court ruling, see Joseph P. Tomain, *Nuclear Power Transformation* (Bloomington: Indiana University Press, 1987), 14–17.

106. "California: One Down," *Nuclear Industry,* 8.

107. This assessment is true for all activists interviewed for this article. For activist comment on Proposition 15's defeat, see Mary Ann Eriksen, "Southern California: Proposition 15—Losing a Battle but Winning the War," *Sierra Club Bulletin* 61 (July–August 1976): 14–15; Tom Turner, "Prop. 15: When Is a Loss a Gain?" *Not Man Apart,* July 1976, 1–3: and Leary, "Best Possible Defeat," 104–7. For a less positive assessment, see John W. Gofman, "But Did They Really Want to Win?" *Mother Jones* 2 (February–March 1977): 9–10.

108. James M. Jasper, *Nuclear Politics: Energy and the State in the United States, Sweden, and France* (Princeton: Princeton University Press, 1990); Elizabeth Nichols, "U.S. Nuclear Power and the Success of the American Anti-Nuclear Movement," *Berkeley Journal of Sociology* 32 (1987): 167–92; and Daniel Pope's chapter in this volume.

109. California activists played a decisive or substantial role in the defeat of a half dozen proposed projects. The issues at each site varied, but only in the shutdown of the Rancho Seco plant in the late 1980s was a nuclear defeat due to finances. Safety, aesthetics, and regional antagonisms were usually critical issues.

110. Carroll, *Nothing Happened,* 321.

111. Teller's view of the link between ample energy and the American Dream is best illustrated in *Energy from Heaven and Earth,* chap. 10.

Antinuclear Activism
in the Pacific Northwest
WPPSS and Its Enemies

Daniel Pope

Conceived in the atmosphere of growthmanship and technological enthusiasm that characterized the electric power industry of the late 1960s, the Washington Public Power Supply System's nuclear projects pointed the Pacific Northwest toward an energy future that was jarringly at odds with the realities of the next two decades. WPPSS itself, motivated by a combination of public power idealism, organizational hubris, and external pressure, took on immense construction projects without the organizational capacities to carry them successfully to conclusion. As the economics of nuclear energy became more and more dubious in the late 1970s and early 1980s, the failure of the WPPSS projects loomed as virtually inevitable.

The Washington Public Power Supply System, a Joint Operating Agency under Washington State law, had formed in 1957. Its founders wanted an organization to undertake electrical power projects that were too large for individual public utility districts (PUDs) to pursue on their own. The Supply System's first project was a small dam at Packwood Lake in the Cascade Mountains. In 1962, after intensive maneuvering by Washington Senator Henry M. Jackson, Congress designated WPPSS to construct and operate turbine-generators attached to the Atomic Energy Commission's plutonium-producing reactor, the N-reactor, at the Hanford Nuclear Reservation.

The full commitment of WPPSS to nuclear power development came with the promulgation of a Hydro-Thermal Power Program for the Pacific Northwest in 1968.[1] Public and private utilities in the region, under the leadership of the Bonneville Power Administration, based the plan on forecasts which showed the region needing twenty large thermal generating plants by 1990. By May 1974, WPPSS had accepted the responsibility for building five large nuclear plants, three on the Hanford Reservation and two at Satsop in Grays Harbor County in western Washington.

Throughout the rest of the 1970s, the WPPSS nuclear projects faced a seemingly endless series of delays and cost escalations. The Supply System developed a voracious appetite for borrowed money and became the largest issuer of municipal bonds in the nation by the end of the decade. Its projects inched toward completion while their expected dates of operation receded into the future. Meanwhile, in the aftermath of the energy price shock of the early 1970s and spotty regional growth, electricity demand grew much more slowly than the utilities had forecasted. Still, the projects continued, and still the Supply System and its backers continued to insist that they were vital to the Northwest's energy future.[2]

What efforts were there to protest the WPPSS nuclear juggernaut? What were the strategies? How effective were the protests? This article will describe some of the shifting patterns of opposition to the Supply System's projects and will attempt some explanation of the nature and impact of antinuclear protest in the Pacific Northwest.

Assessing the impact of protest movements is never simple. Especially during and after the mass mobilizations of the late 1970s in the United States and Western Europe, activists hoped and conservatives feared that the antinuclear protest, exemplifying the "new social movements" that had supplanted traditional class politics, had the potential to disrupt some of the fundamental forces of what is variously called late capitalism or postindustrialism. Thus, for example, French sociologist Alain Touraine looked to antinuclear protest in his search for a movement that could claim "historicity" in opposition to the "programmed society."[3] Barbara Epstein's intriguing recent work gives antinuclear power activism a position of prominence in the nonviolent direct-action movements she sees as potentially transforming America.[4] Ronald Inglehart identified a large sector of U.S. and Western European citizens whose values "have been shifting from an overwhelming emphasis on material well-being and physical security toward greater emphasis on the quality of life." Although his empirical measures do not focus on environmental or energy issues, he describes the "post-materialists" as hostile to nuclear power.[5] On the right, backers of nuclear energy have in their own way categorized their opponents as part of a new class of postindustrial Luddites. In the words of Stanley Rothman and S. Robert Lichter, "Some liberal or radical members of key strategic elites . . . who are alienated from the social and political system . . . are drawn to concrete issues" like nuclear energy which "serve as a surrogate" for their dissatisfaction with liberal capitalism.[6]

However, in his recent study of *Nuclear Politics* in the United States, France, and Sweden, James Jasper contends that antinuclear protest "had little effect on nuclear energy policies in any country." He concludes, "The antinuclear movement of the mid-1970s had more effect on the public debates than on the eventual outcomes."[7] His conclusion echoes Dorothy Nelkin and Michael Pollak's point: institutional and legal factors in France and Germany were more important than the character of their antinuclear movements in determining the fate of nuclear power in those nations.[8]

There is an irony here. The Pacific Northwest has for some time been known as a center of new social movements, with a notably strong environmentalist presence. Ernest Callenbach's tract dubbing the region "Ecotopia" in 1975 spoke not only of the physical environment but also of the Northwest's social attitudes.[9] Yet the depth and breadth of opposition to WPPSS generally lagged behind the growing problems that the Supply System faced. Meanwhile, at Shoreham, New York, and at Seabrook, New Hampshire, intervenors with concerns ranging from the aesthetic to the apocalyptic dogged such projects almost from their inception, slowed plant construction, and converted the plants into political and perhaps economic liabilities. Without popular antinuclear pressure, Seabrook would have opened sooner and Shoreham would not now be facing dismantling.[10] Moreover, as we shall see, the social basis of the opposition to WPPSS which did develop did not neatly match the pattern of a new social movement. Broad, sustained protest of the environmental and safety implications of the Supply System's plants failed to develop. When popular opposition did emerge in the early 1980s, economic concerns seem to have been central.

Why did antinuclear protest matter less in the Pacific Northwest? No single explanation will suffice, of course, but some historical and structural context may be useful. It is important to note, for instance, that the WPPSS projects were for many years insulated from close public scrutiny. The politics of public power had been heated, to say the least, in the 1930s and 1940s, but by the 1960s their intensity had faded. Public utility districts in Washington (and to a lesser extent Oregon) were fixtures of their local economies and business scenes. Board elections drew little attention, and their actions less scrutiny. WPPSS as a consortium of PUDs (and municipal utilities) was a step further removed. Its board of directors, comprised of a representative from each member utility, ceded major decisions to its Executive Committee. Until a forced restructuring in 1981 added members appointed by the governor to the Executive Committee, therefore, there was no external control over the WPPSS policy-making structure. Sparsely attended by journalists, Executive Committee and board meetings seldom confronted the broader policy issues that the Supply System's problems implied. Thus, there was no steady stream of information about the projects and the obstacles they encountered.

Moreover, WPPSS had financial independence from ratepayers and voters. It could finance its capital investments by issuing tax-exempt revenue bonds without voter approval. As far back as 1968, the managing director had pointed to this autonomy: "Ability to issue bonds by action of the controlling body and the consent of the parties to the arrangement without referring to a vote of any electorate or other third party veto" was one of the Supply System's organizational virtues.[11]

Location was also a factor in protecting WPPSS from public anger. The Supply System was headquartered in Richland, adjacent to the Hanford Reservation. The Tri-Cities (Richland, Pasco, Kennewick) near Hanford had grown from tiny settlements to substantial towns as creations of the nuclear age, and local opposition there was virtually nonexistent. Over 200 miles from the state's population and political action center in Seattle, Hanford was a difficult target for protest. In the late 1960s, WPPSS had intended to build at Roosevelt Beach on the Pacific near Hoquiam. When the state fisheries agency threatened to require extensive study of possible shellfish damage from thermal pollution, WPPSS quickly decided to relocate the plant to the friendly confines of the Hanford Reservation. This is the one operating plant, numbered, confusingly enough, WPPSS Nuclear Project-2 (WNP-2). WNP-1 and WNP-4 were sited nearby at Hanford. Plants 3 and 5, twinned at Satsop west of Olympia, were also placed where local opposition was likely to be muted, especially in economic slumps, when the promise of economic benefits to nearby timber-dependent communities outweighed nuclear fears. (WNP-4 and WNP-5 were terminated in 1982, leading to WPPSS's default on $2.25 billion in municipal bonds in 1983. After construction suspensions of over a decade, WPPSS canceled WNP-1 and WNP-3 in 1994.)

It is also notable that for some, especially in the early years of reactor planning, nuclear energy was an idealistic cause which would preserve the region's quality of life while enhancing the standard of living. From the standpoint of longtime public power activists, the wppss projects were a boon to the citizens and consumers of the Northwest. When Glenn Seaborg, chairman of the Atomic Energy Commission, came to speak at Richland's twenty-fifth anniversary celebration in 1968, his call for a "nuplex" of nuclear-powered industries reprocessing waste materials and removing factories from big cities was as thoroughly utopian as any Ecotopian manifesto.[12] Antinuclear activists thus had no monopoly on visionary schemes for the Pacific Northwest.

The financing arrangements of the first three wppss plants may have had dual effects. Under the plan known as net billing, publicly owned utilities which purchased shares in the projects assigned their shares of the plants' output to the Bonneville Power Administration. bpa, which sold vast quantities of hydroelectric power to these utilities, would, in exchange for the assignment of the nuclear output, deduct the cost of the wppss power from the bills bpa sent to the utilities each month. Net billing had the effect of regionalizing the plants' costs and spreading them among all bpa users. Bonneville customers would all receive a mixture of hydro and nuclear kilowatts and would all pay a rate that melded the higher cost of nuclear with the low-cost power from the federal hydro system. Net billing also provided an implicit federal guarantee for the tax-exempt bonds that wppss issued. On the one hand, regionalization meant that all bpa customers, not just the members of wppss, had a stake in avoiding problems with the net-billed plants. On the other hand, the federal guarantee probably delayed the onset of financial anxiety attacks by dispersing the costs of these facilities throughout the region.[13]

Antinuclear forces in the Northwest did grow apace in the 1970s with a national and international movement. They began, in fact, with a substantial victory. In 1968 the Eugene Water and Electric Board easily won voter approval for a $225 million bond issue for a nuclear plant in Oregon's Lane County. Slated as one contribution to fulfilling the Hydro-Thermal Power Plan, the eweb plant was nevertheless blocked in 1970 when the city's voters reversed themselves and imposed a moratorium on the utility's participation in a nuclear plant. Although some of the opposition to the eweb plant was of the nimby ("not in my back yard") variety, the leaders of the Eugene Future Power Committee articulated a broad critique of nuclear solutions on environmental, safety, and economic grounds.[14]

The region's nuclear activists, despite this victory, evinced little interest in WPPSS in its early years. There were some opponents of Portland General Electric's Trojan plant, completed at Rainier, Oregon, along the Columbia in 1975. The first civilian nuclear plant in the region (other than the steam generator attached to the Hanford Reservation's N-reactor), Trojan was visible from Interstate 5, a short drive from Portland, and about two hours by car from Seattle. Yet opposition to Trojan itself never reached massive proportions. The plant encountered only "normal" cost overruns and construction delays. Its construction came during the energy shocks of the early 1970s, when policy makers were still emphasizing the need for domestic energy production and contending that nuclear power was a crucial element of the nation's energy future.

For those who were observing Northwest nuclear development in the early 1970s, some warning signs about WPPSS were already visible. After 1973, Bonneville Power Administration could no longer offer net billing arrangements to utilities participating in WPPSS plants. The credits were limited to slightly less than the amount the utilities paid to BPA for the federal power they purchased. The first three WPPSS plants, according to cost predictions, would exhaust the available credits. Moreover, an IRS ruling in 1972 held that interest payments on bonds for future net billed projects could no longer be exempt from federal income tax. Without this municipal bond tax exemption, WPPSS would lose its ability to finance projects at competitive interest rates. Faced with this situation, convinced of the continued need for large-scale power development, and pressured by Donald Hodel, Bonneville Power administrator, in May 1974 WPPSS undertook to build two more nuclear plants without net billing. Participating utilities (which came to number eighty-eight) agreed to purchase shares of the plants' generating capability. Although there were indications that Bonneville might find a way to support WPPSS plants 4 and 5, the utilities ended up on their own, pledged to pay for their shares of the projects whether or not they successfully produced electricity.

These new projects caused many utilities to think twice about participation. In most communities, PUDs and municipal utilities saw no alternative to subscribing to shares of the projects. In Seattle, however, citizen opposition blocked the path toward nuclear commitment. Well analyzed elsewhere by political scientists J. Gregory Hill and Wayne Sugai, the debate in Seattle can be rather quickly summarized.[15] When Seattle City Light prepared to sign option agreements on shares of plants 4 and 5, the Washington Environmental Council intervened, and the city undertook a major Energy 1990 study of its power needs and resources. A Citizens' Overview Committee in April 1976 recommended that Seattle not participate in the additional plants, and a broad coalition of environmentalist and consumer groups joined in opposition. After broad public debate, the City Council that July turned down proposals to buy a 5 percent or even a token 1 percent share of the projects. Eugene's Water and Electric Board had changed substantially since the moratorium campaign, and that city also said no to the blandishments of WPPSS and Bonneville.[16]

While other utilities in the Pacific Northwest signed on with plants 4 and 5, antinuclear forces in Oregon and Washington were taking a different tack. Encouraged by a Ralph Nader national organization, Critical Mass, activists put ballot measures before the public in seven states. Dubbed the Nuclear Safeguards Initiatives, these stressed the dangers of reactor design and radioactive waste disposal and the limits Congress had imposed on utility liability for nuclear accidents. In Washington, the Nuclear Safeguards Initiative (I-325) gained its impetus from a local group, Coalition for a Safe Environment, which had formed to oppose Puget Sound Power and Light Company's plans to build two nuclear plants in the Skagit Valley northeast of Seattle and drew upon a spectrum of environmental and antinuclear organizations.[17] Although proponents disclaimed a desire to eliminate all nuclear power, utility and construction companies recognized the initiatives as a dire threat to the industry's future and spent heavily to defeat them. Outspent by pronuclear forces, I-325 backers in Washington State saw their proposal go down to a two-to-one defeat.[18] In Oregon, the equivalent ballot measure fared somewhat better, receiving 42 percent approval, but this was the best result of any of the referenda for the safeguards movement. National public opinion polls in the 1970s, before Three Mile Island (March 1979), consistently showed solid pluralities, usually majorities, for expanding nuclear energy supplies, and the 1976 ballot results thus coincided with survey findings.[19]

Nationally, the late 1970s saw a shift in mobilization against nuclear power. In Robert Cameron Mitchell's words, antinuclear protest grew from an "elite quarrel" to a "mass movement."[20] The huge demonstration at Seabrook in April 1977 was the clearest example of this escalation. In the Northwest, however, the Crabshell Alliance never came close to duplicating the size and fervor of New England's Clamshell Alliance. In July 1977, a crowd of 700 gathered for a peaceful and legal protest at the Satsop WPPSS site (clearly an easier place to assemble for antinuclear protest than at Hanford), and one Crabshell organizer predicted, "This is just the first of many actions."[21] However, the next year when the Crabshell Alliance mobilized another demonstration near the plant site, the *Seattle Times* reported the crowd at a disappointing 190. The Alliance soon withered away, even as the Supply System's problems mounted and public doubts crystallized into anger.

Internal management problems at the Supply System caused cost escalations and construction delays throughout the late 1970s. Between 1976 and 1978, a series of audits and consultants' studies had explored problems in relations between WPPSS and its architecture and engineering contractors, in handling change orders to revise construction processes, and in the relationship between Bonneville Power Administration, as implicit financial backer of the net-billed plants, and WPPSS. This last became the subject of a major study by Theodore Barry & Associates (TBA), released in January 1979.[22] The TBA report found many shortcomings in internal control and in coordination with Bonneville, and received substantial coverage in regional media.

Perhaps more important than the studies in generating opposition, an 88 percent Bonneville wholesale rate increase in December 1979 made it clear that the WPPSS projects were likely to end rather than prolong the Northwest's era of cheap electricity. The need to begin debt repayment on the net-billed plants (WPPSS nuclear plants 1, 2, and 3)— still years away from operation—was the reason for BPA's largest rate increase ever.

By the end of the 1970s, WPPSS had acquired some bitter opponents in the Northwest's political circles. The Three Mile Island accident harmed nuclear energy's reputation nationally, and the WPPSS plants' estimated cost grew to $15.9 billion. Congressman Jim Weaver (Democrat, Oregon) was the most important foe at the national level. Weaver, convinced for years that nuclear power was dangerous and that Northwest power policies were designed to line the pockets of corporate interests (notably the direct service industries, or DSI, primarily aluminum companies), waged protracted battles against the various regional power bills that Congress debated from 1977 to 1980. When his filibustering failed to stop the version that became law in December 1980, Weaver continued his struggles against WPPSS, the BPA, and related targets. And when, in 1983, he became chair of the House Interior and Insular Affairs Committee's Subcommittee on Mining, Forest Management and the Bonneville Power Administration, he held a series of hearings in which he angrily lambasted WPPSS, BPA, and their allies and denounced the projects as monstrous giveaways to corporate interests. In the state of Washington, State Senator King Lysen emerged as the most formidable WPPSS critic at Olympia. He pressed for a 1980 investigation of the "Causes of Cost Overruns and Schedule Delays" on the nuclear projects, which remains one of the broadest critiques of the WPPSS ventures. The next year, in a legislative compromise that fended off more restrictive legislation, the Washington legislators mandated an *Independent Review* of plants 4 and 5.[23]

Just as WPPSS itself was a product of the progressive tradition in Northwest politics, so too was the initiative process which its opponents employed in order to stymie it. By the 1970s, both the public power movement and the crusade for direct democracy had lost much of their populist ardor. Many public utility leaders had adopted a business-oriented growth mentality. Progressive reformers' hopes for direct democracy had also been compromised. Although the record was mixed, voter-sponsored initiatives had seldom proved to be (as conservatives had feared) leveling devices. Moneyed interests, though rarely able to get pet initiatives passed, could usually defeat measures they considered threatening.[24] The failures of the 1976 Nuclear Safeguards Initiatives paralleled the passage in 1978 of California's Proposition 13, "The Revolt of the Haves" in Robert Kuttner's pointed phrase.[25]

However, the ineffectual efforts for direct action, post–Three Mile Island anxiety about nuclear power, and the growing unhappiness with WPPSS made energy activists look again at using the initiative process. When, in 1979, they began to discuss campaign strategies, they found themselves divided. One group of activists wanted to fight WPPSS on economic grounds by proposing an initiative that would require voter approval of bond issues for publicly owned electric power projects.[26] Jim

Lazar, an energy economist, and Charles Caldart, an Olympia attorney, argued that the dollars-and-cents case against WPPSS was the one that could win public support. Other activists disagreed. They pressed for a measure that would ban importation of nuclear waste into the state. With the example of Three Mile Island and an apparent political paralysis in solving long-term waste storage problems, defending Washington against ecological and health dangers seemed a promising approach. During the 1980 season for collecting petition signatures, the two factions could not agree; each pursued getting its own initiative measure on the ballot. As the deadline neared, the bond approval measure had collected only about a third of the necessary signatures, so its backers shelved it and joined with the nuclear waste opponents to put Initiative 383 over the top and onto the November 1980 ballot.[27]

Using the slogan "Don't Waste Washington," campaigners for Initiative 383 found themselves faced with only token opposition. Pronuclear interests in the state had no direct stake in the importation of wastes from elsewhere, and out-of-state forces apparently did not see one state's proposal as a threat. Moreover, the U.S. Supreme Court in the Northern States Power Company case of 1972 had let stand a circuit court ruling that the federal government had almost exclusive regulatory authority over radioactive emissions and wastes. Industry forces could reasonably expect that even if the measure passed it would be overturned in the courts. Thus it came as little surprise that I-383 passed by a three-to-one margin—nor that a Federal District Court judge invalidated it the following June.

Meanwhile, the Supply System's problems worsened. In February 1980, WPPSS directors had forced the removal of Managing Director Neil O. Strand and, after a six-month search, replaced him with Robert Ferguson, a well-regarded industry professional. Ferguson brought a new degree of realism to WPPSS leadership, and by the spring of 1981 he had concluded that bond financing of plants 4 and 5 could not continue along its escalating path. In early June, Moody's Investor Services belatedly lowered its rating of WPPSS 4 and 5 bonds from gilt-edge to a medium (Baa1) grade. (Standard and Poor's soon followed suit.) Upon Ferguson's recommendation, the Supply System board voted the next week to impose a construction moratorium on these two plants, although it continued to budget and plan on the assumption that the system would eventually resume work and complete the plants.

Even as Wall Street's reluctance to invest in the unprotected securities of WPPSS 4 and 5 was stopping progress on these plants, activists were trying to give the Northwest a means of halting the headlong rush to financial disaster. Another hefty increase in BPA wholesale rates, 53 percent, announced in February 1981, had brought home to ratepayers the impact of massive WPPSS spending.

Backers of Initiative 394 hoped to stymie the WPPSS projects through requiring public approval of bond issues for utility financing. The measure also required a cost-effectiveness study for each project. Adopting the slogan "Don't Bankrupt Washington," they paralleled the 1980 "Don't Waste Washington" motto but identified the nuclear threat as primarily pecuniary. They prided themselves on hardheaded economic logic, criticizing the faulty demand projections, construction delays, and cost overruns of nuclear plants, and deemphasizing questions of safety and environment. Jim Lazar says he was involved with the initiative, and with antinuclear protest since the 1970s, "strictly as an economist." Indeed, he attributes the measure's success in part to the fact that "it wasn't an antinuclear initiative." Steve Zemke, official sponsor of the initiative, made the same claim: "We're not against building nuclear plants, we're just trying to control the spending."[28]

Unlike the preceding year's campaign, the I-394 contest elicited support from both sides. Under the leadership of Zemke, backers recruited volunteers to staff telephone banks and call supporters of past environmental initiatives, urging them to sign the I-394 petition. Although an exceptionally rainy spring hampered signature collection, petition circulators in shopping centers and on street corners garnered 186,000 signatures by the July deadline.

Even before the petitions were submitted, initiative opponents had organized in June a group eventually named Citizens Against Unfair Taxes (CAUT). The Western Environmental Trade Association, a business group despite the green "e" on its letterhead, plotted opposition strategy with the help of a Los Angeles campaign management firm. Spending was heavy. CAUT raised $1,277,267 in cash contributions, more than five times the Don't Bankrupt Washington receipts of $239,779.[29] Paradoxically, the largest contribution to CAUT probably harmed its cause; this was a $200,000 loan from Idaho-based Morrison-Knudsen, Inc., a major construction contractor on WPPSS's Satsop plants. Morrison-Knudsen's construction change orders had been identified in the State Senate's 1980 study as among the important reasons for WPPSS's cost overruns. Other contributions from contractors and building trades unions to CAUT had a similarly self-interested flavor.

Supporters of I-394 tapped contributions from both environmentalist and economic sources, but fund-raising was not easy. At the end of September, the committee had raised only $53,000, while the opposition had already amassed three-quarters of a million. Zemke embarked on an East Coast tour to raise money. At the same time, he commissioned a professional poll and employed the well-known advertising specialist Tony Schwartz, who had created the famous "daisy" commercial for Lyndon Johnson's campaign against Barry Goldwater. The largest donor was Alida Rockefeller Dayton of New York, a backer of environmentalist causes, who gave $45,000 for media advertising time.[30] However, the campaign also got a $10,300 gift from International Association of Machinists' Lodge 751, representing Boeing aerospace workers.[31] Lazar recalls that the group's research indicated voter animosity to both contractors and unions, but the Machinists' involvement steered the campaign rhetoric to an anticorporate focus.[32]

Wayne Sugai in his excellent study of anti-WPPSS mobilization emphasizes the contrasts between the unsuccessful Nuclear Safeguards Initiative (I-325) of 1976 and the Don't Waste Washington campaign (I-383) of 1980, on the one hand, and, on the other, I-394 with its pocketbook orientation. Like Lazar, he points out that the rhetoric of the 1981 campaign stressed the costliness of huge investments in nuclear energy instead of the environmental and safety concerns highlighted in the earlier contests. An analysis of voting statistics suggests two revisions of this contrast.[33] First, in terms of the geographic distribution of voter support, there was a good deal of overlap among the three initiatives. Second, neither the earlier two measures nor the later one drew heavily on the "new class" constituencies associated with the new social movements. It would appear that at the county level, support for *each* was associated with some indices of more conventional political and economic liberalism.

Given the overwhelming support for the 1980 nuclear waste initiative, the absence of concerted opposition to it, and the low degree of voter attention it received, this analysis will concentrate on the 1976 Nuclear Safeguards vote and the 1981 Don't Bankrupt Washington election. These two nuclear initiative campaigns used substantially different rhetoric, and the results differed sharply. The 1976 effort failed by a two-to-one margin while I-394 passed with 58 percent of the vote. Yet the counties that gave the greatest backing to the first initiative were also likely to give strong majorities to the Don't Bankrupt Washington measure, while strong opponents of the first were also likely to reject the second. The correlation coefficient is a striking +.87.[34]

Antinuclear voting on both issues also correlated strongly with county tallies in the 1980 presidential race. The correlation coefficient between support for each measure and the share of the county's vote going to Ronald Reagan is −.79. Thus, whether the issue was posed as an environmental or an economic one, the more hostile a county was to nuclear energy, the more likely it was to be among the more liberal ones in the state.

To examine whether antinuclear voting was related to socioeconomic conditions, we consider four variables: the 1981 unemployment rate, per capita income, the proportion of the labor force in manufacturing, and the share of the adult population with sixteen years or more of schooling. For both the 1976 and 1981 votes, the only significant correlation links support for the antinuclear initiatives with the manufacturing share of the labor force. Contrary to arguments that antinuclear sentiment is a postindustrial phenomenon, however, the correlation is positive (+.43, significant at the one percent level) between the county vote on the Nuclear Safeguards Initiative and the degree of manufacturing employment. The correlation of manufacturing's share and the yes vote on the economically oriented Initiative 394 is almost precisely the same (+.44, also significant at the one percent level). Correlations of both votes with levels of income and education, although not statistically significant, are in fact slightly negative, and the association of antinuclear voting with county unemployment rates is positive.[35] It may well be that the region's economic slump in 1981 converted years of antinuclear activists' frustration into triumph.

Heartening as the I-394 vote was to WPPSS opponents, the projects' supporters took quick steps to nullify its effects. Three banks serving as bond trustees for the net-billed plants 1, 2, and 3 went to U.S. District Court in December 1981. The U.S. Department of Justice filed a similar complaint on behalf of the BPA. On June 30, 1982, the day before the bond approval requirement was scheduled to go into effect, Judge Jack E. Tanner declared it unconstitutional on the grounds that it impaired existing contracts regarding the net-billed plants. Early in 1983, a U.S.

Court of Appeals ruling upheld Tanner's decision, and the Supreme Court that spring refused Don't Bankrupt Washington's appeal petition, thus closing the case.

Although passage of I-394 appeared to pose a formidable barrier to WPPSS's continued growth, it was more symptom than cause of the multifarious problems besetting the Supply System's nuclear ambitions. WPPSS's own huge managerial problems, a worsening recession in the Northwest, a sharp slowdown in electrical demand growth, interest rates at record heights, and Wall Street's growing doubts about the projects' viability were the forces that doomed plans to complete the five plants.

During the initiative campaign, the Supply System had groped for a way to raise the funds needed for maintaining plants 4 and 5 in their mothballed status; the scheme was complex, and ultimately untenable. In January 1982, in rapid succession, Clark County PUD, owner of 10 percent shares of the projects, decided not to pay into the preservation fund; Moody's suspended credit ratings for the plants' bonds; and the legislature-mandated *Independent Review* suggested that resuming construction after a substantial delay would be very costly. By January 15, thirty-three of the eighty-eight participants had refused to contribute to mothballing expenses. That day, Robert Ferguson recommended termination of the projects, and the Executive Board agreed a week later.

Participating utilities now faced the staggering prospect of having to begin payments on the municipal bonds worth $2.25 billion that had financed the abandoned plants. According to the 1976 Participants' Agreements, repayment would have to start a year after termination. An "Irate Ratepayers" movement erupted that winter. This ratepayer protest of 1982 is itself a topic worthy of extended treatment, which it cannot receive here. Fortunately, Wayne Sugai's discussion in "Mass Insurgency" of this grass-roots mobilization is both thorough and thoughtful. In terms of social movement theory, however, the ratepayer protest raises some interesting issues. In a sense, the situation of early 1982 brought antinuclear opposition full circle. In its earliest phases, opposition had been local; after a brief period dominated by efforts at direct action, the foes of nuclear power had in 1979 through 1981 adopted a statewide electoral strategy. In 1982, citizens once again looked at their local situation and focused their anger on the utilities that had marched into the Supply System morass and seemed unwilling to extricate themselves and their ratepayers. Although utility activist Dan Leahy claimed in February 1982 that "we have a statewide movement going," local interests and personalities predominated.[36] In part as a corollary of this localism, it appears that the Irate Ratepayers lacked strong ties to the environmentalist movement.

A second point is that the Irate Ratepayers traded off the centralized focus and structure of concentrating on a single goal characteristic of the initiative campaigns in favor of a broader offensive against the utility and financial malefactors they faced. Their programs ranged from turning out hidebound PUD commissioners to withdrawing funds from Seattle's SeaFirst Bank, because of its involvement with WPPSS bonds, to supporting State Senator King Lysen's rather quixotic race for the U.S. Senate against incumbent Senator Jackson. Although the ratepayer movement did have experts such as Dan Leahy engaged in the cause, it seems—especially in the winter and spring of 1982—to have been borne on a current of popular fury at the WPPSS debacle. Lazar's comment that the ratepayer protest "had no agenda" and thus "couldn't be held together" reflects one side of the picture.[37] It might be equally correct to say that the initial anger at the likelihood of huge electric rate increases propelled them toward a broad anticorporate agenda that was too far-reaching for many of them to accept.

While it would be foolish to generalize from the experience of WPPSS, in this case at least the grander claims of new social movement theorists about the importance of the antinuclear movement seem less applicable than James Jasper's skepticism. The opposition to WPPSS in 1981, as measured in voting figures at the county level, came from the same areas that had supported nuclear safety and environmental measures. Yet the social and economic settings of these votes were likely to be conventionally liberal blue-collar counties with significant economic grievances. As we have seen, broad-based opposition to the Supply System's ventures emerged slowly, fully a decade after WPPSS began to make its nuclear commitments. When it did appear, as in the 1981 Initiative 394 campaign and the ratepayer revolt of 1982, external challenges and internal weaknesses muted its successes. Six months after the I-394 victory, the courts threw out its central provision. The ratepayer movement unseated some PUD leaders who had gone along with WPPSS and frightened a few others into a more judicious stance, but it was unable to sustain mass insurgency for more than a few months in the winter and spring of 1982.

Yet, after all, the Supply System's nuclear dreams shriveled up in the early 1980s. Two plants canceled, two mothballed for a decade and then terminated, and one fitfully producing electricity for a region until recently (and perhaps now again) with an energy surplus—this is a far cry from the lofty aspirations of power planners a generation ago. When we seek to find out why, we will have to turn to the misguided nature of their dreams and to the fatal flaws in their efforts to realize them. Ultimately, we must conclude, WPPSS was its own worst enemy.

NOTES

1. U.S. Department of the Interior, Bonneville Power Administration, *A Ten Year Hydro-Thermal Power Program for the Pacific Northwest* (January 1969). The plan was announced to the public on October 22, 1968.

2. General accounts of WPPSS include: James Leigland and Robert Lamb, *WPPSS: Who Is to Blame for the WPPSS Disaster* (Cambridge, Mass.: Ballinger, 1986); D. Victor Anderson, *Illusions of Power* (New York: Praeger, 1985); Daniel Jack Chasan, *The Fall of the House of WPPSS* (Seattle: Sasquatch, 1985); David Myhra, *Whoops!/WPPSS* (Jefferson, N.C., and London: McFarland, 1984). Anderson's book contains a useful chronology of major events (pp. 145–53). A very detailed chronology of the events surrounding the 1983 default can be found in United States Securities and Exchange Commission, Division of Enforcement, *Staff Report on the Investigation in the Matter of Transactions in Washington Public Power Supply System Securities* (Washington, D.C.: Securities and Exchange Commission, 1988), 33–41. This article relies on the works cited above and other research for the story of WPPSS's activities.

3. Alain Touraine, *Anti-Nuclear Protest: The Opposition to Nuclear Energy in France* (Cambridge: Cambridge University Press, 1983), and *The Voice and the Eye: An Analysis of Social Movements* (Cambridge: Cambridge University Press, 1981). For other studies of antinuclear power protest which generally stress its post-industrial character, see Jerome Price, *The Antinuclear Movement* (Boston: Twayne Publishers, 1982); Dorothy Nelkin and Michael Pollak, *The Atom Besieged: Antinuclear Movements in France and Germany* (Cambridge, Mass.: MIT Press, 1982); Dorothy Nelkin, *Nuclear Power and Its Critics: The Cayuga Lake Controversy* (Ithaca: Cornell University Press, 1971); on Seabrook, see Henry F. Bedford, *Seabrook Station* (Amherst: University of Massachusetts Press, 1990). Christian Joppke, *Mobilizing against Nuclear Energy* (Berkeley: University of California Press, 1993), contends that new social movement theory applies more to West German than to U.S. antinuclear protest.

4. Barbara Epstein, *Political Protest and Cultural Revolution* (Berkeley: University of California Press, 1991), especially chaps. 2 and 7.

5. Ronald Inglehart, *The Silent Revolution: Changing Values and Political Styles among Western Publics* (Princeton: Princeton University Press, 1977): 3 and passim.

6. Stanley Rothman and S. Robert Lichter, "Elite Ideology and Risk Perception in Nuclear Energy Policy," *American Political Science Review* 81 (June 1987): 398–99.

7. James M. Jasper, *Nuclear Politics: Energy and the State in the United States, Sweden, and France* (Princeton: Princeton University Press, 1990), 8, 267–68.

8. Nelkin and Pollak, *Atom Besieged,* 196–97.

9. Ernest Callenbach, *Ecotopia: The Notebooks and Reports of William Weston* (Berkeley, Calif.: Banyan Tree Books, 1975).

10. David P. McCaffrey, *The Politics of Nuclear Power* (Dordrecht: Kluwer Academic Publishers, 1991), esp. 191–202. For a highly critical view of Shoreham, see Karl Grossman, *Power Crazy* (New York: Grove Press, 1986). On Seabrook, see Bedford, *Seabrook Station.*

11. Owen W. Hurd to Supply System Board of Directors, "BPA Power Purchase Plan Implementing Entity," April 26, 1968. Document in possession of attorney Martha L. Walters, lent to author.

12. Glenn T. Seaborg, "Large-Scale Alchemy—25th Anniversary at Hanford-Richland," U.S. Department of Energy Coordination and Information Center Library, Las Vegas, Nevada, no. 0148580 (Washington, D.C.: U.S. Atomic Energy Commission, June 7, 1968). Thanks to Dr. Michele S. Gerber for a copy of this address. "Richland Is Human Bonus, Spin-Off of Nuclear Efforts, Says Seaborg," *Tri-City Herald,* June 9, 1968.

13. For a detailed description of net billing, see Kai N. Lee and Donna Lee Klemka, with Marion E. Marts, *Electric Power and the Future of the Pacific Northwest* (Seattle: University of Washington Press, 1980), 75–82.

14. For a more complete account, see Daniel Pope, " 'We Can Wait. We Should Wait.' Eugene's Nuclear Power Controversy, 1968–1970," *Pacific Historical Review* 59 (August 1990): 349–73.

15. Joseph Gregory Hill, "The Public Interest and the Evaluation of Public Policy" (Ph.D. diss., University of Washington, 1981), esp. chap. 1, "The Politics of Energy 1990." Wayne Sugai, "The WNP 4 & 5 Decision: Seattle and Tacoma—A Tale of Two Cities," *Northwest Environmental Journal* 1 (1984): 45–95.

16. A more detailed treatment of WNP-4 and 5 is Daniel Pope, "Seduced and Abandoned? Utilities and WPPSS Nuclear Plants 4 and 5," *Columbia: The Magazine of Northwest History* 5 (Fall 1991): 12–20.

17. Papers of the Coalition for a Safe Environment (also apparently sometimes known as Coalition for Safe Energy) are in the University of Washington Libraries, Manuscripts and Archives, Seattle, Accession no. 3096.

18. Wayne Hideo Sugai, "Mass Insurgency: The Ratepayers' Revolt and the Washington Public Power Supply System Crisis" (Ph.D. diss., University of Washington, 1985), 206–16, discusses the I-325 campaign.

19. Stanley M. Nealey, Barbara D. Melber, and William L. Rankin, *Public Opinion and Nuclear Energy* (Lexington, Mass.: D. C. Heath, Lexington Books, 1983), 31 for a summary table. See also William R. Freudenburg and Eugene A. Rosa, eds., *Public Reaction to Nuclear Power: Are There Critical Masses?* American Association for the Advancement of Science Symposium 93 (Boulder: Westview Press, 1984), for studies of public opinion and nuclear energy issues.

20. Robert Cameron Mitchell, "From Elite Quarrel to Mass Movement," *Society* 18 (July–August 1981): 76–84.

21. "700 March in Nuclear-plant Protest at Elma," *Seattle Times,* July 17, 1977, G6.

22. Theodore Barry & Associates, *Management Study of the Roles and Relationships of the Bonneville Power Administration and the Washington Public Power Supply System,* report submitted to the Bonneville Power Administration (Los Angeles: Theodore Barry & Associates, January 1979).

23. Washington Energy Research Center, Office of Applied Energy Studies, *Independent Review of Washington Public Power Supply System Nuclear Plants 4 and 5: Final Report to the Washington State Legislature* (Seattle: Washington Energy Research Center, March 15, 1982).

24. On public power, see, e.g., Bruce Marvin Haston, "From Conflict Politics to Cooperative Politics: A Study of the Public-Private Power Controversy in the Pacific Northwest" (Ph.D. diss., Washington State University, 1970); Erwin C. Hargrove and Paul K. Conkin, *TVA: Fifty Years of Grass-Roots Bureaucracy* (Urbana and Chicago: University of Illinois Press, 1983). On initiatives, see, e.g., Hugh A. Bone and Robert C. Benedict, "Perspectives on Direct Legislation: Washington State's Experience, 1914–1973," *Western Political Quarterly* 28 (June 1975): 347–48; Thomas E. Cronin, *Direct Democracy: The Politics of Initiative, Referendum, and Recall* (Cambridge: Harvard University Press, 1989), 109.

25. Robert Kuttner, *Revolt of the Haves: Tax Rebellions and Hard Times* (New York: Simon and Schuster, 1980).

26. The strategic debates are covered in David C. Schmidt, "Winning an Initiative Big: How They Whipped 'Whoops' in Washington State," *Campaigns and Elections* 4 (Fall 1983): 4–19, and in Sugai, "Mass Insurgency," chap. 3, passim.

27. Sugai, "Mass Insurgency," 237–47, explores the 1980 initiative.

28. Jim Lazar, Olympia, Washington, telephone interview by author, August 3, 1992. Zemke quoted in "Initiative 394 on Energy-project Spending Off to Stormy Beginning," *Seattle Times,* July 9, 1981, B5.

29. Cited in Sugai, "Mass Insurgency," 269.

30. David D. Schmidt, *Citizen Lawmakers: The Ballot Initiative Revolution* (Phila-

delphia: Temple University Press, 1989), 77–95, offers a detailed description of the Initiative 394 campaign effort.

31. House Committee on Interior and Insular Affairs, Subcommittee on Mining, Forest Management and Bonneville Power Administration, *The Bonneville Power Administration* [BPA] *and Washington Public Power Supply System* [WPPSS], Hearings, 98th Cong., 2d sess., 1984, serial 98–48, part I, 428–31, lists contributors of at least $250 to each side.

32. Lazar, interview.

33. Data on election results by county come from Office of the Secretary of State, Washington (State), *Abstract of Votes: General Elections* (Olympia: Secretary of State): 1976, p. 14 (for I-325); 1980, p. 5 (for presidential election); 1981, p. 2 (for I-394). Socioeconomic data are from U.S. Bureau of the Census, *County and City Data Book, 1983* (Washington, D.C.: Government Printing Office, 1983), 612–14.

The statistical evidence does not conclusively demonstrate that voters who favored the 1976 measure also favored the 1981 initiative, nor that the I-394 initiative was especially popular with liberal, Democratic, or blue-collar voters. This is because the data presented represent correlations of county voting percentages, not individual voting behavior. To assume that individuals' votes were similarly correlated would be to commit what is known as the "ecological fallacy."

34. They were also the counties giving the strongest support to the 1980 initiative to block the importation of nuclear waste, I-383. Although this initiative passed handily, it was soon ruled unconstitutional in federal court as a violation of the commerce clause. The correlation of the 1980 nuclear waste initiative with the 1976 vote was .75; with the 1981 measure, .78.

35. Lettie McSpadden Wenner and Manfred W. Wenner, "Nuclear Policy and Public Participation," *American Behavioral Scientist* 22 (November–December 1978): 277–310, find that the proportion of college graduates in a county is positively related to support for the 1976 Safeguards Initiatives in Oregon and Ohio. Thus, the Washington findings cannot be extended automatically to other states. I examined one additional variable: I hypothesized that the presence of a county public utility district (PUD) or major municipal utility which was a participant in plants 4 and 5 might affect the vote on the Don't Bankrupt Washington measure, but in fact there was no difference between counties with and without participating utilities. Correlations of socioeconomic variables with the Initiative 383 vote were not significant, but the signs pointed the same way as on the other initiatives—positively associated with unemployment and manufacturing's share, negatively with higher education and income.

36. Sugai, "Mass Insurgency," 336, for Leahy quote; chaps. 4 and 6 for discussion of ratepayer protest.

37. Lazar, interview.

Air Force, Western Shoshone, and Mormon Rhetoric of Place and the MX Conflict

Matthew Glass

D uring the Cold War decades, "the Bomb" came to play a fundamental symbolic role in American culture. For both supporters and foes,
nuclear weapons represented far more than a pragmatic response to the
bifurcated postwar political order. As Robert Oppenheimer recognized in
the searing heat and light emanating from the Trinity explosion, nuclear
weapons seemed to bridge the gap between the human and the divine.
Such power challenged existing views of the sacred, requiring Americans
to incorporate the new destructive power into their religious worldviews.
Nuclear weapons may even have given rise to new religious symbols and
practices.

Many Americans envisioned the invention and deployment of nuclear weapons as the embodiment of either providential blessings or
curses. President Truman, for instance, put a distinctly theological reading on the Manhattan Project when he told the nation in the wake of
the Hiroshima and Nagasaki bombings, "We thank God it has come to
us instead of to our enemies, and we pray that He may guide us to use it
in His ways and for His purposes."[1] In popular culture, in art, in intellectual reflections, and in the musings of policy makers, nuclear weapons
have been imagined to be either our salvation or our damnation.[2] In
what follows I want to examine one way in which the American West
itself has been touched by this imaginative need to find order and purpose in the new human capability to create atomic chaos.

For better or worse, imagination has always contributed to shaping
the American West. We can see it in the creation and migration stories
of indigenous tribal peoples, or in such mirages of conquest as Quivira,
Cibola, and the Northwest Passage. Donald Worster provides a more
modern example in his history of western irrigation, a story of settle-

ment infused with the visionary desire to make the Great American Desert bloom like the Garden of Eden.[3]

In the years since World War II a new imaginative exercise has pinpointed the American West, arising from federal efforts to develop and deploy nuclear weapons across public lands, and from competition between cities and states to garner a portion of the consequent regional economic boom.[4] Here I want to focus on one episode taken from the larger story of American imaginative responses to the creation and deployment of nuclear weapons, the Great Basin opposition to MX mobile-basing which arose in the fall of 1979. In particular, I will examine the ways in which various players in that conflict—the U.S. Air Force, the Mormon Church, and the Western Shoshone Nation—imagined the West, and will argue that the rhetoric of place voiced by opponents affected the controversy's political outcome.[5]

On September 7, 1979, when President Jimmy Carter announced his decision to deploy MX missiles across the valleys of eastern Nevada and western Utah, he was acknowledging the completion of a lengthy imaginative process. The MX missile system culminated two decades of ICBM research. The mobile-basing proposal that earmarked Great Basin lands was itself the end result of Air Force concerns over missile mobility dating back to the "missile gap" of the late 1950s. In its earliest incarnations, a mobile ICBM had been envisioned rolling down the nation's rail lines or highways. Among the thirty-seven alternative plans for the ICBM considered by the Air Force during the early 1970s were to suspend it from balloons, to fly it around in special transport planes, or to float it on sequestered inland waters.[6]

The MX described in Carter's announcement was an imposing technological feat. Planners envisioned a missile larger than anything in the U.S. arsenals, although still smaller than the 121-foot Soviet SS-18. The MX, 70 feet long and 92 inches in diameter, would weigh in at 192,000 pounds, over twice the weight of Minuteman III. The missile would be fitted with three solid fuel booster stages and a final warhead-ferrying, liquid-fueled stage. "The bus," the final stage, would carry between ten and twelve warheads, with a yield of 300 to 500 kilotons, depending on the warhead model.[7]

Carter and his planners envisioned the MX as based in a series of shelters spread across forty-seven Great Basin valleys. The two hundred missiles called for initially were to be shuttled on specially constructed

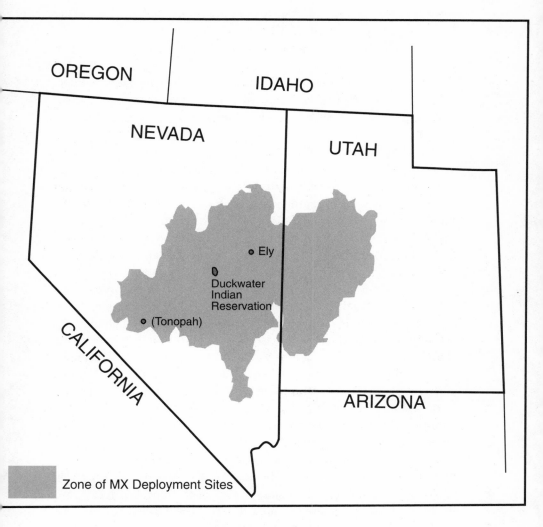

MAP 3. Proposed MX sites in the Great Basin

roadways, designed to hold the titanic weight of the combined missile, launcher, and transporter—1,600,000 pounds. According to Air Force publicity sheets, the transporter, 201 feet long, would become the largest rubber-tired vehicle in the world. The amount of roadway required was also enormous, totaling close to 10,000 miles. Each MX missile was to have its own loop connecting the twenty-three shelters. The shelter clusters were to be connected with a main roadway, some 8,500 miles of it, which would link the clusters with maintenance facilities, the two main operational bases, and rail lines.[8]

In the course of the two years of intense debate, back-room politicking, and media blitzing that followed Carter's announcement, the federal government projected a number of images of the West and its citizens in order to secure mobile-basing's future. They initially portrayed the West of the MX in idyllic terms. Carter told the American people that MX would be "based in a sheltered, road-mobile system to be constructed in our western deserts, the total exclusive area of which will not exceed 25 square miles." He emphasized that the system "minimizes the impact on the environment."[9]

Aware that local support would be essential, the Air Force launched a $24 million campaign to placate the worries of residents in the region, working out of the Ballistic Missile Office at Norton Air Force Base in southern California. Air Force personnel assigned to public relations echoed Carter's claim that the MX would have a minimal impact on western public lands. Air Force publicity sketches of the completed project showed cattle grazing next to security fences, and buckaroos on horseback contemplating the view across valleys dotted with cattle, sagebrush, and unobtrusive MX shelters. In a dinner with the Ely, Nevada, Chamber of Commerce, the room well supplied with flags, Brigadier General Guy Hecker told the 250 people present: "You can still mine around these [missile] sites, you can rockhound, you can shoot rabbits." Seeking to allay the fears mentioned by one diner concerning fallout or nuclear strikes on the area, Hecker claimed: "I'd be happy to retire here, move my family here. Ely would be one of the safest places in the U.S."[10]

The idyllic image rapidly sank from view as the press began covering the Air Force public relations campaign, and as Great Basin residents and local officials uncovered holes in federal statements and promises. The Air Force saw its missile system as simply one more facet of the Bureau of Land Management's multi-use policy, for the BLM was administrative agency for much of the land slated for the MX. However, as a "shocked" Senator Jake Garn (Republican from Utah) discovered in hearings, the proposal required the entire area to be "segregated" during the ten-year construction period.[11]

A more fundamental image of the region, the Great Basin as a wasteland or sacrifice area, emerged in the course of various press conferences and environmental impact statement (EIS) hearings stemming from the project's placement on public lands. Federal environmental law (NEPA and FLPMA) required the preparation of an extensive environmental review of the project. This opportunity, with its two tiers of public hearings held across the affected area, gave citizens and local officials at least some chance to learn the specifics of MX deployment, and to harangue and question Air Force officials in person.[12]

In December 1979, Mormon activist Edwin Firmage, a professor of international law at the University of Utah, wrote an editorial for the *Salt Lake Tribune* in which he attacked Air Force Chief of Staff General Lew Allen's comment that the MX would function as a "nuclear sponge" to absorb the major portion of the Soviet arsenal. Firmage concluded that "the administration evidently considers Utah and Nevada to be the most expendable part of our nation."[13]

As if to call attention to Firmage's editorial, Air Force undersecretary Antonia Chayes had a reply hand-delivered to the *Tribune* from the Pentagon. Contending that Firmage was simply mistaken in his understanding of the nature of U.S. strategic doctrine and the functions of the MX, Chayes concluded:

> We are making every effort to consult with the leaders and citizens of the potentially affected areas so as to devise approaches to this vital national undertaking which are compatible with local concerns and values. After all, the Air Force's mission in strategic defense, as in all other areas, is to protect our way of life.[14]

Chayes's comments indicate the logic by which the image of the West as a wasteland became incorporated into the modern national security worldview, which assumes a particular relationship between local and national priorities.

When pushed to acknowledge the enormous environmental and social effects that MX construction would have generated, Air Force officials resorted to the language of national purpose, and a moral rhetoric which sought to play off the disadvantages of the few against the benefits to the many. In spite of efforts to retract the idea of "nuclear sponge," this tactic depended on the logic of viewing the Great Basin as something of a national sacrifice area. Within the worldview of strategic planners, the national good would best be achieved through a construction process that Air Force brochures spoke of as "man's largest project." And while sacrifices involved in such a work might be substantial, federal officials urged patriotic westerners to make them willingly, and played up the economic boost that construction would bring to the region.[15] The *Draft Environmental Impact Statement* prepared for the Air Force spoke of the MX as "the highest national priority."[16] Following the release of the DEIS, Antonia Chayes said to an interviewer: "While the impacts may appear severe when viewed from the perspective of a little-developed area, when viewed from a national perspective . . . they are not that large."[17]

To minimize the costs attending the highest national priority, Air Force personnel issued photographs of the region emphasizing its desolate character. A brochure distributed by the Boeing Aerospace Company, which had been awarded several key MX contracts, juxtaposed a black and white photo of a desolate, nameless Nevada valley with the text: "This is the land chosen for the new MX strategic deterrent missile."[18] As one opponent put it, the Air Force wanted to convey to the public and Congress that there was "nobody out there but sagebrush and Indians." Members of House and Senate subcommittees controlling MX appropriations were flown over the deployment area at sufficient altitudes to make them wonder if anything at all lived down there. In Congress itself, those representatives from Nevada or Utah who played a role in slowing down the mobile-basing steamroller were labeled soft on communism, and unwilling to shoulder the burden necessary for the good of the nation. Congressman Joseph Addabbo from New York, for example, told Utah's governor Scott M. Matheson that the MX "has to go somewhere" and therefore Utah.[19]

The MX controversy differs in many ways from other chapters in the public reception of nuclear weapons deployment in America. For one thing, opponents were successful in overturning the project. Certainly the EIS process opened up the possibility for public scrutiny and perhaps the construction of legal hurdles which otherwise would not have threatened to slow down its IOC (initiation of construction) date.[20] The political clout of Nevada's Senator Paul Laxalt, Reagan's 1980 campaign manager, and the ultimate denunciation of the proposal by the Mormon Church's First Presidency were perhaps the most crucial factors leading to Reagan's abandonment of mobile-basing in October 1981.

But at the level of public debate, the MX controversy also differed from other antinuclear campaigns in the kind of rhetoric that was adopted by local opponents, a point to which I will return in my conclusions. If mobile-basing proponents sought to amass national support by portraying the Great Basin as land to be sacrificed for the good of the country, local opponents sought to emphasize the profound depth of human ties to the region.

Opponents within the basin were an unusually wide-ranging group: ranchers, environmentalists, academics, priests, and nuns. Generally, political conflicts among Great Basin residents are such that many of the groups involved in a coalition have little in common, often resorting to the courts to press their conflicting agendas about how to manage the public lands upon which their livelihoods and lifestyles depend. But confronted with the national security arguments, which most people expected would be well received in the Great Basin, opponents of various stripes actively sought to join forces with members of two cultural groups, Mormons and Western Shoshones.

What is it that made these subcultures within the Great Basin seem particularly valuable in the effort to derail the MX? Opponents turned to both Native Americans and Mormons not simply to amass group strength, or to suggest that there was some kind of ideological unity, for the environmental politics of the Great Basin often find ranchers and Native Americans on opposite sides of the fence over BLM land, and Native Americans on reservations at odds with urban dwellers over water rights.

What opponents gained at a rhetorical level through the participation of Mormons and Western Shoshones was the way in which members of these groups spoke about their commitments, their loyalties to the land and people of the region, in short the way their traditions uphold images of the region in which they live. Members of both groups seemed to opponents to speak with a moral voice that was not tempered by subjectivity or masked self-interest.

The fragility of the coalition, "the Great Basin MX Alliance," meant that opponents could not directly challenge the national security argument advanced by the administration and the Air Force. Instead, they focused on the social and environmental impacts. In public statements issued by the coalition, in media campaigns, and during a rapid-fire speaking tour of East Coast cities financed by the national antinuclear

261

movement, Great Basin opponents played up the cultural and religious history which enabled them to draw on the imaginative view of the region contained specifically in Mormon and Western Shoshone traditions. While Mormons and Shoshones certainly differ in political interests, economic power, and worldview, activists from both cultures were able to portray their links to the Great Basin in ways that opponents in general could mobilize behind. Consequently, it is well worth considering these elements of the Shoshone and Mormon worldviews.

Archaeologists claim that Western Shoshones have lived in the Great Basin for approximately 4,500 years.[21] Early ethnographers found that unlike many other Native American tribes, Great Basin Shoshones did not have any myths of migration from another place.[22] Modern Shoshones speak of their people as having always been in the region.

Traditional Shoshone life in the Great Basin was undoubtedly hard. The arid landscape and relatively extreme climate meant that Shoshones could not depend on a steady food supply. Organized in small family units, they regularly traveled over areas as wide as 100 miles in diameter in search of seasonally available plants and scarce game. White settlers and early ethnographers regarded the Shoshones with disdain, as when John Wesley Powell rated them at the bottom of the ladder of social evolution. Yet, as twentieth-century ethnographies have shown, they adapted by necessity to the environmental rigors of life in the Great Basin.

Scholars such as Ake Hultkranz argue that the traditional Shoshone worldview developed out of the efforts necessary for survival in a harsh environment.[23] Native American religions often embody aspects of the culture's environmental relations. Subsistence activity tends to generate a two-pronged understanding of the relationship between land and people which figures prominently in the rituals, stories, and moral practices of a culture. On the one hand, the land is the source of life, calling for responses of thankfulness and respect. On the other hand, it remains indifferent to human purpose, and requires manipulation in order for humans to survive. For the Shoshones, survival in a precarious setting intensified this dual characterization of the land.

The basic concept found in Great Basin tribal religions is power (*puha* in Numic). Tribal groups conceived of the Great Basin as a "web" of power, embracing landforms, such as mountains, trails, uplands, water sources; and various living things, such as plants, animals, and people.

The human task was to maintain connections with the sources of power found in the environment, and to use the power in ways that benefited the community.[24] Thus the land itself played a crucial role in defining who the Shoshone people were.

Modern Shoshones active in the MX controversy drew on this traditional understanding to counter the Carter administration's view of national priorities. They saw the MX as the culmination of the federal government's efforts to deprive them of their traditional lands. Air Force plans called for deploying MX sites across most of the 24 million acres recognized as Shoshone territory under the 1863 Treaty of the Ruby Valley.[25] Indeed, the 7,000-acre Duckwater Reservation was shown on Air Force maps as the probable site of three missile shelters.

Shoshones were able to speak of the project as destroying not simply their livelihoods but their lives, which they saw defined by access to the sources of power available on numerous sites spread across the deployment area. As one elder put it:

> If our land is taken—where will we go as Indian people? For the non-Indian it is different, [because] non-Indians can go back to their home country, where their ancestors are. But we, as Indians, if we do not have the land we have no where else to go. The land is part of us, it is tied to our lives. You cannot take this away from the Shoshone people.[26]

Shoshone creation stories speak of their people being placed in the Great Basin by the Creator. A strong link is forged between the homeland and personal and social identity. This connection is clear in the public discourse offered by Shoshones working against deployment. The declaration condemning Carter's MX decision issued in the fall of 1979 by the Western Shoshone Sacred Lands Association claimed that the Shoshone Nation had a duty to protect the homeland given to them by the Creator.[27]

In a region known for its boom-or-bust history, where populations ebb and flow with the promise of wealth, Shoshones spoke about their commitment and responsibilities to those who would live in the Great Basin decades or centuries in the future. The Association appealed to Shoshones to put aside considerations of land claims awards or compensation for transfers to the Air Force: "Are we willing to sell? Do we have the courage of our ancestors to provide for future generations of Shoshones? One hundred years from now, if there are any Shoshones left, how will they look at our generation as ancestors? . . . How will our own children view us when they become adults and have no land on which to raise their families?"[28]

This responsibility to future generations, as Jerry Millett, chair of the Duckwater tribe, has said, means that when the Shoshones make a decision, "it's gonna be for the Shoshones for on and on. I don't think the U.S. does that." Thus during the course of the MX controversy, Shoshone people found themselves and their lands pulled in contrary directions: they were faced with the national security image of an enormous Soviet threat requiring them to sacrifice some of their traditional lands for the good of the nation; but there was also the traditional cultural responsibility to live rightly on the land. Shoshone responsibilities conflicted with what Air Force personnel said they should do as good American citizens. As Millett explained: "What they're telling me to do is not what the Shoshones are instructed to do by their Creator."[29]

Mormon opponents were also able to marshal a distinctive image of the region to counter those advanced by the Carter administration and the Air Force. Given the fervent anticommunism which Mormon leaders had preached throughout the Cold War, and their consequent strong support of U.S. military and strategic policy, Air Force officials assumed that there would be little problem in convincing the Saints that the MX was a national priority as well as an economic windfall for Utah defense firms such as Hercules or Morton Thiokol. However, an early meeting with church leaders yielded nothing more than a cautious statement about church neutrality, given that the MX was "not a moral issue."[30]

But church leaders, along with a sizable portion of the membership, were very concerned about the MX. A poll conducted by Salt Lake's *Deseret News* in April 1980, after the issue had been public for about seven months, showed that 67.9 percent of the residents in the deployment area opposed the MX. In Utah itself, Republicans and Mormons were overwhelmingly opposed, while Democrats remained evenly split.[31]

For over a year Edwin Firmage singlehandedly had been trying to persuade the First Presidency to come out in opposition to the MX. Writing to Richard Lindsay, then the executive director of the church's Special Affairs Committee in March 1980, Firmage urged the church to counter its reactionary image and to speak with the vision of Brigham

Young and J. Reuben Clark. Clark, onetime ambassador to Mexico and undersecretary of state for Franklin Roosevelt, was an influential voice for isolationist foreign policy in the 1930s and 1940s.[32] For Firmage, Clark reflected the best features of the church's traditional view of the political arena, and Firmage hoped to remind its leaders of this tradition of political and moral critiquing of state power.[33]

In the spring of 1981 the First Presidency finally issued a strong statement, culminating in a declaration starkly contrasting the region as envisioned in Mormon sacred history with the one embodied in the national security worldview.

> Our fathers came to this western area to establish a base from which to carry the gospel of peace to the peoples of the earth. It is ironic, and a denial of the very essence of that gospel, that in this same general area there should be constructed a mammoth weapons system potentially capable of destroying much of civilization.[34]

Although the First Presidency spoke of the land along the Wasatch front being a base from which to spread the gospel of peace around the world, within the Mormon heritage the region has been envisioned most frequently as a refuge or shelter from the outside world. Mobile-basing thus rekindled dark Mormon memories of the U.S. Army's invasion of Utah in 1857. In addition, within Mormon country there are many who have not forgotten the blithe federal assurances that accompanied the Atomic Energy Commission's aboveground atomic testing of the 1950s.[35]

But at the same time, the First Presidency's statement grounded opposition in the strongest images available within the Mormon experience. In Mormon tradition the Great Basin literally was Zion, the Promised Land. And the Great Trek leading to its Mormon settlement was a sacred migration, in which the chosen people, like the Jews of old, were led out of an American Egypt and into their own Canaan.[36] If the Great Basin was comparable to Zion, it could not serve as a nuclear sponge. Those who placed their hopes in deterrence may well have believed that the MX's deployment would make the region the safest in the country, as General Hecker said. But in the eyes of Mormon activists, deployment looked like one more Gentile attempt to blot out the Lord's chosen people.

While Shoshone and Mormon activists comprised only a small portion of the MX opposition in the Great Basin, their rhetoric played an important role in mobilizing public opinion and in presenting an image of the region that could circulate in the national press. Shoshone references to the arid sage and piñon valleys as their dwelling place for thousands of years, a land entrusted to them by the Creator, or Mormon language about the Zion of God's chosen and the importance of remaining stewards of that land—all had currency in the public remarks of the opposition as a whole. Thus, leading non-Mormon MX opponents took upon themselves the task of rebuking the LDS church for its perceived tardiness in responding to the MX threat. The Reverend Steven Sidorak, a Salt Lake Methodist minister involved in the MX movement, told those gathered at the 1980 Mormon Theological Symposium: "The Church of Jesus Christ of Latter-Day Saints has been conspicuously quiet, neither hot nor cold." Drawing on Mormon views of the Great Basin as sacred space, he commented on the paradox of church silence when confronted with "the prospects of [the church's] promised land being abruptly turned into a wasteland." More pointedly, he said: "The air force has recently reiterated the celebrated LDS belief that indeed: 'This is the place.' Why all it would take is for the institutional Church of Jesus Christ of Latter-Day Saints to say: 'This is NOT the place'—to send the air force flying away into the wild blue yonder."[37]

It is this rhetoric of place, what I call a religious localism, which seems to me distinctive about the activism of Great Basin MX opponents. Shoshone and Mormon images of what the Great Basin was really all about gave opponents the rhetorical means to counter the national security worldview. While MX supporters continually spoke of opponents as being simply self-interested NIMBYs ("not in my back yard"), Shoshone and Mormon images enabled the coalition to express their opposition with a religious and moral depth. Those who spoke to the MX issue from a perspective drawing on Shoshone or Mormon language appeared to be articulating a vital loyalty to the land and communities of the region—a loyalty that was more than mere intransigence.

National security logic requires the mobilization of individuals and communities, and the transformation of landscapes into whatever forms are envisioned as most suitable to strategic missions. In the first year of the nuclear era, James Forrestal, President Truman's secretary of the Navy, said that American national security depended on taking "into

266

account our whole potential for war, our mines, our industry, manpower, research, and all the activities that go into normal civilian life."[38] National security would thus be achieved not only through the readiness of government bureaucracies and defense forces but also by the infusion of the same spartan spirit of mobilization into the population at large.

Air Force personnel working the MX campaign were asking no more of Great Basin residents than had been required of the rest of the nation. General Hecker, upon hearing poll results indicating that many basin residents were suspicious of the MX, said he was not concerned, because "39% of the people care about a strong defense . . . especially in these troubled times."[39] In the wake of the statement by the LDS First Presidency, General Richard Ellis of the Strategic Air Command blasted Mormon leaders as overlooking their members' responsibilities to defend the United States. From his Omaha office Ellis said SAC felt that "our defense responsibilities don't conflict with our moral responsibilities. To enjoy the latter we must provide the former."[40]

The riddle in all this becomes clear when we compare the rhetoric of MX foes with that of the national antinuclear weapons movement. The nuclear anxieties sweeping across America as a whole during the early 1980s were articulated in two very different rhetorical styles, both producing little in the way of effective mobilization and change. One style, common among groups such as Physicians for Social Responsibility or the nuclear freeze movement, sought to provide an overwhelming array of facts concerning nuclear war and its consequences, and the various scenarios about its aftermath. This rhetoric of facts and fears was expressed perhaps most eloquently in Jonathan Schell's book *The Fate of the Earth* (1982) and the movie *The Day After* (1983). The underlying assumption in such works seemed to be that if people were sufficiently terrorized by depictions of the end of the world they would do something about it.[41]

The other approach sought to persuade by urging American citizens and policy makers to follow the moral high ground. Most typically, this was the goal of the numerous liberal and evangelical religious groups whose members made up such a large portion of the antinuclear movement nationwide. While denominational and theological differences resulted in countless variations, religious opponents basically sought to persuade the public and the strategic weapons community that people had higher obligations than those enshrined in the national security state.[42]

Nuclear opponents urging the moral high ground generally ignored the forms of loyalty and commitment to the modern nation-state which sociologists and others have referred to as "civil religion."[43] Although Americans in the post-Watergate years may have become more suspicious of government operations on a domestic level, they have remained susceptible to appeals to national defense. If Americans were incapable of digesting mountains of facts, and if their media-produced nightmares were soothed easily, they were also not inclined to embrace unilateral disarmament because some minister said it was the right thing to do.

Much of the national antinuclear weapons movement asked Americans to imagine the unimaginable—the apocalyptic destruction of life as we know it, a radically reorganized global political order, or simply a world in which everyone did the right thing and followed the golden rule. Great Basin MX opponents required far less from the citizens they sought to mobilize and the policy makers they tried to influence. They portrayed a future that was quite imaginable: a region quickly bloated with an enormous population of transient workers, fragile landscapes scarred not so much from incoming Soviet warheads as from Caterpillar tractors and survey crews, scarce water resources depleted not by vaporization in a nuclear exchange but from the mixing of cement, and sovereign native nations severed from homelands so that cement could be poured. In short, the West they already knew, but more so.

The national antinuclear weapons movement worked by trying to get Americans to imagine something bigger than the picture of the world painted by weapons proponents, to fix their ultimate loyalties to something bigger than the nation-state, and they failed.[44] Great Basin MX opponents drew on Shoshone and Mormon traditions to help them paint a picture of the West that was in some sense smaller than that of MX supporters, and they succeeded.

In this they accomplished something that Josiah Royce, the great American philosopher, thought was crucial for America and especially the West itself. Royce, born in a California gold camp in 1852, wrote his first book on the American conquest of California. In that book and others he portrayed American civilization as a kind of empire, gobbling up its own variety of lands and peoples, and then turning to others. To counter what he called "imperialistic" developments, and what we might more accurately call nationalism, he urged citizens to adopt a provincial outlook. In the years prior to World War I, Royce cautioned that "the nation by itself, apart from the influence of the province, is in danger of becoming an incomprehensible monster."[45] The central dilemma faced by American citizens, as Royce saw it, was that their local environments and ways of life, which in effect made them who they were, were being swallowed up by nationalizing political and economic tendencies. The growth of the national security state in the years after World War II, especially in the American West, likely would have come as no surprise to Royce.

Great Basin opponents were able to resist the exercise of the national security imagination, or what Royce might have called the imperial imagination, which rationalized the destruction of the region's environments and subsumed its way of life into a cost-benefit analysis of the nation's good.[46] They were compelled to do so in a manner that could overcome historical conflicts as well as ideological and cultural differences. But that requirement seems to have been their good fortune. Great Basin opponents had to avoid the standard forms of antinuclear rhetoric, which would prove ineffective anyway during the course of the Reagan presidency, and find other ways of speaking about their region and their commitment to its preservation. If Cold War Americans could imagine nuclear weapons only as symbols of damnation or salvation, and if such limits on imagination constrained political mobilization, then Great Basin MX opponents were able to succeed in their own resistance to deployment by not bothering with such imaginative exercises. Instead, in the course of drawing upon local images of what the region had been, they countered the image of their future as fashioned by the nation's guardians.

NOTES

1. Quoted in Paul Boyer, *By the Bomb's Early Light: American Thought and Culture at the Dawn of the Atomic Age* (New York: Pantheon, 1985), 211.

2. In recent years several authors have offered studies of the cultural impact of nuclear weapons. Boyer's history of the first Cold War decade, *By the Bomb's Early Light,* is an excellent example. Others include A. G. Mojtabai, *Blessed Assurance: At*

Home with the Bomb in Amarillo, Texas (Boston: Houghton Mifflin, 1986); Paul Loeb, *Nuclear Culture: Living and Working in the World's Largest Atomic Complex* (Philadelphia: New Society, 1986); and Spencer R. Weart, *Nuclear Fear: A History of Images* (Cambridge: Harvard University Press, 1988). From the standpoint of comparative religion, nuclear weapons make an obviously interesting topic of study. See, for instance, Ira Chernus and Edward Tabor Linenthal, *A Shuddering Dawn: Religious Studies and the Nuclear Age* (Albany: State University of New York Press, 1989); Ira Chernus, *Dr. Strangegod: On the Symbolic Meaning of Nuclear Weapons* (Columbia: University of South Carolina Press, 1986); and G. Simon Harak, "One Nation under God: On the Soteriology of SDI," *Journal of the American Academy of Religion* 56, no. 3 (1988): 497–528.

3. See Donald Worster, *Rivers of Empire: Water, Aridity, and the Growth of the American West* (New York: Pantheon, 1985).

4. See Gerald Nash, *The American West Transformed: The Impact of the Second World War* (Bloomington: Indiana University Press, 1985), and Robert Gottlieb and Peter Wiley, *Empires in the Sun: The Rise of the New American West* (Tucson: University of Arizona Press, 1985), for the effects of science, urbanization, and the emergence of the nationally integrated economy, including military development, on the region. Patricia Nelson Limerick, *The Legacy of Conquest: The Unbroken Past of the American West* (New York: Norton, 1987), 78–89, 134–52, traces the paradoxical ideology of boosterism and resentment in relation to federal efforts to develop the West's resource base. See also William Cronon, George Miles, and Jay Gitlin, *Under an Open Sky: Rethinking America's Western Past* (New York: Norton, 1992), and Patricia Nelson Limerick, Clyde A. Milner II, and Charles E. Rankin, *Trails: Toward a New Western History* (Lawrence: University Press of Kansas, 1991), for recent directions in the study of the American West.

5. Some portions of this chapter appear in different form in my *Citizens Against the MX: Public Languages in the Nuclear Age* (Urbana and Chicago: University of Illinois Press, 1993).

6. Most of the academic study of the MX by social scientists has focused on the role of nonstrategic factors in its development. See John Edwards, *Superweapon: The Making of MX* (New York: Norton, 1982), for an account of the MX's early history, and Gregory C. Tarbell, "Congress, Counterforce and the Genesis of the MX, 1974–76" (M.A. thesis, Brown University, 1983), for congressional reception during the Ford administration. Robert Hoover, *The MX Controversy: A Guide* (Claremont, Calif.: Regina, 1982), offers a useful guide to sources. Lauren Holland and Robert Hoover, in *The MX Decision: A New Direction in Weapons Procurement Policy?* (Boulder: Westview, 1985), make a sustained analysis of extrastrategic factors, and give some attention to the role of Great Basin citizens themselves. Janice Maureen Kroll, "Arms Control and the MX" (Ph.D. diss., University of Southern California, 1985), proceeding from the assumption of mobile- basing's

strategic necessity, offers a critique of the roles played by other institutions and other political actors in tabling the Carter proposal.

7. The MX is described well in Herbert Scoville, *MX: Prescription for Disaster* (Cambridge: MIT Press, 1981), and Jonathan Medalia, "MX Intercontinental Ballistic Missile Program," Issue Brief IB 77080 (Washington, D.C.: Congressional Record Service, 1980).

8. Opponents of MX liked to compare the amount of road required with the federal highway projects begun after World War II, totaling some 40,000 miles. MX would have concentrated one-fourth of this within a geographical area the size of Pennsylvania. Features of the mobile-basing proposal are described in many places. See U.S. Office of Technology Assessment, *MX Missile Basing* (Washington, D.C.: Government Printing Office, 1981); Department of the Air Force, Ballistic Missile Office, *MX and the Environment* (Washington, D.C.: Government Printing Office, 1979); and the Air Force's draft environmental impact statement, *Deployment Area Selection and Land Withdrawal/Acquisition DEIS* (Washington, D.C.: Government Printing Office, 1980). For critiques of the proposal, see David Gold et al., *Misguided Expenditure: An Analysis of the Proposed MX Missile System* (New York: Council on Economic Priorities, 1981), and Scoville, *MX: Prescription for Disaster.*

9. "MX Missile System," in *Public Papers of the Presidents of the United States: Jimmy Carter,* vol. 2 (Washington, D.C.: Government Printing Office, 1979), 1600.

10. *Reno Evening Gazette,* July 16, 1979.

11. *Salt Lake Tribune,* November 21, 1979.

12. See Holland and Hoover, *The MX Decision,* for an extended analysis of MX in terms of environmental law. For good treatments of public lands issues, see Marion Clawson, *The Federal Lands Revisited* (Washington, D.C.: Resources for the Future, 1983); Paul Culhane, *Public Lands Politics* (Baltimore: Johns Hopkins University Press, 1981); Phillip O. Foss, ed., *Federal Lands Politics* (New York: Greenwood, 1987), John Francis and Richard Ganzel, *Western Public Lands* (Totowa, N.J.: Rowman and Allanheld, 1984); and for MX itself, see Paul Culhane, "Heading 'Em off at the Pass: MX and the Public Lands Subgovernment," in *Federal Lands Policy,* ed. Phillip O. Foss (New York: Greenwood, 1987), 91–110.

13. *Salt Lake Tribune,* December 2, 1979.

14. *Salt Lake Tribune,* February 10, 1980.

15. The pork barrel aspects of MX are intriguing in their own right. Those who supported the project in the region, including a number of state and civic political leaders, unions, and construction firms in Las Vegas, tended to argue that patriotic sacrifice and economic booms went hand in hand. For instance, one letter to the editor of the *Ely Daily Times* urged Nevadans: "Back up the President and be loyal Americans, even if we have to sacrifice a little to keep America free. Let's do it. . . . If everyone felt the same [as opponents] we could wake up saying

271

good morning to the Russians. We need something here to build up the economy of the county" (*Ely Daily Times,* January 15, 1980).

16. Department of the Air Force, Ballistic Missile Office, *MX Environmental Technical Report* (Washington, D.C.: Government Printing Office, 1980), 1.

17. Kennedy Maize, "Air Force Bares MX's Ugly Side," *Defense Weekly,* December 22, 1980.

18. "MX" brochure, Boeing Aerospace Company, n.d., MX Information Center Collection, MS527, box 41, folder 1, Manuscripts Division, Special Collections, University of Utah Marriott Library.

19. Scott M. Matheson, *Out of Balance* (Layton, Utah: Gibbs M. Smith, 1986), 67.

20. However, as Holland and Hoover point out in *The MX Decision* (p. 111), the EIS process also provided the Air Force with legal grounds to avoid addressing any environmental impacts not specifically brought up in the course of public hearings. For an insightful analysis of the limits to the public hearing process, see Ray Kemp, "Planning, Public Hearings and the Politics of Discourse," in *Critical Theory and Public Life,* ed. John Forester (Boston: MIT Press, 1985), 177–201.

21. David Hurst Thomas, "An Archeological Perspective on Shoshonean Bands," *American Anthropologist* 76, no. 1 (1984): 11–23.

22. Robert Lowie, "The Northern Shoshone," *Anthropological Papers of the American Museum of Natural History* 2 (1909): 165–306.

23. Ake Hultkranz, "Religion and Ecology among Great Basin Indians," in *The Realm of the Extra-Human: Ideas and Actions,* ed. Agehananda Bharati (The Hague: Mouton, 1976), 137–50.

24. Jay Miller, "Basin Religion and Theology: A Comparative Study of (Power)—*Puha,*" *Journal of California and Great Basin Anthropology* 5, no. 1/2 (1983): 79.

25. The Western Shoshones have been involved in protracted litigation over their traditional lands for many years. An earlier settlement, negotiated by the law firm of Wilkinson and Barker, was rejected by the Shoshones but upheld by the courts, which agreed to award them the 1872 value of their traditional lands. This disputed settlement provided the Air Force with grounds for its assumption that the Shoshones no longer held a valid claim to their traditional lands. For statements of Shoshone difficulties, set in the context of claims brought before the Indian Claims Commission, see Robert T. Coulter and Steven M. Tullberg, "Indian Land Rights," in *The Aggressions of Civilization: Federal Indian Policy since the 1880s,* ed. Vine Deloria and Sara Cadwalader (Philadelphia: Temple University, 1984), 204–5; and Omer C. Stewart, "The Shoshone Claims Cases," in *Irredeemable America: The Indians' Estate and Land Claims,* ed. Imre Sutton (Albuquerque: University of New Mexico Press, 1985), 187–206. Joshua D. Reivman presents a good analysis of the limiting factors for Native Americans seeking land returns in the wake of recent Supreme Court rulings in "Judicial Scrutiny of Native American Free Exer-

cise Rights: *Lyng* and the Decline of the *Yoder* Doctrine," *Boston College Environmental Law Review* 17, no. 1 (1989): 169–99.

26. Dagmar Thorpe, "The MX Missile and the Western Shoshone: The Destruction of a People," in *Western Shoshone Sacred Lands Association,* Spring 1981, 9.

27. *Western Shoshone Sacred Lands Association,* April 1980.

28. Ibid.

29. Jerry Millett, interview by author, Duckwater, Nevada, November 6, 1987.

30. Robert Gottlieb and Peter Wiley, *America's Saints: The Rise of Mormon Power* (New York: Putnam's, 1984), 65.

31. *Deseret News,* April 21, 1980.

32. Firmage to Richard P. Lindsay, March 17, 1980, Citizen Alert MX Missile Papers, box 3, folder 11, Special Collections, University of Nevada Reno Library.

33. Edwin Firmage, interview by author, Salt Lake City, Utah, November 3, 1987.

34. Spencer Kimball, N. Eldon Tanner, and Marion G. Romney, "Statement of the First Presidency of the Church of Jesus Christ of Latter-day Saints on Basing of the MX Missile," MX Information Center Collection, MS527, box 163, folder 5, Manuscripts Division, Special Collections, University of Utah Marriott Library.

35. For an overview of relations between the Utah Mormons and the federal government, including the 1857 invasion, see Leonard J. Arrington and Davis Bitton, *The Mormon Experience: A History of the Latter-day Saints* (New York: Knopf, 1979), 161–84. Despite the hostilities and prejudices underlying the perceptions many of their fellow citizens continued to hold of Mormons, Arrington and Bitton note that by the end of the First World War, "Mormons were more American than most Americans. Patriotism, respect for the law, love of the Constitution, and obedience to political authority reigned as principles of faith" (*The Mormon Experience,* 184). For useful overviews of the tensions Mormonism has undergone in its efforts to remain distinctive within the realm of American culture, see Thomas F. O'Dea, *The Mormons* (Chicago: University of Chicago Press, 1957); Klaus J. Hansen, *Mormonism and the American Experience* (Chicago: University of Chicago Press, 1981); Jan Shipps, *Mormonism: The Story of a New Religious Tradition* (Urbana and Chicago: University of Illinois Press, 1985); and Gordon and Gary Shepherd, *A Kingdom Transformed: Themes in the Development of Mormonism* (Salt Lake City: University of Utah Press, 1984). For accounts of the atomic testing program in Utah, see Philip L. Fradkin, *Fallout: An American Nuclear Tragedy* (Tucson: University of Arizona Press, 1989), and John Fuller, *The Day We Bombed Utah* (New York: New American Library, 1984). Howard Ball, *Justice Downwind: America's Atomic Testing Program in the 1950s* (New York: Oxford University Press, 1986), and A. Costandina Titus, *Bombs in the Backyard: Atomic Testing and American Politics* (Reno: University of Nevada Press, 1986), provide important studies of the program's impact on citizens in the region; and Robert A. Divine,

Blowing on the Wind: The Nuclear Test Ban Debate, 1954–1960 (New York: Oxford University Press, 1978), examines the history of the debate over aboveground testing.

36. Shipps, *Mormonism,* 120.

37. Stephen Sidorak, "Address to the Mormon Theological Symposium," n.d., MX Information Center Collection, MS527, box 117, folder 20, Manuscripts Division, Special Collections, University of Utah Marriott Library.

38. Quoted in Daniel Yergin, *Shattered Peace: The Origins of the Cold War and the National Security State* (Boston: Houghton Mifflin, 1977), 204.

39. *Nevada State Journal,* February 17, 1980.

40. *Nevada State Journal,* May 7, 1981.

41. Paul Boyer's "From Activism to Apathy: The American People and Nuclear Weapons, 1963–1980," *Journal of American History* 70, no. 4 (1984): 821–44, offers a critical reading of recent antinuclear activists' lack of historical sense, with the result that their efforts basically replayed the work of nuclear opponents during the early years of the Cold War. For an extensive treatment of the antinuclear concerns of scientists connected with the Manhattan Project and other early critics, see Alice Kimball Smith, *A Peril and a Hope: The Scientists' Movement in America* (Chicago: University of Chicago Press, 1965). For important discussions of the continuities between nuclear activists in the 1980s and traditional apocalyptic thinking in American culture, see Edward Tabor Linenthal, *Symbolic Defense: The Cultural Significance of the Strategic Defense Initiative* (Urbana and Chicago: University of Illinois Press, 1989), and "Restoring America: Political Revivalism in the Nuclear Age," in *Religion and the Life of the Nation: American Recoveries,* ed. Rowland A. Sherrill (Urbana and Chicago: University of Illinois Press, 1990), 23–45.

42. Religious opposition to nuclear weapons has spawned a voluminous literature in the decades since Hiroshima. For the most part, the movement has not been studied by historians or other scholars. For studies of Catholic concerns, see William A. Au, *The Cross, the Flag, and the Bomb: American Catholics Debate War and Peace, 1960–1985* (Westport, Conn.: Greenwood, 1985); Jim Castelli, *The Bishops and the Bomb: Waging Peace in a Nuclear Age* (Garden City, N.Y.: Image Books, 1983), and Robert Heyer, ed., *Nuclear Disarmament: Key Statements of Popes, Bishops, Councils and Churches* (Ramsey, N.J.: Paulist Press, 1982). For a collection of historical documents in a long-running debate among mainstream Protestants and members of the "historic peace churches" such as Mennonites and Quakers, see Donald Durnbaugh, ed., *On Earth Peace: Discussions on War/Peace Issues between Friends, Mennonites, Brethren and European Churches, 1935–1975* (Elgin, Ill.: Brethren Press, 1978). For another historical collection from the mainstream Protestant National Council of Churches, see Harold L. Lunger, ed., *Facing War / Waging Peace: Findings of the American Church Study Conferences, 1940–1960* (New York: Friendship Press, 1988). Milton S. Katz studies SANE in *Ban the Bomb: A*

History of SANE, *the Committee for a Sane Nuclear Policy, 1957–1985* (Westport, Conn.: Greenwood, 1986), and Robert D. Holsworth provides a well-done case study of religious activists in the early 1980s in *Let Your Life Speak: A Study of Politics, Religion and Antinuclear Weapons Activism* (Madison: University of Wisconsin Press, 1989).

43. See Wilbur Zelinsky, *Nation into State: The Shifting Symbolic Foundations of American Nationalism* (Chapel Hill: University of North Carolina Press, 1988), for the most recent extended treatment.

44. For a sampling of literature on the American peace movement and nuclear weapons, see Boyer, "From Activism to Apathy"; Charles DeBenedetti, *The Peace Reform in American History* (Bloomington: Indiana University Press, 1980); Lawrence S. Wittner, *Rebels Against War: The American Peace Movement, 1933–1983* (Philadelphia: Temple University Press, 1984); and Katz, *Ban the Bomb*.

45. Royce's first book was *California, from the Conquest in 1846 to the Second Vigilance Committee in San Francisco, 1856: A Study of American Character* (New York: Macmillan, 1886). His remarks on American imperialism appear in *The Philosophy of Loyalty* (New York: Macmillan, 1908), 239. See also his essay "Provincialism" in his *Basic Writings*, vol. 2 (Chicago: University of Chicago Press, 1969), 1067–88.

46. My understanding of rationalization, an important concept in modern social theory, comes from the work of Juergen Habermas, particularly *The Theory of Communicative Action*, vol. 1, *Reason and the Rationalization of Society* (Boston: Beacon, 1984) and vol. 2, *Lifeworld and System: A Critique of Functionalist Reason* (Boston: Beacon, 1987), and *The Structural Transformation of the Public Sphere: An Inquiry into a Category of Bourgeois Society* (Cambridge: MIT Press, 1991).

Contributors

CARL ABBOTT is professor of urban studies and planning at Portland State University. He is the author of several books on urban growth and regional planning in the American West and serves as coeditor of *Pacific Historical Review* and *Journal of the American Planning Association.*

ROBERT E. FICKEN, an independent scholar of Pacific Northwest history, resides in Issaquah, Washington. His books include *The Forested Land: A History of Lumbering in Western Washington* (1987), *Rufus Woods, the Columbia River, and the Building of Modern Washington* (1995), and, with Charles P. LeWarne, *Washington: A Centennial History* (1988). He was the 1997 recipient of the Pacific Northwest Historians Award.

JOHN M. FINDLAY, a professor of history at the University of Washington, also serves as director of the Center for the Study of the Pacific Northwest and managing editor of *Pacific Northwest Quarterly.* He is the author of "Atomic Frontier Days: Richland, Washington, and the Modern American West" (*Journal of the West,* July 1995).

MATTHEW GLASS is associate professor in the Department of Philosophy and Religion at South Dakota State University, where his teaching includes religion in American culture and environmental ethics. He is interested in the role of religion in debates over land use in the American West. The author of *Citizens against the MX: Public Languages in the Nuclear Age* (1993), he is currently working on a manuscript on Mount Rushmore in American culture, for which he has received an NEH fellowship.

STANLEY GOLDBERG at the time of his death in 1996 was at work on a biography of General Leslie Groves, the Manhattan Project commanding officer. His published work includes *Understanding Relativity: Origin and Impact of a Scientific Revolution* (1984) and a coedited volume of essays, *The Michelson Era in American Science, 1870–1960* (1988). He was a longtime consultant to both the National Museum of American History and the National Air and Space Museum of the Smithsonian Institution. His work on the history of the Manhattan Project resulted in a number of articles, including "Inventing a Climate of Opinion: Vannevar Bush and the Decision to Build the Bomb" (*Isis*, September 1992).

BARTON C. HACKER joined the Smithsonian as curator of armed forces history collections in 1998, ending his two decades of research and writing on the history of radiation safety in nuclear weapons testing and related issues, which included a prize-winning article in *Public Historian* (1992) and a prize-winning book, *Elements of Controversy: The Atomic Energy Commission and Radiation Safety in Nuclear Weapons Testing, 1947–1974* (1994).

GREGG HERKEN is a historian and curator at the National Air and Space Museum, Smithsonian Institution. His specialty is nuclear history and U.S. foreign relations during the Cold War. His books include *The Winning Weapon: The Atomic Bomb in the Cold War, 1945–1950* (1980), *Counsels of War* (1985), *Cardinal Choices: Presidential Science Advising from the Atomic Bomb to SDI* (1992), and *Inside the Wire: Physics, Politics, and the Cold War* (forthcoming).

BRUCE HEVLY teaches history of technology and science at the University of Washington. With John M. Findlay he is writing a history of Hanford and the Tri-Cities in Washington state.

DAN O'NEILL is the author of *The Firecracker Boys* (1994). An independent researcher and writer affiliated with the oral history program at the University of Alaska Fairbanks, he was named Alaska historian of the year in 1994 by the Alaska Historical Society.

DANIEL POPE is associate professor of history at the University of Oregon. He is working on a book on the history of the WPPSS nuclear projects and has written several articles on nuclear power in the Pacific Northwest, including " 'We Can Wait. We Should Wait.' Eugene's Nuclear Power Controversy, 1968–1970" (*Pacific Historical Review*, August 1990).

FERENC M. SZASZ is professor of history at the University of New Mexico in Albuquerque. He has written several articles and two books on the Atomic West, *British Scientists and the Manhattan Project: The Los Alamos Years* (1992) and *The Day the Sun Rose Twice: The Story of the Trinity Site Nuclear Explosion, July 16, 1945* (1984; rev. ed, 1994).

THOMAS WELLOCK, a former nuclear engineer for naval and civilian reactors, is assistant professor of history at Central Washington University. He is the author of *Critical Masses: Opposition to Nuclear Power in California, 1958–1978* (1998).

Index

Bureau of Reclamation, U.S., 23–24, 30, 32

Bush, Vannevar, 39, 42, 43–44, 45, 68–69, 70, 81

Byrnes, James F., 66–70

California, 119–30 *passim,* 200–225 *passim;* energy needs, 215–16; initiative process, 203, 206–8, 210; legislation to regulate nuclear power industry, 218–19, 221–23, 224–25; regulatory agencies, 203–4, 214–15, 216–17. *See also* Proposition 15; University of California

Californians for Nuclear Safeguards (CNS), 210, 213, 218, 221

Cape Thompson, Alaska, 181–82, 187–88, 190–91, 193

Carter, Pres. Jimmy, and MX missile basing, 256–58

Christensen, Sherman, 163–65

Church of Jesus Christ of Latter-day Saints. *See* Mormon Church; Mormons

CIF. *See* Creative Initiative Foundation

class divisions: at Los Alamos, N.M., 98, 105–6; at Richland, Wash., 102–3

Clay, Gen. Lucius, 44, 86

Columbia Basin Project, 21–32

Columbia River, 10, 21–32; Hanford Reach of, 31; water for Hanford reactors, 54

Commoner, Barry, 192–93

Compton, Arthur Holly, 3, 45, 47, 49

Conant, James B., 3, 39, 43, 45, 47, 68, 70, 79, 81

controlled fusion: prospects for as energy source, 146–47, 152–53

Creative Initiative Foundation (CIF), 211–13, 219–20

Department of Energy, U.S. (DOE), 4, 130; and 1950s sheep deaths, 164

DOE. *See* Department of Energy

Dunning, Gordon M., 160, 166–68

Du Pont Company (E.I. du Pont De Nemours and Company, Inc.), 21, 27; Richland, Wash., 95, 98; as Manhattan Project contractor, 47–48, 78, 80; and plutonium production at Hanford, 61–65

Durkin, Martin, 59–60

environmentalism: and attitudes toward nuclear power, 190, 192–93, 202–3. *See also* Friends of the Earth; opposition to nuclear power; Sierra Club; Wilderness Society

Eskimos, 181, 182, 186–89; and radioactive fallout, 191. *See also* Alaska Natives

Eugene, Ore.: and proposed nuclear power plant; 240–41; rejects additional participation in WPPSS, 242

federal government. *See names of specific agencies*

Fermi, Enrico, 3, 49, 80, 94, 141

Fermi, Laura, 98

Firmage, Edwin, 259, 264–65

Foote, Don Charles, 186–87, 191

Forrestal, James, 266–67

Friends of the Earth, 209–10

fusion. *See* controlled fusion; Tuck, James L.

General Electric (GE), 103; public attitudes toward, 100, 109; and Richland, Wash., 99

Germany, and the race to build an atomic bomb, 71, 87

Gordon, Bishop William, 185–86